P9-CMX-974

INDUSTRIAL WORKERS IN THE U.S.S.R.

THE CONTEMPORARY SOVIET UNION SERIES: INSTITUTIONS AND POLICIES

Each volume in the Contemporary Soviet Union Series examines in detail the facts about an important aspect of Soviet rule as it has affected the Soviet citizen in the 50 years since the Bolshevik Revolution of 1917.

Subjects include industry, culture, religion, agriculture, and so on. A careful examination of official Soviet material in each field provides essential basic reading for all students of Soviet affairs.

Robert Conquest is a former Research Fellow in Soviet affairs at the London School of Economics and Political Science and Senior Fellow of Columbia University's Russian Institute. His works include *Power and Policy in the USSR*, *The Pasternak Affair: Courage of Genius*, *Common Sense About Russia*, *The Soviet Deportation of Nationalities*, and *Russia after Khrushchev*.

THE CONTEMPORARY SOVIET UNION SERIES:
INSTITUTIONS AND POLICIES

EDITED BY ROBERT CONQUEST

Industrial Workers in the U.S.S.R.

FREDERICK A. PRAEGER, *Publishers*
New York · Washington

BOOKS THAT MATTER
Published in the United States of America in 1967
by Frederick A. Praeger, Inc., Publishers
111 Fourth Avenue, New York, N.Y. 10003

Library of Congress Catalog Card Number: 67–27315

This book is Number 196 in the series
Praeger Publications in Russian History and World Communism

Printed in Great Britain

Contents

Editor's Preface

In any advanced society, the relationship between the government and the industrial proletariat is a major element in the political and social scene. But in the USSR this is particularly so. For it is there a matter not merely of the practical conduct of a large part of the nation's affairs, but also of doctrinal issues crucial to the entire position of the ruling party. And, moreover, in the Soviet system, the concept of industrial planning, with State control and supervision at every level, also plays an important doctrinal as well as an important practical rôle.

The position of the industrial working class in Russia constitutes a paradox. That class lacks any real voice in deciding State, or even industrial, issues. But at the same time, it has always been, *theoretically* speaking, the ruling element in the Soviet Union.

Karl Marx foresaw a 'dictatorship of the proletariat' coming into being in the industrialised societies of the West, at a time when the vast bulk of production had been turned into a large-scale, social affair by mature capitalism; and when as a result the proletariat constituted the great majority of the population. When the Bolshevik Party came to power in Russia, these conditions were not, of course, fulfilled. The Bolsheviks regarded themselves as the party of the proletariat, but the proletariat was itself a minority, and a politically immature one, by Marxist standards, at that.

The Party, about a third of whose members—and almost all of whose leaders—were intellectuals, came to regard itself as the trustee of a future proletarian majority, rather than as arising in the ordinary Marxist way from the existing economic situation. Even in 1917, the crucial meeting of the Central Committee nine days before the October Revolution received numbers of reports from the factories that the idea of the rising was 'not popular', that 'the masses received our call with bewilderment'. The seizure of power was a fairly small-scale operation carried out by a small number of Red Guards, only partly from the factories, and a rather larger group of Bolshevised soldiery while the masses were generally neutral. The following January the Constituent Assembly was dispersed by force, and Lenin proclaimed that 'the workers' would not submit to a peasant majority. But as early as 1919 he found it necessary to make a remark crucial to the whole Communist attitude to the working class: 'We recognise neither freedom, nor equality, *nor labour democracy* [my italics] if they are opposed to the interests of the emancipation of labour from the oppression of capital.'*

Next year, he was insisting that 'revolutionary violence' was essential 'against the faltering and unrestrained elements of the toiling masses themselves'.† It had become clear that the working class was thoroughly disenchanted with the Party. Mensheviks and other moderates had been elected to the leaderships of the great unions, only to be expelled by force. A Communist leader put the case clearly to a Party audience:

'The Party is the politically conscious vanguard of the working class. We are now at a point where the workers, at the end of their endurance, refuse any longer to follow a vanguard which leads them to battle and sacrifice . . . Ought we to yield to the clamours of working-men who have reached the limit of their patience but who do not understand their true interest as we do? Their state of mind is at present frankly reactionary. But the Party has decided that we must *not* yield, that we must impose our will to victory on our exhausted and dispirited followers.'‡

In February, 1921, came the wave of strikes and demonstrations in Petrograd leading up to the sailors' and workers' rebellion in the naval base at Kronstadt, which was put down in blood. Henceforward the Party, cut off from genuine working-class roots, rested on its ideas alone. Its justification came no longer from the politics of actuality but from the politics of prophecy.

But in its phraseology, the idea of the proletariat remained important. And for a time the Communist leadership imposed on the reluctant Trade Unions still made some attempt to

* Lenin, Speech of May 19th, 1919.

† See *Kommunist*, No. 5, 1957, page 21.

‡ Karl Radek, addressing the War College in 1921. Alexander Barmine: *One Who Survived*, New York, 1945, p. 94.

express their membership's wishes, under the guidance of one of the few workers to reach high Party position, Mikhail Tomsky.

But a further disjunction was now to take place. In 1929–30 Stalin, who had defeated all his rivals for power, resurrected in an extreme form the 'Leftist' policies originally urged by Trotsky and rejected by Lenin. The Soviet Union was to be industrialised and proletarianised by a crash programme based essentially on force. The capital required was to be extracted from the peasantry by forced collectivisation and the seizure of a predetermined amount of their produce—regardless whether that left them subsistence. This is not the place to discuss the damage inflicted on Russian agriculture, nor the appalling famine which ensued as a direct result. But in the industrial field too, the new policy involved minimal rations and harsh discipline.

Tomsky and his followers were removed in April, 1929. As Kaganovich was to say at the XVIth Party Congress in 1930, 'The greater part of the leadership, both of the Central Council and of the individual Unions, has been replaced. It could be said that this was a violation of proletarian democracy, but, Comrades, it has long been known that for us Bolsheviks democracy is no fetish.' Over the following years came the Draconian laws against absenteeism and other breaches of labour discipline, and the rigorous 'norm' system. These were for the next generation to be between them the basis of Soviet policy towards the industrial worker which, in milder and less complete form, survives to this day.

The 'Plan', which now became central to the whole Soviet economic effort, had not the rationality that its name implies. It is a curious fact that none of the Five-Year Plans under which Russia theoretically operated after 1929 received final form and approval till anything up to 22 months after its official starting day, until the Sixth Plan was approved on time in 1956, only to be revised within a year and scrapped within two, a fate shared by the Seven-Year Plan which then replaced it.

Nor were the Plans comprehensive. In earlier days they consisted of little more than a set of unintegrated, and unrealistic, targets for each branch of industry. The Party press has lately censured Stalin for suppressing all attempts of the economists to examine the Plans properly,* and, in fact, in the struggle which ensued, almost all of the economists perished, leaving the field to the creators of economic myth. All this is to say that the 'Plans' were in effect something else: the vehicles of an unco-ordinated crash programme. Under these pressures considerable results were nevertheless achieved in industrialisation, as they were not in agriculture. But from the workers' point of view, the Plan became the sole determinant of his condition. The theory of the Party attitude to the proletariat found practical expression.

Any worker who set out to defend his own interests, or the interests of his fellows, as against the inordinate demands of a management itself under extreme pressure from the centre, was regarded as acting against the proletariat. For, it continued to be argued, the Party, and its State, and its Plan, represented the true interests of the working class. Any workman failing it, or acting against it, was therefore a traitor. What would elsewhere have been normal Trade Union activity was totally suppressed, and with a good conscience, by those who believed themselves to 'represent' the proletariat. As a result, Stalin's industrialisation was carried through under conditions less tolerable than those which had attended the capitalist phase in Russia, or elsewhere. A system became established which, again, has relaxed but shown no essential change.

From a Marxist point of view the proletarian party which had achieved power without an adequate proletariat was an anomaly. But it was an anomaly which some Communists hoped to correct by creating *ex post facto* the necessary industry and proletariat. Thereupon, it might be hoped, the bonds between the hitherto self-sufficient Party and the people might be re-established and something resembling the socialist democracy to which Marx had looked forward might emerge. Russia, the fourth industrial power before World War I, is now the second (though in national product *per capita* it still appears to rank in about the same position as in 1914—around twentieth). The industrial proletariat is not yet a majority of the population, but it is about as large as the peasantry: at the same time it has been held since 1961 that the country is no longer a Workers' State but 'a state of the whole people', since

* *Pravda*, December 1, 1963.

the collectivised peasantry has also supposedly developed to a high political and civic level.

But, so far at least, one looks in vain for any true re-integration of the working class into the Soviet polity. During the 1956 thaw there were stormy meetings in the factories at which even members of the Presidium were howled down as representative of the new wealthy 'They'. Strikes, developing, as in Novocherkassk in 1962, into major riots, have marked every relaxation. The Marxist optimists of the 'twenties do not seem to have taken into account the fact that over decades a close-knit ruling element, whomever it may think it represents, develops its own interests and resists all attempts to destroy or limit its powers or privileges. The Soviet proletariat appears to be more 'alienated' in Marx's sense than in most other countries. The question of its future rôle and of its future relations with the government is one of the most important of various Soviet problems which await solution. Meanwhile we can look at the origins, development and nature of the system.

Robert Conquest

Acknowledgements are due to Messrs. I. I. Stepanov, L. Levine, H. S. Murray and M. Friedman for their invaluable collaboration.

Introduction

Since the initiation of the First Five-Year Plan new generations of Soviet citizens have grown up. These people, and even their elders who were, say, 16 years old in 1928 and are now 55, have spent their entire working lives under the succession of Five- and Seven-Year Plans which have determined Soviet industrial development for the last three and a half decades. The bright hopes of the Revolution itself, the rigours of war Communism (1918–21) and the relaxations of Lenin's New Economic Policy (NEP) remain no more than childhood memories or parents' tales: only through school history books or current ideological propaganda do these events still live in people's minds. The Soviet worker of today judges his position against a background not of 1917 and the 1920s, but of the 1930s and 1940s.

For this reason, and for brevity's sake, this chapter will deal cursorily with the first decade of the Soviet régime, adducing facts from this period only in so far as they are essential to the understanding of what followed. For the rest, the treatment will be predominantly systematic, under headings that represent the main forces—economic, political, legal or social—which together determine the position of the Soviet working man or woman. Within most of these sections, however, three broad chronological periods may be discerned: first, from about 1928 to 1940, being the period when the Soviet working class first felt the full impact of planning and industrialisation; second, 1940 to 1953, when the war and its aftermath outweighed most other factors; and lastly, current developments.

The general pattern of Soviet economic evolution is not treated in this chapter. It should, nevertheless, always be borne in mind, since it is fundamental to the legal and institutional features here described. Since the decision to industrialise the country was taken in 1925, the Soviet economy has been going through a process of ruthless capital accumulation in the Marxist sense. The rate of investment in the economy has been extremely high, with preference given to heavy industry; the needs of today have continually been left unsatisfied in the name of greater plenty or greater power tomorrow; and laws have been made and institutions devised to ensure that all protest against the exploitation involved in this policy is stifled before it finds expression. What this has meant in human suffering and deprivation cannot be reckoned in statistics; but it may safely be said that the cost of the Soviet experiment, in these terms, has been higher than the population of any other industrialising country has had to sustain.

When Marx described the accumulation of capital in England in the nineteenth century, he was able to document his analysis in horrifying detail from British official sources, particularly Factory Inspectors' and Public Health Reports. The student of Soviet Russia has no such advantages: such data are not published in the Soviet Union, except in scattered fragments in the Press. The material on which this study rests is therefore drawn chiefly from Soviet Laws and from Government and Party documents, collated where possible with facts from Soviet life as they emerge in newspapers and periodicals.

The basis of Soviet labour legislation is found in the Labour Codex of the RSFSR of 1922, on which the Codices of the Union Republics are closely based: for example, nearly every section of a Collection of Legislative Acts on Labour published in 1961 begins with an extract from the Codex of 1922, followed by subsequent enactments.[1] The Soviet authorities have long recognised—at least since 1938—that the Labour Codex needs 'radical supplementation and revision'.[2] Voroshilov said at the XX Party Congress in 1956 that

> 'it is necessary to raise the question of revising and putting into order the legislation on labour. This must be done . . . because the Union Republics' current Codices, adopted many years ago, do not now, in spite of many supplements, reflect the socio-economic changes that have taken place in [the] State since that time . . .'[3]

But little has been done. In October 1959, the Draft Principles of Labour Legislation of the USSR and Union Republics were published for nationwide discussion: they were for the most part a recapitulation of earlier legislation. Perhaps for this reason the Draft Principles were never presented to the USSR Supreme Soviet for approval. The post-Khrushchev régime has shown no inclination to revive them or substitute alternative comprehensive legislation on labour.

I

Employment: The 'Right to Work'

Of all the factors that determine the position of the Soviet worker one that has changed least over the years is the legislation on the Labour Contract, which regulates the normal procedure of 'hiring and firing' in the Soviet Union. Apart from the introduction of Labour Books in 1938 and the Draconian laws stemming from the imminence of war in 1940 (these fall rather under the heading of Labour Discipline, and are so treated here), the amendments and additions to the original legislation relate to particular points such as part-time work, privileges for workers in distant parts of the USSR, or the position of pregnant women, and introduce no fundamental alterations into the Law.

THE LABOUR CONTRACT: ENGAGEMENT, TRANSFER AND DISMISSAL

According to the RSFSR Labour Codex of 1922, the Labour Contract was an 'agreement between two or more persons whereby one side (the employee) offers his labour power to the other side (the employer) for remuneration'.[4] The definition has, however, been refined by more recent Soviet legal commentators, since, as they put it, in the USSR 'society is not divided into sellers and buyers of labour power'.[5] The term 'employer' is therefore replaced by 'enterprise (or establishment)', and a corresponding change is made in the word for 'employed'.[6]

The Parties to a Labour Contract are an organisation on the one hand and an individual worker or employee on the other. Under the 1922 Labour Codex contracts may also be concluded with a group of workers (an *artel*); since 1960, however, when 1,400,000 members of industrial co-operative *artels* were incorporated in the system of State enterprises,[7] *artels* have ceased to exist. Minors over the age of 16 have a legal 'capacity to conclude a labour contract' on a par with adults.[8] For many years adolescents over the age of 14 were allowed to conclude labour contracts 'in exceptional circumstances, and with the permission of the labour protection organs',[9] but a 1956 decree raised the absolute minimum age to 15.[10] Since 1936 the law has been that no worker may be refused engagement on the grounds of his social origin, past court conviction, parents' or relatives' conviction or other similar reasons, 'except in so far as is envisaged by special laws';[11] nevertheless, 'managements must be guided by the principle of selecting cadres according to political as well as practical criteria'.[12] Since 1937 pregnant women,[13] and since 1949 nursing mothers, may not be refused work because of their condition.* [14] A probationary period may be required: for workers this must not exceed six days; for employees, two weeks; for employees in responsible posts, one month.† [15] The results of the trial are assessed by the management, and if they are unsatisfactory the labour contract is annulled; the employee is then paid the wages due to him according to his 'wage-scale rate'‡ and dismissed.[16] He may then appeal to a court or other body§ for settling labour disputes;[17] but he can, of course, look for no unemployment relief while his appeal is pending,‖ though up to 20 days' average wages will be paid retrospectively if his appeal is sustained.[18]

When a labour contract is concluded, the parties thereby automatically become subject to the provisions of Soviet labour legislation. Other obligations, which arise from the terms of the contract itself, are worked out by the parties concerned. Some of these—the fact of entry and acceptance of the worker into the enterprise concerned, and the definition of the labour function to be performed—are regarded as 'essential', and no contract is possible without them. Supplementary conditions—for instance, to define the worker's task more exactly or to give him extra rights such as housing or crèche facilities—may also

* Refusal of employment or dismissal of women on these grounds is punishable under Article 139 of the RSFSR Criminal Codex by up to one year's corrective labour, or dismissal.[19]

† The words 'workers' and 'employees' are used in the Russian sense of manual workers and office workers respectively. Similarly, the word 'enterprise' denotes a factory, and 'establishment', an office, or Government department.

‡ *See* pp. 53f. § *See* p. 180. ‖ *See* pp. 21, 34ff.

be added to the contract.[20] Wages, being regulated by law, are not normally part of the contract.

No term in the contract must contravene the law 'or other normative act'.[21] The 1922 Codex specified only that the terms of the contract should not bind the worker to any conditions *worse* than those fixed by labour legislation, collective agreements,* or the *Rules of Internal Labour Order*†; but a Soviet authority has pointed out that the text of this article is 'obsolete', and that 'Socialist planning' does not permit, for example, wage-scale rates to be fixed at the discretion of 'individual economic executives contracting with individual workers'.[22] The same authority concludes:[23]

> 'Hence today all conditions of a labour contract will be void which either reduce the worker's range of duties or raise the norms of payment or other legal guarantees in comparison with the rules established by law and other normative acts.'

However, in their desire to fulfil the plan, undertakings bid against each other to obtain scarce labour.‡ The Soviet Press in recent years has severely criticised workers who change jobs to obtain higher wages, and managements often depart from the letter of the law by giving workers higher grades than they warrant or by upgrading posts arbitrarily.[24]

Labour contracts are normally concluded verbally and are of indefinite duration.[25] They may also, in cases covered by law or governmental decree, be concluded for definite periods, normally for not more than a year.[26] Finally, a contract may be made to cover the time necessary to complete a specific job of work.[27] It is only these contracts of definite duration which have to be in written form.[28]

There are, however, two documents which play a part in the Labour Contract, although they are not the contract itself. The first is the worker's Labour Book, without which he cannot be accepted for work (unless it is his first job), and which is kept by the management during his employment.[29] An entry in the Labour Book may be used, in the case of dispute, as

* *See* pp. 176ff. These collective agreements are to be distinguished from the group contracts mentioned earlier.

† *See* pp. 111ff.

‡ e.g. *Pravda* reported on February 2, 1965, that highly skilled workers often transfer from large to small enterprises where wages are higher.

evidence that a labour contract was in fact concluded.[30] The second document is the worker's Pay Book. Pay Books are mentioned in the 1922 Codex, and again in a source of 1941;[31] but during or after the war they apparently fell out of use, for in 1947 Ministries and Departments were ordered to 'resume' their issue to workers.[32] In current practice the Pay Book is issued to the worker by the management within five days of his starting work; a contract can be concluded without issue of a Pay Book only if it is for less than a week.[33] The Pay Book contains the information necessary for determining the worker's basic wage (i.e. his wage-scale rating, etc.) and every month a note is made in it of the amount and make-up of his earnings (e.g. basic rate, bonuses, overtime, etc.).[34]

Once the Labour Contract is concluded, there are certain circumstances in which the management may transfer the worker to other work. The 1922 Codex provided that only in case of temporary shortage of the type of work for which the worker was engaged might he be transferred to other work 'corresponding to his skill', and dismissed if he refused; otherwise transfers were permitted only 'in exceptional cases, when it is necessary to ward off imminent danger',[35] presumably in case of fire, flood, etc. In 1931, however, a new article was added to the Codex, granting managements the right, in case of 'production necessity', notably idle-standing, to transfer workers or employees for up to one month to other work in the same or another enterprise in the same locality: refusal without valid reason was to be treated as a violation of labour discipline.[36] Permanent transfer to other work not mentioned in the Labour Contract was permitted only with the consent of the worker. In four types of situation, however, the worker could be dismissed for refusal to accept permanent transfer[37]:

(1) if the transfer was caused by the enterprise closing down or reducing staff;
(2) if it was caused by the worker's unfitness for his work;
(3) if it was caused by his persistent output of spoiled goods;
(4) if the worker was being transferred to the same type of work on another lathe or in another shop in the same enterprise.

No *general* provision in law was made for the compulsory transfer of workers or the direction of labour to other localities until the war*; according to the Codex of 1922, such transfers

* *See* p. 33.

require the consent of the worker[38]; and the abolition of the *NKT* (People's Commissariat of Labour) in 1933 removed the organisation through which such planned manpower allocation might have been effected.[39] But the system of Organised Recruitment, introduced in 1931, provided a lever for shifting unskilled labour from the country to the towns, and later from one area to another; subsequently skilled labour has also been recruited through this system (*see* p. 30).

The conditions in which the Labour Contract may be terminated by the enterprise (i.e. in which the worker may be sacked) are laid down in law. In addition to the cases where the worker may be dismissed for refusal of transfer (referred to above) there are eight legal grounds for dismissal:[40]

(1) 'whole or partial liquidation' of the enterprise (or establishment) or 'reduction of work' therein;
(2) 'hold-up of work' for more than one month 'for reasons of production';
(3) discovery of the worker's 'unfitness' for his job;
(4) 'systematic non-fulfilment' by the worker without good reason of duties imposed on him by contract or *Rules of Internal Labour Order*;
(5) commission by the worker of a criminal act directly connected with his work and confirmed by a court sentence, or his detention in custody for over two months;
(6) absenteeism without valid reason;
(7) absence from work for over two months because of temporary disability;
(8) restoration of a predecessor to his job according to established legal procedure.

A recent Soviet publication on labour law points out that 'Soviet labour legislation, which is called on to secure stable labour relations and guarantee the right to work, permits the dismissal of a worker by management only with the agreement of the factory and local trade union committee and on grounds stipulated by law'.[41] There are, however, exceptions to this general rule. These were clarified in September, 1965, by a decision of the Presidium of the USSR Supreme Soviet.[42] In addition to those holding jobs specified in a 1957 decree[43]* there are five other categories of workers and employees whom

* This includes managers and deputy managers of enterprises, administrations, warehouses, etc.; chief engineers, chief accountants and their deputies, chief designers, mechanics, electricians; shop and department heads of factories and enterprises.

managements may dismiss without the prior agreement of the trade union: those holding positions filled by competition and not re-engaged for a further term; those dismissed under the statutes on labour discipline if the statutes do not require consultation with the unions; those holding more than one job; those sentenced to terms of imprisonment or corrective labour or other punishment other than at their place of work. Frequent reports in the Soviet Press of the illegal dismissal of workers, however, make it clear that managements are prone to interpret some of the above legal provisions with considerable elasticity or simply to ignore them. In 1961 a case was reported of an exemplary worker dismissed for alleged unfitness for work, when in fact the manager had to find a job for a former department head.[44] There have been cases where a worker has been dismissed because of 'being on bad terms' with a fellow employee[45] and where a worker's dismissal has been a 'camouflaged form of removal from the staff of persons whom the management did not like'.[46] In 1960 alone members of the Kirgiz republican prosecutor's office appealed against some 300 cases of illegal dismissal.[47] In the previous year the People's Courts of Kuibyshev *oblast* examined 'hundreds' of cases of illegal dismissal. The *oblast's* public prosecutor held workers' ignorance of labour legislation, of the functions of Labour Disputes Commissions and of the rights of trade unions responsible for many of the cases being brought to court.[48] In 1960 in Moscow 49 per cent, and in 1961, 54 per cent of workers and employees who appealed against illegal dismissal were reinstated by the People's Courts.[49] In 1965 the courts in Leningrad reinstated 392 people[50] and those in the whole Soviet Union reversed more than half the decisions on dismissal.[51] In 1964 the courts in the Georgian and Uzbek Republics reinstated more than 70 per cent of those who appealed against wrongful dismissal, and in the Azerbaidzhan, Kirghiz, Tadzhik and Armenian Republics the courts reinstated more than 60 per cent of such people.[52] Trade unions are frequently not informed of dismissals or agree to them when they are illegal.[53] In January, 1965, the Presidium of the AUCCTU issued a resolution calling on trade union committees to exercise their rights more vigorously in this connection.[54]

Dismissal may also result from an 'expression of will' of organs not party to the Labour Contract. One instance of this type of dismissal is when a worker is called up for service in the Armed Forces, or volunteers himself.[55] Another is found in the provision of the 1922 Codex that a labour contract may be annulled at the demand of a trade union (at *raion* or higher level). A Soviet handbook on civil and labour law has explained that this gives trade union bodies the right 'to demand from the administration the dismissal of malicious disorganisers of production, violators of labour and State discipline, and persons damaging the interests of workers and employees'.[56] A further instance is the power of the State Trade Inspectorate, which is responsible for supervising the observance of trading rules, to demand the dismissal of workers in internal trade.[57]

In certain cases the dismissed worker has the right to two weeks' notice or to a discharge gratuity (*vykhodnoe posobie*) of two weeks' average wages instead of notice. If he is discharged on his refusal of work in another enterprise or another locality, or when a predecessor is restored to his job, or when he is called up for service in the Army, the management is obliged to pay him a gratuity of twelve working days' average wages; if the reason for his discharge is the closing down of the enterprise or staff reduction, or cessation of work for more than one month, or the discovery of his unfitness for the job, the management is legally bound to give him twelve working days' notice, or failing this, a gratuity of twelve working days' average wages. If, on the other hand, he is dismissed for systematic non-fulfilment of duties, for committing a criminal act connected with his work, for absence from work because of prolonged disability, or absenteeism without valid reason, or if he is dismissed by request of a trade union, or by sentence of a court, no gratuity is payable. Nor may a worker leaving a job of his own accord claim a gratuity.* [58]

INDUSTRIAL LABOUR SHORTAGE AND ORGANISED RECRUITMENT

Overt large-scale unemployment, which had been characteristic of the Soviet Union in the 'twenties, reaching a maximum official registered figure of 1,741,000 in April, 1929,[59] began to decline sharply after that date; the last official figure published was 240,000 on October 1, 1930.[60] Less than three weeks later the Central Committee of the Party declared:[61]

* On leaving jobs, *see* pp. 98–108.

'The enormous success of Socialist industrialisation of the country and the rapid tempo of collective and State farm construction have led to the total liquidation of unemployment in the Soviet Union.'

This swift transformation may partly be explained by the fact that on October 9 the *NKT* issued a decree by telegram 'suspending unemployment benefit payments'.[62] According to this decree, sickness attested by a medical certificate was the only excuse that would be accepted for refusing work, and people who declined work without such reasons were to be struck off the labour exchange registers.[63] This reduced their chances of getting new employment; from the point of view of the labour exchanges they ceased to exist, and the official register of unemployed was correspondingly reduced. The fact that some ten weeks later the *NKT* introduced two additional valid reasons for refusal of work—lack of dwelling space at the new place of work and separation from one's husband (in the case of married women)[64]—suggests that the decree proved impossible to enforce in its full severity.

These measures also reflected a real change in the supply of labour on the Soviet market, and it was a scarcity of certain forms of labour rather than a pool of unemployed which soon became the main problem of the Soviet authorities: in the words of a Marxist economist, there was a 'state of labour shortage that was to become increasingly acute from 1930 onwards'.[65] The main reason for this was doubtless the investment in heavy industry undertaken in the First Five-Year Plan. Productivity of labour, moreover, failed to rise as fast as the planners had anticipated,[66] and the process of expansion entailed a much larger increase of the labour force in industry than had been envisaged over the whole five years (1928–32) the total of wage and salary earners rose from 10,800,000 to 22,600,000,[67] an increase of more than double the 4,500,000 proposed in the Plan.[68] Most of these new recruits came from the countryside, some of them preferring to change to an urban life rather than be collectivised.[69] But the labour shortage in the cities was aggravated by a certain reflux of workers—notably those who had been accustomed to take seasonal industrial employment (*otkhodniki*)—back to their villages in the hope of 'saving the farm' and rejoining their families; according to *Trud*, the trade union newspaper, 'hordes of excited miners [ran] for home'[70] on hearing that their plots were being expropriated as *kulak* property.

The policy of forcing industrialisation as a necessary condition of the advance towards Socialism, clearly formulated at a Central Committee Plenum in 1926,[71] and enforced in the First Five-Year Plan, thus ran up against an unexpected obstacle. The planners were faced with the task of bringing the labour supply under control, and ensuring that industry got the men required for expansion. This involved a transformation of the Government organs concerned with labour. Already in 1930 the *NKT* had been castigated by the Central Committee for bureaucratism and for 'paying out tens of millions of roubles in relief 'for unemployment' while waging no struggle against self-seeking elements, floaters who refuse work, etc.'[72] The immediate result of this was the *NKT's* telegraphic decree of October 1, already quoted, in which, apart from stopping unemployment benefit, it instructed labour exchanges to 'take all steps necessary to send unemployed persons to work immediately', and ordered that the unemployed 'should be given jobs not only within their vocational qualifications but also other work requiring no special skills'.[73]

Since the list of acceptable excuses was severely limited, this amounted to a high degree of power to direct labour. The labour exchanges, which in the conditions of the 'twenties had given some semblance of reality to the existence of a free labour market and freedom of choice of employment, were now to be 'reorganised within 20 days for the purpose of the training and planned allocation of manpower'.[74] In the event, this proved impossible: the exchanges were quite unsuited to act as recruiting agencies, and soon ceased to exist.*

In fact, without going as far as overt industrial conscription, the Soviet Government adopted 'new forms of planned supply of manpower to enterprises',[77] which enabled it to put con-

* One Soviet version has it that the labour exchanges ceased to exist in 1928–9—some two years before unemployment was officially claimed to have come to an end.[75] This can be reconciled with the sources quoted above only by supposing that 1928–9 was the date when the labour exchanges lost their name and began to be known as 'labour organs'. It has not been possible to establish the exact date, but it must have been before 1933, when *NKT*, whose organs the labour exchanges were, was itself abolished. The 'Information Bureaux' which appeared in Moscow in 1935 discharged some of the functions of labour exchanges, but they seem to have had only a brief existence, and have not been heard of since that date.[76]

siderable pressure on rural workers to move into industry. The first step, in March, 1931, was to remove recruitment of workers on collective farms from the jurisdiction of the labour authorities, so that it could be 'integrated with the work of the economic organs'[78] (i.e. the enterprise, trusts, combines, etc., would negotiate directly on their own behalf). Next came a pronouncement by Stalin, on June 23, in which he noted that the spontaneous rural exodus that had supplied industry with its labour in previous years had dried up[79]:

> 'We must no longer count on a spontaneous influx of manpower [to industry]. This means that we must pass from the "policy" of waiting for the spontaneous influx to the policy of *organised* recruitment of workers for industry.'

What was needed, he said, was 'to recruit labour in an organised way'; the method was to be by 'concluding contracts with the collective farms'.[80] In September, 1931, plant managements were authorised to hire men 'directly without recourse to agencies of the labour administration'.[81]

Gradually a new system of 'Organised Recruitment' (*organizovanny nabor rabochikh*, or *orgnabor*)—which survives to this day—was given legislative basis. Already in March, 1930, collective farms had been obliged to free labourers for seasonal industrial work in numbers to be determined by State planning agencies; the selection of the men to fill the quotas was left to the collective farm managements, and they were obliged to go if ordered.[82] A year later Stalin's speech prompted a new decree 'On Migration' (*Ob otkhodnichestve*), dated June 30, 1931. By this enactment *kolkhozniki* who left the farms to work in industry were afforded a number of guarantees, notably re-employment on their return, work for their families while they were away, and no loss of status *vis-à-vis* the other farm members.[83] Collective farms releasing members for industrial employment were to receive from the 'economic organs' 'special means of increasing production, corresponding to the number of members withdrawn from the farm'.[84] Other Government agencies were also to give priority to such farms, for instance in allocating agricultural supplies, in school building and social institutions.[85]

To qualify for the guarantees laid down in the decree, peasants had either to go 'by agreement with the appropriate economic organs' or to 'present a certificate from the economic organ about their work'.[86] The decree does not make it clear whether the 'agreements' were to be made with the individual peasant or directly between the economic organ and the collective farm without the participation of the peasants concerned. But the latter method accords most nearly with Stalin's words on the subject, and seems to be the principle behind the instructions issued in March, 1930. The Fourth Five-Year Plan used the phrase 'contracts between economic organisations and collective farms and collective farmers'[87]—a form of words found in a 1956 monograph on Organised Recruitment with reference to the early 'thirties.[88] Subsequent events suggest that it was the agreement with the farm, rather than with the *kolkhoznik*, which really counted. Although the official position was that contracts should be concluded on a voluntary basis, some industrial managers tended to expect ' "delivery" of manpower from the collective farms'.[89] By August, 1931, it had become necessary to issue a further decree to ensure that besides the agreement between the recruiting body and the collective farm there must also be an individual labour contract signed by the peasant himself.[90] It may be thought, nevertheless, that if the peasant could be persuaded to leave the farm, he could be persuaded to sign a contract, particularly since the recruiting agents were not over-scrupulous in making promises of housing, specialised employment, etc., to attract the *kolkhozniki*.[91]

During the next few years policy oscillated between discouraging and encouraging migration other than that covered by agreements between economic organs and farm managements. In March, 1933, the decree On Migration was repealed and replaced by another, which apparently represented the interests of collective farms, which found themselves stripped of their labour force by peasants moving into industry and then claiming the privileges of farm members. According to the new law *only* those peasants who migrated on the basis of a special contract registered with the farm management could enjoy *kolkhoznik's* privileges for themselves and their families; moreover, peasants who departed 'wilfully' without a contract were now to be expelled from the collective farm.[92] But by April, 1938, 'in spite of frequent warnings from the *SovNarKom* and the Central Committee [of the Party]' there had been many instances of unfounded expulsion of *kolkhozniki* from collective farms, chiefly because members of their families had left to work in State enterprises, and a new decree was issued to curb such excesses.[93] The relaxation in the great purges, just beginning at this time, can be seen reflected in the decree: its first directive was that 'purges in collective farms on any pretext should be forbidden'.[94] The second point was that expulsions on the grounds that one member of the family had gone off to work permanently or temporarily in State enterprises should cease. Chairmen and members of the collective farm boards who allowed such practices were to be treated as criminal offenders.[95]

These legislative *volte-faces* were manifestations of a lack of organisation inherent in the system from its inception. Although it was termed 'Organised Recruitment', it was organised only in comparison with the relatively free play of the labour market that had preceded it. It operated without reference to the general planning mechanism: the initiative was left to the local economic bodies—trusts, enterprises and so forth—to enter into negotiations with the collective farms. Only in the first few years had there been, at least on paper, a degree of co-ordination by the organs of the *NKT*, which were to 'assign recruitment districts to the economic organs';[96] but the *NKT* was abolished in 1933 in view of the fact that a 'number of its functions (regulation of the labour market and distribution of manpower) had disappeared';[97] and no other central regulating body took its place in this function. As a result, by 1938 the *SovNarKom* noted that there was 'disorganisation' in the recruitment of manpower from the collective farms: recruitment orders were compiled on the basis of obsolete data, and issued to farms where there was a labour shortage, but not to those where there was a surplus; further, owing to bad organisation by the People's Commissariats, there were 'numerous instances where dozens or often hundreds of representatives of economic organisations were sent to one and the same *raion* [district] or one and the same *oblast* [province] to recruit workers'.[98] Competition between various organisations produced a situation in which a worker could be given the cash advance to which he was entitled, first by one and then by another organisation which hoped to entice him from the first; and *oblast* executive committees were inclined to favour the interests of loal industry at the expense of All-Union industry.[99]

All this pointed to the need for tighter central control. Accordingly, 'groups for planning the recruitment of workers' were set up, attached to the local *Gosplan* (State Planning) organs of some five autonomous republics and 32 *oblasts*, where the greatest number of migrant workers were to be found: similar groups were set up in the Summary Plant Sections of the USSR, RSFSR, Ukrainian and Belorussian *Gosplans*.[100] For the operational control (as opposed to planning) of recruitment a hierarchy of 'Commissions for Organised Recruitment' was established in the USSR *SovNarKom's* Economic Council, in the RSFSR, Ukrainian and Belorussian *SovNarKoms*, and in subsidiary Government bodies in the areas concerned.[101]

At the same time conditions of recruitment were laid down. It was to take place 'by the conclusion of agreements';[102] travel allowance was to be paid, and also an advance of wages of 100 roubles (half on leaving and half on arrival; both travel allowance and advance were increased in the case of recruitment for work in the Far Eastern *krai* [territory]). Recruited workers were to be sent off in groups, for which it was made obligatory to select 'politically screened and reliable workers as escorts'.[103] Provision was also made for the reception of the recruits, including 'mass political and explanatory work among [them] about the significance of the building site (enterprise) and their future work, the rules of internal order, safety regulations and Stakhanovite methods of work. . .'.[104]

Broadly similar features of organisation and practical arrangements have survived both the war and a subsequent interlude during which organised recruitment was run by the Ministry of State Labour Reserves.[105] When the system was again reconstructed in 1953 its new forms were very similar to those laid down in 1938. In about 1957 Chief Administrations for Organised Recruitment of Labour attached to Councils of Ministers of union republics became Chief Administrations for the Resettlement and Organised Recruitment of Labour, and resettlement of workers in the developing eastern regions of the country appeared to become one of their prime concerns. Each Chief Administration has subordinate Departments (formerly Administrations) attached to Soviet Executive Committees in the larger administrative areas (*oblasts, krais* and autonomous republics) and there is a system of representatives and inspectors (formerly sections) in *raions*. The 'planned guidance' of organised recruitment, for which the State Economic Commission was responsible until its abolition in 1957, now presumably devolves upon USSR and republican *Gosplan*, though republican Councils of Ministers appear to be responsible for approving plans for organised recruitment, which are implemented by the Chief Administrations.[106]

Although Soviet sources insist that Organised Recruitment is not a form of direction of labour, but is carried out 'on strictly voluntary principles',[107] the indications are that a good deal of pressure is involved. Some of these indications have already been mentioned in connection with contracts between economic organisations and collective farms. Others stem from the position of Organised Recruitment as part of the planning system. Organised Recruitment is described as 'one of the methods of planned distribution of manpower'.[108] And although 'planning must rest on the creative initiative of the masses',[109] nevertheless the 'plans for the distribution of manpower are normative acts, and have obligatory force for the organs which carry them out'.[110] Moreover, the plans' 'obligatory nature is guaranteed by State coercion . . .'.[111]

More specifically:[112]

> 'The State Economic Commission of the USSR [now presumably replaced in this function by USSR *Gosplan*] compiles operational plans for the direction of workers from one Union Republic to another. . . . The operational plans . . . are acts of government, which the Chief Administrations (Administrations) for Organised Recruitment of Workers . . . are bound to execute. . . . The local Section for Organised Recruitment of Workers is obliged to carry out the recruitment on the scale established by the Plan.'

In the February 11, 1965, issue of *Komsomolskaya Pravda* the public prosecutor of Orenburg *oblast* said that unsupervised *orgnabor* representatives recruited labour in the smaller towns of central Russia by giving a totally false impression of conditions in developing regions. Their recruiting drive included fixing job advertisements on every telegraph pole, writing articles for newspapers, making announcements over local radio stations and visiting factories. The 'undiscriminating and credulous man' thus recruited would find that the town to which he had moved was merely 'a dot on the map, people living in tents and barracks'.

A remark by Shelepin, then leader of the *Komsomol*, at the XX Party Congress, gives some more definition to the phrase 'planned distribution of manpower'. 'Many heads of enterprises', he said with reference to Organised Recruitment, 'avoid responsibility for the selection of cadres . . . *because they know in advance that they will be sent as many workers as they ask for.*'[113]

The scale on which Organised Recruitment has been applied in the USSR has varied at different times. During the First Five-Year Plan Organised Recruitment 'played an important part in supplementing the working class with new cadres'[114] and in the Second and Third Plans accounted for more than half of all the new workers industry.[115] From 1940, when the system of State Labour Reserves was introduced, less was heard of Organised Recruitment for some years, though it continued to exist beside the new system.[116] The Fourth Five-Year Plan (1946) called for its 'resumption' so as to attract labour from the countryside into industry, transport and building.[117] At the same time the net was cast wider than before: now not only *kolkhozniki* were recruited, but also the 'non-working town population'[118]—that is to say, 'persons released from certain branches of the national economy . . . , persons engaged in household work, demobilised from the ranks of the Soviet Army' and so forth.[119] The increased pressure on the agricultural labour market reduced the scope of Organised Recruitment in the countryside,[120] and it was not mentioned in the Fifth Five-Year Plan. Subsequently it reappeared, particularly to recruit men from the urban population for work in the North, the Urals, Siberia and the Far East,[121] a task in which it was expected to play an important part in the Sixth Five-Year Plan.[122] A suggestion at the XX Party Congress,[123] that the time had come to abolish the system of Organised Recruitment, was soon dealt with by Khrushchev. 'How are we to get people for the new construction sites?' he asked a meeting of the *Komsomol* and youth of Moscow. He answered his own question: 'This problem is solved by the Organised Recruitment of labour.'[124]

Since its inception in the early 'thirties, therefore, the rôle of Organised Recruitment has been radically changed. Instead of shifting manpower from the countryside into the towns, it now chiefly pumps the town surplus off to the new 'frontier' areas beyond the Urals and in the North. Its functions have been defined as the re-location of labour on an industrial and territorial basis as a result of changes in technology and the location of industry, and the recruitment into the State labour system of self-employed persons and young people previously unemployed.[125]

Organised Recruitment appears to be no longer exclusively concerned with providing an untrained labour force, as Press advertisements indicate,[126] though the provision of fresh supplies of trained labour remains primarily the concern of the vast training system known as the State Labour Reserves. At the same time there have been indications that the system of Organised Recruitment may be discontinued. As long ago as 1961 a Soviet authority stated that 'it has now outlived its usefulness', and revealed that in 1959 and 1960 the number of persons recruited for the RSFSR *oblasts* through this system declined by 75 per cent.[127] More recently *orgnabor*, together with other labour recruitment agencies, has been criticised as 'ineffective'[128] and likened more to a travel bureau than an organised recruitment organ.[129] Since Khrushchev's fall from power the proposal has been widely canvassed that all labour recruitment should be combined in a single, new central organisation.*[130]

THE SPECIAL POSITION OF THE SKILLED WORKER

Besides the State Labour Reserves, whose main purpose has been to ensure a steady supply of young trained labour into those parts of the economy where it is most needed and a system of directing young managerial and technical specialists for three years after their graduation, there have at various times been other methods whereby the State has distributed skilled labour in accordance with its aims—specifically to serve the needs of the Plans. In 1930, for instance, when the First Five-Year Plan was beginning to make extraordinary demands on skilled labour, the NKT was given the right,[131]

> 'in agreement with trade unions and on the application of business institutions, to remove and transfer skilled labour and specialists from less important branches of the economy to the more essential, and from one district to another. . . .'

The disappearance of the *NKT* in 1933 left a gap which was not filled until the approach of war in 1940, and during the intervening years there was no agency competent to direct skilled labour. In October, 1940, however, People's Commissariats were authorised to order the transfer of 'engineers, constructors, technicians, foremen, draughtsmen, economists,

* *See* section on The Right to Work: pp. 34f.

workers in accountancy, finance and planning, and also qualified workers of the sixth and higher grades',[132] as a measure of compulsion without the consent of the worker concerned; nor was there any question of reference to the trade unions. The main consolations for the uprooted worker were that if he were sent to another district he was paid expenses plus a lump sum equal to one month's wages, and that one year was added to his period of service for pension.[133] The validity of the decree was subsequently extended to various categories of workers not covered by its original wording.[134]

A curious feature of this legislation was that it did not make clear whether People's Commissariats could move workers only within their own spheres of jurisdiction, or whether they could cede or trade them to other Commissariats. On general grounds, the latter seems the more probable, and, if this is so, the co-ordinating body (apart from the *SovNarKom* itself) was presumably the *SovNarKom's* Committee for the Accounting and Distribution of the Labour Force, which also dealt with Labour Mobilisation during the war.[135]

This decree, with most of the other labour legislation passed just before or during the war, was repealed in April, 1956[136]; according to one 1954 authority, it had been 'scarcely applied' since the war.[137] Emphasis is now laid rather on the 'series of substantial privileges and advantages in the sphere of labour conditions' which the Government establishes to attract labour into the most important branches of the economy.[138] Khrushchev stated that skilled workers 'must have definite privileges, they must have priority in getting accommodation'.[139] Wage policy, too, is naturally brought into play so as to shift labour, skilled and unskilled alike, where it is most needed.

According to figures quoted in 1966 for average *nominal* wages per head of population in the economic regions of the RSFSR, for instance, the Far East led all others by 35 per cent, followed by Eastern Siberia, the North-West, the Urals and Western Siberia. Figures for 1962 put actual average income per head of population in the Far East 20 per cent above that for the Central Region and 44 per cent higher than in the North Caucasus.[140] However, these higher money incomes were largely cancelled out by a higher cost of living. In Western Siberia, for instance, the cost of living is nine per cent higher than in central Russia and 20 per cent higher than in the North Caucasus. In Eastern Siberia the corresponding figures are 20 and 31 per cent and in the Far East 28 and 41 per cent.* [141] Under a 1960 decree[142] bonuses may be up to 80 per cent, and in other remote areas 50 per cent, of basic wages (reductions on previous upper limits). This decree was attacked in the USSR Supreme Soviet in October, 1965, by a deputy from Magadan, as resulting from 'unjustified haste' on the part of the State Committee for Labour and Wages.[143] It was also obliquely criticised at about the same time by the First Party Secretary of the Primorsky *Krai*[144] and more recently by a leading Soviet economist.[145] The whole question of bonuses for work in the Far North and other remote regions is apparently under review,[146] but to date no modifications of existing legislation have been introduced.

LABOUR SERVICE AND MOBILISATION

Besides the measures outlined above, exceptional powers to direct labour may be granted for certain purposes or under certain conditions. Among these is the power of conscription for Labour Service (*trudovaya povinnost*). Introduced during the period of War Communism (1918–21), when it was very widely used,[147] Labour Service found its way in a more limited form on to the Labour Codex of 1922, by which it has been regulated ever since, with amendments from time to time as occasion demanded. The relevant article of the Codex reads:[148]

> 'In exceptional cases (struggle against natural disasters, insufficiency of labour power for the execution of very important State tasks) all citizens of the RSFSR, with certain specified exceptions, may be put to work under Labour Service. . . .'

Additional paragraphs name some of the tasks for which Labour Service has been used in the past:[149]

> 'Earthquakes, catastrophes, train wrecks, fires, floods, epidemics, clearing snow and ice from railways, struggle against mass attacks

* The high cost of living in Siberia and the Far East, coupled with inadequate housing and other facilities (and the desire of some people to make money out of resettlement grants), has led to a high rate of re-migration from these areas to European ones. From 1959 to 1963, for instance, there was a net loss of 230,000 people from Western Siberia (*Literaturnaya Gazeta*, September 4, 1965). In Siberia and the Far East, labour turnover is two to two-and-a-half times higher than in European areas (E. S. Lazutkin, *Voprosy Filosofii*, 1966, No. 3).

of pests—locusts, beasts of prey—. . . logging, timber rafting . . . getting the grain harvest to the railway stations . . . attacks by wolves . . . help with the sowing [in 1930] . . . improving the roads.'

The main categories of persons exempt from Labour Service are young people under 18, men over 45, women over 40, those suffering from a disability or disease which prevents them from working, women during periods of eight weeks before and after confinement, nursing mothers, disabled ex-servicemen and ex-workers, and women with children of less than eight years old who have nobody to look after them.[150] Conscript labour must be paid, 'except in cases where all the citizens taking part have an interest in forestalling or removing a natural disaster . . . '[151]—a provision which plainly permits of elastic interpretation; and in one instance—logging and timber-rafting—it was explicitly stated that '*kulak* elements' labour' should be paid at a lower rate.[152] Evading Labour Service during time of war is punishable under Article 82 of the RSFSR Criminal Codex by from 5 to 10 years' deprivation of freedom or the death penalty.

During the war the principle of Labour Service was much extended and generalised in the form of Labour Mobilisation. Mobilisation for work in production and construction was permitted in February, 1942, 'for the duration of the war' and covered men aged 16 to 55 and women of 16 to 50; students, young people liable to be called up into the State Labour Reserves, and women with young children were the only classes exempted. Responsibility for these operations was given to the USSR *SovNarKom's* Committee on the Accounting and Distribution of the Labour Force. As a general rule, mobilisation was for work within the district of residence, but, 'in particular cases', the State Committee for Defence could draft labour to other areas.

Shortly afterwards, in April, 1942, similar provisions were made for mobilisation for work in collective farms, State farms and machine tractor stations (MTSs): only here the minimum age was 14 and certain classes of students and schoolchildren were liable, and employees in the governmental and public services (who had been exempt, with those already employed in industry and transportation, from the draft for production and construction) were specifically required to be called up so far as possible without disrupting the services.[153]

Seasonal mobilisation of town population for harvest work, an example of which occurred in July, 1962, when it was decided to send 11,500 town workers and 4,000 technical school students of Alma-Ata *oblast* to help with the harvest,[154] appears to have been the only use made of this legislation since the war. Collections of Labour Laws published in 1956 and 1961 omit all reference to Labour Service, although it is included in an encyclopaedic dictionary on labour law published in 1963.[155]

THE RIGHT TO WORK: UNEMPLOYMENT TODAY

The first Soviet (RSFSR) Constitution of 1918 enunciated only the Pauline[156] principle, 'He who does not work, neither shall he eat',[157] which has been retained in Article 12 of the USSR Constitution of 1936. In the first RSFSR Labour Codex of 1918 there was a mention of the 'right of all able-bodied citizens to put their labour to use'; but this has since been dismissed in Soviet legal thought as no more than a 'programmatic proposition' or 'slogan'[158] in the conditions of the time. In the 1936 Constitution, however, which is taken much more seriously, Article 118 declares:[159]

> 'Citizens of the USSR have the right to work, that is, the right to guaranteed employment. . . . The right to work is ensured by the Socialist organisation of the national economy, the steady growth of productive forces of Soviet society, the elimination of the possibility of economic crises, and the abolition of unemployment.'

Although the quick tempo of industrial expansion has so far provided a steady demand for labour in the Soviet Union, there are a number of points which suggest that, although large-scale unemployment has not been in evidence, forms of 'partial', 'concealed', or 'frictional' unemployment, together with frequent periods of idle-standing in factories, have all played their part in the life of the Soviet working man.

The Soviet worker may find himself unemployed if he has been dismissed for redundancy or because the plant at which he works has had to shut down for more than one month. The salient fact in such a case is that he can, since 1930, expect no unemployment relief payments: when chronic large-scale unemployment disappeared in the USSR, *all* unemployment relief was abolished, no allowance being made for temporary unemployment as a result of economic development. The dismissed worker is entitled to no more than two weeks' wages *or* two weeks' notice. Managements are obliged to inform the Trade Union Committee 'in good time' of their intention to reduce staff; and the worker, if he so wishes, must be given some 'other sort of work', *if there is any*, in the same enterprise or in another enterprise in the same trust and in the same area.[160] The list of vacancies to be filled by the dismissed workers is established by the management 'in agreement with the local Trade Union Committee'[161]—a provision the full weakness of which is appreciated only when it is understood how ready trade unions have been to yield to managements.

Until recently, however, the existence of this type of unemployment was not officially recognised. In the words of one authority, writing in the late 'forties and early 'fifties:[162]

> 'In the USSR, where unemployment has been abolished fully and for ever, and Socialist enterprises, continually expanding the scope of their production, are always feeling the need for new cadres, the dismissal of workers by the management . . . can occur only in rare cases, and amounts essentially to the worker's transfer to work in another enterprise or establishment.'

The post-Khrushchev period has been characterised by more public realism and frankness about economic and social problems. The existence of unemployment is now more freely admitted, though some Soviet writers still cling to the outworn maxim that 'the Socialist system has completely excluded unemployment from the life of society'.* [163] Shortly after Khrushchev's removal *Trud*[164] admitted that 'in certain regions of the country, particularly in small towns, surpluses of labour have appeared'. This theme was later taken up in many articles in the Soviet Press.[165] At a Plenum of the CPSU Central Committee[166] in September, 1965, Kosygin, Chairman of the USSR Council of Ministers, referred euphemistically to 'considerable reserves of labour in small towns, especially in western regions of the Ukraine, Belorussia, a number of areas in the Transcaucasus and also in certain central regions of the RSFSR'.† He blamed the over-concentration of industry in large towns, and called upon *Gosplan* to study regional labour resources in order to promote a more rational allocation of industrial de-

* Soviet external propaganda still claims that there is no unemployment in the USSR (e.g. *USSR Questions and Answers, Novosti* Press Agency, 1965, p. 146).

† There is also evidence of unemployment in Uzbekistan, Moldavia, Kazakhstan, Lithuania and the Far North.

velopment. The acute need for this is borne out by the fact that in Pskov *oblast* in 1966 there were 26,500 unemployed.[167] A leading Soviet economist has stated[168] that because of the inadequate development of industry in many medium and small towns many workers have to engage in private farming or home work. In an attempt to alleviate this situation the USSR Council of Ministers in October, 1966, issued a decree on the development of local industry and handicrafts. This was intended to 'further the attraction into social production of the able-bodied population engaged in private and domestic work, particularly in small towns and workers' settlements'.[169] But, according to the economist, even in Moscow and Leningrad the percentage of the able-bodied population not employed in the public sector is as high as six or seven. The figure for the whole Soviet Union was 20 per cent and for Siberia 26 per cent. The percentage in some towns was even higher. This may be partly accounted for by unemployment among women, now recognised as a serious problem in areas of heavy industry inadequately provided with light industry employing women.[170] But the same writer pointed out that even at the beginning of the Seven-Year Plan (1959) there were unused labour resources in Moscow, Leningrad, Odessa and other large towns, where this qualification would not apply to the same extent.

The Soviet authorities have also adopted a more realistic approach to social problems created by technical progress, particularly mechanisation and automation, and recognise the need for the redeployment of labour.[171] It has also been acknowledged that 'the placement of these workers is not always accomplished without suffering and does not always meet the needs of those released'.[172] An indication of the effect of unemployment on the individual worker was given by *Izvestiya* in October, 1965.[173] An inquiry among newly-engaged workers at four large factories in Gorky revealed that 15 per cent had been unemployed for up to three days; 33 per cent for three to 10 days; 15 per cent for up to 20 days; 16 per cent for up to 30 days; and 12 per cent for more than a month. A study conducted in Sverdlovsk[174] showed that workers who changed jobs of their own volition 'took no part in social production' for an average of 23 working days. Similarly, each of the workers made redundant by a Moscow transport undertaking in 1966 spent an average of more than a month looking for another job.[175] To remedy this situation, many Press articles, including one in the Party theoretical journal *Kommunist*,[176] suggested the creation of an organisation which would 'constantly be informed of requirements for workers and employees in the mass trades at all factories, enterprises and institutions . . . and which would send them those wanting employment'. One economist has even suggested paying dole to workers made redundant by technical progress.[177] (At present, unemployment may be compensated only when 'enforced absenteeism' is caused by unjust dismissal or by a worker being arrested on a criminal charge of which he is acquitted. Compensation in these cases is up to 20 days' pay[178] for the former and up to two months' pay[179] for the latter.)

The Soviet Government has not acted upon any of the many workable proposals to promote better deployment of labour and to ease the position of the redundant worker.* The virtual lack of labour exchanges may be expected to make itself more acutely felt as the economic reforms and the greater rights accorded to managements begin to take effect. Under the reforms, managements are encouraged to increase efficiency and productivity by shedding surplus labour. In October, 1966, the Moscow Public Prosecutor criticised managers who used their newly-granted independence to dismiss staff illegally. He reminded them that under the Criminal Code the penalty for such offences could be dismissal or up to a year's corrective labour.[180]

One form of unemployment, which had been prevalent in the 1920s, reappeared in the 1950s and continues to pose serious problems. In the absence of a youth employment service in the USSR the transition from the status of a schoolboy (even from a technical school) to that of worker was often a long one with a period of unemployment and frustration. In 1952, according to one report, 7,600 Labour Reserve School pupils had no jobs ready for them when they finished their training;

* In December, 1966, only two embryonic labour exchanges were known to be operating. One, in Gorky, developed from a district Soviet Commission for the Affairs of Minors (*Izvestiya*, October 7, 1965); the other, in Armenia, known as the republican Department for Employment, is officially stated to be the only organisation of its kind in the Soviet Union. It replaced the *orgnabor* department. Some 45–50 people are said to register in each of its 12 departments every day (*Komsomolskaya Pravda*, October 22, 1966).

in 1953 14,000 were in this position and in 1955 more than 18,000.[181] Legislation in 1956 introducing a shorter working week for the same pay for juveniles from 16 to 18[182] made them disadvantageous for managements to employ. As a result managements resorted to many expedients and frequently flouted the laws; sometimes the young worker was made to work the full adult working day,[183] sometimes his wages were reduced,[184] but more often—which was not strictly illegal—managements refused to take on young people, who had to be paid full wages for less work. Cases of juvenile unemployment were reported from widely scattered areas of the USSR.[185] It was largely the difficulties in employing school-leavers in production which prompted the 1958 educational reform, which made 'production training' an important part of school curricula. This laid down, *inter alia*, that the USSR and union republican Councils of Ministers were to draw up long-term and annual plans for vocational training and 'the placing in jobs of graduates from eight-year schools, professional-technical institutes and secondary vocational schools in order to establish a quota at factories for the employment of young people'. This appears to have had some effect but unemployment among school-leavers persists. Factory managers continue to employ young people under 18 only with reluctance, and some seek every opportunity to dismiss them.[186] In July, 1965, *Pravda* said in a leading article,[187] that in 1964 the plan for placing school-leavers and youths in jobs was fulfilled by only a third in Rostov *oblast*, and by less than half in Kursk *oblast*. In 1965, RSFSR planning organs had underestimated the number of jobs needed for young people by more than 100,000.[188]

The problem of finding jobs for increasingly better educated young people (a problem exacerbated in the mid-1960s by the steep rise in the birthrate immediately after the Second World War) was highlighted by the publication of the results of a study conducted among school-leavers in Novosibirsk.[189] The study found a great disparity between the training young people received at school and the jobs available. Only 11 per cent of those who left secondary schools in Novosibirsk *oblast* in 1963 went to jobs for which they had been trained at school. The rest had to be retrained for other jobs. 'Production training' had been organised on a haphazard basis, no regard being paid to the availability of jobs or to the pupil's job preferences. Therefore, school-leavers who wanted work for which they had been trained at school could not find it, and those who could find work for which they had been trained did not want it.

The CPSU Central Committee and the USSR Council of Ministers[190] issued a decree at the beginning of 1966 to provide a large increase in the number of places available to school-leavers in colleges of further education and to make special provision for the immediate employment of school-leavers. The decree was intended to counter the effects of the simultaneous release from the schools of an extra age group, following the Government's decision in the autumn of 1964 to cut the length of complete secondary education from 11 to 10 years.[191] In addition to raising the quota of school-leavers that managements were obliged to recruit, the decree established what amounts to a youth employment service. Article 14 of the decree recommended republican Party Central Committees and Governments to establish, within one month, commissions for arranging employment for young people in union and autonomous republics, *krais, oblasts*, towns and *raions*. These commissions are headed at republican level by a Deputy Chairman of the Council of Ministers, and at lower levels by a deputy chairman of the Soviet executive committee. The commissions include representatives of Party, trade union, Komsomol and economic organisations, and of the education authorities.

Insufficient time has elapsed to assess the success of these new bodies. But their establishment marks an important departure in Soviet labour policy. The formation of a large network of labour exchanges for adult workers—so strongly advocated in the Soviet Press—is, however, a politically much more sensitive issue which the Soviet Government has so far not seemed ready to consider.

SOURCES

N.B.—Undated citations of works of which more than one edition is listed in the bibliography refer to the most recent edition there listed; earlier editions are cited with the date in brackets.

1. *Sbornik, passim.*
2. *B.S.E.*, 1st edn., Vol. 33, col. 225.
3. *XX Sezd K.P.S.S.*, Vol. 1, p. 560.
4. *KZoT (1922)*, art. 27; cf. *Sbornik*, p. 69.
5. Aleksandrov, p. 145.
6. *Ibid.*, p. 146; cf. *Sbornik*, p. 69.

7. *Pravda*, January 26, 1961.
8. *KZoT*, art. 31, in *Sbornik*, p. 69; Aleksandrov, p. 151.
9. *Loc cit.*, *KZoT*, art. 135, in *Sbornik*, p. 403.
10. *Pravda*, December 14, 1956.
11. USSR Laws, 1936, 31: 276.
12. Aleksandrov, p. 155.
13. *Sbornik* (1956), p. 24.
14. *Sbornik*, p. 404.
15. *KZoT*, art. 38, in *Sbornik*, p. 70.
16. Aleksandrov, p. 157; *KZoT*, art. 39, in *Sbornik*, p. 70.
17. Aleksandrov, p. 157.
18. *Sbornik*, p. 462.
19. *Sbornik*, p. 404.
20. Aleksandrov, pp. 153f.
21. *Ibid.*, p. 154.
22. *Loc. cit.*
23. *Loc. cit.*
24. e.g. *Pravda*, May 15, 1965.
25. See Aleksandrov, pp. 149, 157.
26. *KZoT*, art. 34, in *Sbornik*, p. 70.
27. *Ibid.*
28. Aleksandrov, p. 149.
29. *Ibid.*, p. 155, Sbornik, p. 88.
30. Aleksandrov, p. 149.
31. *KZoT* (1922), art. 29; *B.S.E.*, 1st edn., Vol. 48, col. 284.
32. *Sbornik*, p. 97.
33. *KZoT*, art. 29, in *Sbornik*, p. 69.
34. *B.S.E.*, 2nd edn., Vol. 36, p. 100.
35. *KZot* (1922), art. 36.
36. USSR Laws, 1932, 59: 262; *KZoT*, art. 37^{1}, in *Sbornik*, p. 98. *Sbornik*, p. 100.
37. *Sbornik*, p. 99.
38. *KZoT* (1922), art. 37; cf. *Sbornik*, p. 102.
39. Schwarz, p. 118.
40. *KZoT*, art. 47, in *Sbornik*, p. 103.
41. *Trudovoe Pravo*, p. 506.
42. *Vedomosti Verkhovnogo Soveta SSSR*, 1965, No. 40.
43. *Ukaz Prezudiuma Verkhovnogo Soveta SSSR*, January 31, 1957, p. 460.
44. *Izvestiya*, March 10, 1961.
45. *Ibid.*
46. *Osnovnye Zakonnodatelnye Akty*, pp. 124, 129.
47. *Izvestiya*, March 10, 1961.
48. *Trud*, June 16, 1960.
49. *Trud*, January 30, 1962.
50. *Pravda*, September 16, 1966.
51. *Trud*, October 1, 1966.
52. *Pravda*, March 12, 1965.
53. *Trud*, January 30, 1962; *Pravda*, October 23, 1966.
54. *Trud*, January 26, 1965.
55. Aleksandrov, p. 188.
56. Yamenfeld, Pavlov and Dvinov, p. 274.
57. Aleksandrov, p. 189.
58. Yamenfeld, Pavlov and Dvinov, pp. 277–8.
59. M. Romanov, in *Voprosy Truda*, July-August, 1930, p. 46, quoted by Schwarz, p. 36.
60. *B.S.E.*, 1st edn., Vol. 47, col. 873.
61. *VKP (b) o Profsoyuzakh*, p. 563.
62. *Izvestiya*, October 11, 1930, quoted by Schwarz, p. 50, cf. Baykov, p. 213.
63. Schwarz, p. 50.
64. *Izvestiya*, December 29 and 30, 1930, quoted by Schwarz, p. 83.
65. Dobb, p. 240.
66. *Ibid.*, p. 239.

67. *Narodnoe Khozyaistvo SSSR v 1960 godu*, p. 633.
68. Schwarz, p. 23.
69. *Ibid.*, p. 16.
70. *Trud*, April 15, 1930, quoted by Schwarz, p. 17.
71. *K.P.S.S. v Rezolyutsiakh*, Vol. 11, pp. 258f.
72. *VKP (b) o Profsoyuzakh*, p. 553.
73. *Izvestiya*, October 11, 1930, quoted by Schwarz, p. 50.
74. *VKP (b) o Profsoyuzakh*, p. 50.
75. *M.S.E.*, 3rd edn., Vol. 1, col. 1038.
76. Schwarz, pp. 52f.
77. *B.S.E.*, 1st edn., Vol. on the USSR, col. 1124.
78. Schwarz, p. 55.
79. Stalin, *Problems of Leninism*, p. 461.
80. *Ibid.*, p. 462.
81. USSR Laws, 1931, 60: 385.
82. *Za Industrializatsiyu*, March 4, 1930, quoted by Schwarz, p. 53.
83. USSR Laws, 1931, 42: 286, art. 1–9.
84. *Ibid.*, art. 12.
85. *Ibid.*, art. 13–16.
86. *Ibid.*, art. 10.
87. *Five-Year Plan*, 1946–50, p. 55.
88. Andreyev and Gureyev, p. 13.
89. V. Revzina, in *Bolshevik*, 1931, No. 13, p. 34, quoted by Schwarz, p. 57.
90. *Izvestiya*, September 10, 1931, quoted by Schwarz, p. 56.
91. *See Za Industrializatsiyu*, April 15 and May 12, 1931; *Trud*, March 3, 1934; all quoted by Schwarz, pp. 58f; cf. also Hubbard, p. 145.
92. USSR Laws, 1933, 21: 116.
93. USSR Laws, 1938, 18: 115.
94. *Ibid.*, art. 1.
95. *Ibid.*, art. 2, 6.
96. Z. Mokhov in *Voprosy Truda*, August-September, 1932, p. 51, quoted by Schwarz, p. 56.
97. *B.S.E.*, 1st edn., Vol. 41, col. 221.
98. *Trudovoe Zakonodatelstvo SSSR*, p. 36.
99. *Loc. cit.*
100. *Loc. cit.* (art. 4).
101. *Loc. cit.* (art. 5).
102. *Ibid.*, p. 37 (art. 11 (a)).
103. *Loc. cit.* (art. 11 (d)).
104. *Loc. cit.*, f. (art. 11 (f)).
105. Andreyev and Gureyev, pp. 52, 102; cf. also *Gosudarstvennye Trudovye Rezervy*, pp. 334 ff.
106. *Byulleten Ispolnitelnogo Komiteta Moskovskogo Gorodskogo Soveta Deputatov Trudyashchikhsya*, 1959, No. 5.
107. B.S.E., 2nd edn., Vol. 31, p. 147; cf. Andreyev and Gureyev, p. 7.
108. Andreyev and Gureyev, p. 8.
109. *Ibid.*, p. 17.
110. *Ibid*., p. 4.
111. *Ibid.*, p. 34.
112. *Ibid.*, pp. 36f. 58.
113. *XX Sezd K.P.S.S.*, Vol. 1, p. 605 (our italics).
114. *B.S.E.*, 2nd edn., Vol. 35, p. 446.
115. *See loc. cit.*
116. *B.S.E.*, 2nd edn., Vol. 31, p. 147.

117. Five-Year Plan 1946–50; p. 55.
118. Andreyev and Gureyev, p. 14.
119. *Ibid.*, p .73.
120. *Ibid.*, p. 13.
121. Aleksandrov, pp. 159f.
122. Andreyev and Gureyev, p. 15.
123. *XX Sezd K.P.S.S.*, p. 605.
124. *Komsomolskaya Pravda*, June 7, 1956.
125. B. Miroshnichenko in *Planovoe Khozyaistvo*, 1960, No. 5, p. 81.
126. *Sovetskaya Moldaviya*, February 7, June 11, July 1, August 20, 1958, January 13, 1965; *Sovetskaya Latviya*, June 21, 1957.
127. V. Moskalenko, in *Ekonomicheskaya Gazeta*, February 7, 1961.
128. V. Nemchenko, in *Voprosy Ekonomiki*, 1965, No. 9.
129. *Sovetskaya Rossiya*, January, 11, 1966; *Komsomolskaya Pravda*, February 11, 1965.
130. e.g. V. Shubkin, in *Kommunist*, 1965, No. 3; Yagodkin and Maslova, and E. Manevich, in *Voprosy Ekonomiki*, 1965, No. 6; V. Nemchenko, in *Voprosy Ekonomiki*, 1965, No. 9; *Literaturnaya Gazeta*, September 4, 1965.
131. *VKP (b) o Profsoyuzakh*, pp. 563f.; cf. Baykov, pp. 213f.; Schwarz, pp. 115f.
132. *Vedomosti Verkhovnogo Soveta SSSR*, 1940, No. 42.
133. Aleksandrov and Moskalenko (1944), pp. 53f.
134. *Ibid.*, p. 54.
135. *Ibid.*, p. 46.
136. *Vedomosti Verkhovnogo Soveta SSSR*, 1956, No. 10:10.
137. Aleksandrov, p. 175.
138. A. Pasherstnik, in *Sotsialistichesky Trud*, 1956, No. 7, p. 5.
139. *Moscow Radio*, home service, March 14, 1961.
140. Milner and Gvozdov, in *Planovoe Khozyaistvo*, 1966, No. 4.
141. A. Gladyshev, in *Planovoe Khozyaistvo*, 1966, No. 10.
142. *Vedomosti Verkhovnogo Soveta*, 1960, No. 7.
143. *Zasedaniya Verkhovnogo Soveta SSSR, Shestogo Sozyva (Shestaya Sessiya), Stenografichesky Otchet*, pp. 160–1.
144. G. Chernyshev, in *Partiinaya Zhizn*, 1965, No. 19.
145. M. Sonin, in *Voprosy Ekonomiki*, 1966, No. 8.
146. *Zasedaniya Verkhovnogo Soveta SSSR, Shestogo Sozyva (Shestaya Sessiya), Stenografichesky Otchet*, p. 161; *Trud*, October 29, 1966.
147. Carr, pp. 208ff.
148. *KZoT* (1931), art. 11.
149. *Ibid.*, art. 11, secs. 2, 3, 4, 6, 9, 12.
150. *Ibid.*, arts. 12, 13.
151. *Ibid.*, art. 11, sec. 4.
152. *Ibid.*, art. 11, sec. 2.
153. *Sbornik Zakonov SSSR i Ukazov Presidiuma Verkhovnogo Soveta SSSR 1938–44*, pp. 148f; Aleksandrov and Moskalenko (1944), pp. 46ff.
154. *Izvestiya*, July 17, 1962.

155. *Trudovoe Pravo*, p. 490.
156. II Thessalonians, Ch. 3, v. 10.
157. RSFSR Laws, 1918, 51; 582, art. 18.
158. Pasherstnik, p. 6; Aleksandrov (1949), pp. 87f.
159. *Constitution (Fundamental Law) of the Union of Soviet Socialist Republics*, art. 118.
160. *Postanovlenie NKT RSFSR*, of February 6, 1928, arts. 1, 4, in *Sbornik*, p. 107.
161. *Loc. cit.*
162. Aleksandrov, p. 175.
163. e.g. V. Nemchenko, in *Voprosy Ekonomiki*, 1965, No. 9.
164. November 3, 1964.
165. e.g. V. Shubkin, in *Voprosy Filosofii*, 1965, No. 5, and in *Kommunist*, 1965, No. 3; M. Sonin, in *Voprosy Ekonomiki*, 1966, No. 8; *Pravda Vostoka*, September 22, 1965; *Sovetskaya Moldaviya*, October 20, 1965.
166. *Pravda*, September 28, 1965.
167. Yu. Chernichenko, in *Novy Mir*, 1966, No. 8.
168. E. Manevich, in *Voprosy Ekonomiki*, 1965, No. 6.
169. *Trud*, October 9, 1966.
170. E. Manevich, in *Voprosy Ekonomiki*, 1965, No. 6.
171. e.g. *Trud*, August 12, 1965; Yagodkin and Maslova, in *Voprosy Eknomiki*, 1965, No. 6.
172. *Trud*, August 12, 1965.
173. October 6, 1965.
174. *Yagodkin*, p. 16.
175. *Literaturnaya Gazeta*, September 22, 1966.
176. V. Shubkin, in *Kommunist*, 1965, No. 3.
177. E. Manevich, in *Voprosy Ekonomiki*, 1965, No. 6.
178. *O meropriyatiyakh po uporyadocheniyu trudovoy distsipliny . . .*, in *Sbornik*, p. 462.
179. *Postanovlenie Plenuma Verkhovnogo Suda SSSR*, September 13, 1957, in *Sbornik*, pp. 463ff.
180. *Pravda*, October 23, 1966.
181. K. Devetyarov, in *Komsomolskaya Pravda*, December 2, 1956.
182. *Sbornik*, p. 418.
183. *See Sovetskaya Kirgiziya*, March 22, 1957.
184. *See* D. Shakirzyanova, in *Molodoy Kommunist*, 1956, No. 11, p. 40.
185. *See Komsomolskaya Pravda*, August 25, 1956; *Trud*, October 7 and November 16, 1956; *Literaturnaya Gazeta*, November 20, 1956; *Uchitelskaya Gazeta*, January 5, 1957; cf. also D. Goryunov, in *Sovetskaya Pechat*, 1957, No. 2, p. 10.
186. *Sovetskaya Rossiya*, October 14, 1965.
187. *Pravda*, July 23, 1965.
188. *Ibid.*
189. *Voprosy Filosofii*, 1965, No. 5.
190. *Pravda*, February 6, 1966.
191. *Pravda*, August 13, 1964.

II
Wages and Norms

THE END OF EGALITARIANISM

In wages policy, as in other things, the end of the decade of the 'twenties marked a turning-point for Soviet Russia: for it was then that the egalitarian tendencies in Soviet economic thinking were finally given their official quietus. Lenin's declaration of April, 1917, that the pay of any official 'must not exceed that of a competent workman',[1] had found expression in legislation immediately after the Revolution: one of the first decisions of the new revolutionary authorities in November, 1917, limited the pay of members of the Soviet of Workers' and Soldiers' Deputies, and of all Party members holding responsible positions, to 400 roubles a month, and the same principle, with a ceiling of 500 roubles (plus 100 roubles for each dependant), was very soon extended to *all* high-ranking employees.[2] But compromise with the realities of economic motive began almost at once, since the few available technical and administrative staff in Russia at the time demanded, and were in a position to exact, relatively high salaries from the new régime. It was this initial differentiation which Lenin described in April, 1918, as[3]

'a retreat from the principles of the Paris Commune . . . [and] a step backward on the part of our Socialist Soviet Government, which from the very outset has proclaimed and pursued the policy of reducing high salaries to the earnings of the average worker.'

By the autumn of 1918 the salaries of the highest grade of specialists had been allowed to rise to more than double that of the highest grade of workers—and therefore to much more than double the wages of the lowest grade of workers.[4] Nevertheless early legislation attempted at least to limit the gap between high and low wages: in a wage scale approved by the Second Trade Union Congress in January, 1919, the highest grade of workers and the highest grade of employees were each given a rate only 1¾ times the lowest grade of each group.[5]

Nevertheless, the dichotomy between principles and practice was unresolved, and indeed continued to widen. The IX Party Conference in September, 1920, explained apologetically that the difficulties that beset the new régime in its first years had made inevitable the 'singling out of "shock" (and in fact privileged) departments and groups of workers', but urged the whole Party 'again and again to struggle to achieve greater equality'.[6] The X Party Congress in March, 1921, at which Lenin introduced the New Economic Policy, resolved that, although 'for a number of reasons' differentiation of wages according to qualification 'must be temporarily retained', policy must nevertheless be based on the 'greatest possible equalisation of wages'.[7] Two months later the IV Trade Union Congress gave instructions for the preparation of a new unified wage system of 17 grades to cover administrators and technicians as well as workers and employees. According to this scale, which survived until 1926, the wage of a highly skilled worker was 3½ times that of the lowest category, and the highest salary 8 times.[8]

The Party line in 1926 was still for the relative equalisation of wage rates: a Party conference that year approved a decision of the Central Committee to raise the wages of the lowest paid workers 'as a further step towards overcoming the abnormal difference in the pay of different categories of workers'.[9] At this point, however, the trade unions, instead of quietly shelving principles as in the past, and getting down to a practical wage policy, attempted to act on the Party's egalitarian hints. Foreign well-wishers, said Tomsky (speaking for the All-Union Central Council of Trade Unions [AUCCTU]), had been shocked that the 'difference between the pay of qualified and unqualified labour is of a colossal magnitude which does not exist in Western Europe'.[10]

Differentials were therefore narrowed: owing to a simultaneous reform in the system of wage-scales, comparisons with the previous scale are risky, but it may be noted, as an instance, that the top grade manual workers were now to be paid only three times as much as the bottom grade.[11] Soon after the reform, morever, the proportion of supplements, bonuses, etc., to basic wages in the workers' earnings was substantially reduced, and the proportion of piece-work in the total industrial work performed also fell sharply.[12] Both these facts, strongly suggest a reduction of factors tending to make for differentiation of earnings; and although many other elements, such as different scales in different industries, piece-work, bonuses, payment of some categories of employees outside the scales altogether, etc., complicate the picture, the general trend is clear. The reversal of policy and principle portended by Stalin's speech to the conference of business executives in June, 1931, is the more striking in that the period immediately before it was one in which a serious attempt had been made to approach Lenin's proclaimed egalitarian ideal.

The change of policy which Stalin proclaimed was forced upon the régime, as the earlier compromises had been, primarily by lack of skills in the labour force. Industry, relying for its recruitment on the 'spontaneous flow' of labour from the countryside, was finding it impossible to keep the men at their jobs when they got them: without an industrial tradition, unused to the constraints of an urban existence,[13] possibly even imbued with something of the 'vagrant instincts of the Russian people',[14] the new industrial worker, finding bad conditions and little help from his trade union, was very ready to move elsewhere in the hope of improving his position. Stalin, however, asking, 'What is the cause of the heavy turnover of labour-power?' answered with characteristic over-simplification:[15]

> 'The cause is the wrong structure of wages, the wrong scales, the 'Leftist' practice of wage equalisation. . . . The consequence of wage equalisation is that the unskilled worker lacks the incentive to become a skilled worker and is thus deprived of the prospect of advancement; as a result he feels himself a "visitor" in the factory, working only temporarily so as to "earn a little" and then go off to "seek his fortune" elsewhere. . . . The skilled worker is obliged to wander from factory to factory until he finds one where his skill is properly appreciated.'

The remedy, according to Stalin,* was to:[16]

> 'abolish wage equalisation . . . [and to] draw up wage scales that will take into account the difference between skilled and unskilled labour, between heavy and light work. We cannot tolerate a situation where a rolling-mill hand in a steel mill earns no more than a sweeper.'

But what gave Stalin's pronouncement special weight, and ensured that his new policy would be enforced with the full

* Other remedies of a harsher and more disciplinary nature are described on pp. 97–106.

driving power of the Party, was his enshrinement of wage differentiation in Marxist dogma:[17]

> 'Marx and Lenin said that the difference between skilled and unskilled labour would exist even under Socialism, even after classes had been abolished; that only under Communism would this difference disappear and that consequently . . . under Socialism "wages" must be paid according to work performed and not according to needs.'

Departure from this was nothing less than heresy. 'It follows', Stalin went on, 'that whoever draws up wage scales on the "principle" of wage equalisation . . . breaks with Marxism, breaks with Leninism.'[18] Six months later he put the point ever more forcibly to Emil Ludwig, who had rashly suggested that equalisation was a Socialist ideal:[19]

> 'Equalitarianism [said Stalin] has nothing in common with Marxist Socialism. Only people who are unacquainted with Marxism can have the primitive notion that the Russian Bolsheviks want to pool all wealth and then share it out equally. That is the notion of people who have nothing in common with Marxism.'

Stalin's justification of wage differentials in the name of Marx and Lenin is broadly the same as that prevailing today. In the words of a popular handbook on industrial wages:[20]

> 'The distribution of the basic mass of material and spiritual benefits intended for the personal consumption of the working people is carried out under Socialism in accordance with the economic law of distribution according to labour, its quantity and quality. At the lowest phase of Communism this objective need is determined by the still inadequate level of development of productive forces which do not yet provide the abundance of material benefits required for distribution according to need, and also by the fact that labour has not yet become the first necessity of life of members of society.'

Since the early 'thirties, in fact, a high degree of differentiation of material and social reward, according to skill, output, and various other indices, has been the rule in Soviet society. The various methods by which this differentiation has been applied will now be examined.

THE WAGE SCALE

The basic determinant of a Soviet worker's wages is his position in the wage scale (*tarifnaya setka*); although other things, notably piece rates and bonuses of various kinds, often eclipse the wage scale in practical importance, they do not exist independently of it.

The reform in 1926–8 of the seventeen-grade wage scale of 1922 in fact replaced the single 'general' scale with a number of scales—one for engineering and technical personnel, one for employees, one for apprentices and one for manual workers. Apart from this, the number of grades in the scales and the differentials between grades varied as between industries and occupational groups.[21] The reversal of policy ushered in by Stalin's speech in June, 1931, could therefore easily be brought into effect piecemeal. The first wage scales to be brought into line with the new (anti-egalitarian) principle were those of the coke and iron and steel industries, and coal, iron and manganese mining. The range between the highest and lowest grades in these industries now varied from 1 : 3·2 to 1 : 3·75. Moreover, besides stretching the scales in this way, the new grades within each scale were set so that, moving up the scale, the differentials between grades remained more or less constant, or even increased.[22]

Some of the effects of the reform may be gauged from a comparison of the wage scales for metal workers in 1927[23] and 1937,[24] which are shown in the table below together with a typical industrial scale for 1956[25] and one introduced in the machine-building industry in 1959, which has six grades instead of the previous eight.[26]

Grade	*1*	*2*	*3*	*4*	*5*	*6*	*7*	*8*
Coefficient 1927 . .	1·0	1·2	1·45	1·7	1·95	2·2	2·5	2·8
Per cent increase over previous grade .	—	20·0	20·8	17·2	14·7	12·8	13·6	12·0
Coefficient 1937 . .	1·0	1·2	1·45	1·75	2·1	2·5	3·0	3·6
Per cent increase over previous grade .	—	20·0	20·8	20·6	20·0	19·0	20·0	20·0
Coefficient 1956 . .	1·0	1·14	1·31	1·52	1·78	2·1	2·5	3·0
Per cent increase over previous grade .	—	14·0	14·9	15·8	17·1	18·0	19·0	20·0
Coefficient 1959 . .	1·0	1·13	1·29	1·48	1·72	2·0	—	—
Per cent increase over previous grade .	—	13·0	14·1	14·7	16·2	16·3	—	—

Generalisation from this table would suggest that over the last 30 years the range between the bottom and top grades first increased and then decreased: incentive to acquire a higher skill was, however, provided by a widening differential between the higher grades. It may reasonably be inferred from the table that the range between the bottom and top grades has been allowed to narrow since 1937, and particularly since the war. In 1946 the ratios of bottom to top grades in the scales used in the machine-building industry were 1 : 3·2 and 1 : 3·6; in 1954 some of these had fallen to 1 : 2 or even less,[27] and although by 1956 they had risen again to 1 : 2·5 and 1 : 2·4,[28] by 1959 they had again generally fallen to 1 : 2.[29] This reappearance of egalitarian tendencies in the wage scales themselves was at first largely due to the fact that when the prices of rationed goods were raised in September, 1946, the lower paid workers were given an addition to their wages, and for piece-workers—that is for the great majority—this was incorporated in their basic wage-scale rate, thus decreasing the bottom-to-top grade ratio.[30]

Reduction of this grade ratio has subsequently become one of the major features of the reorganisation of the wage structure, which began to take effect in 1957. Scales where the top grade exceeded the bottom by 2·5–3·5 times have generally been replaced by new scales with a differential of 1–1·8 or 2.[31] In most industries, beginning in 1959, the eight, ten and twelve grade scales were replaced by six and seven grade scales.[32] It was frequently the case that in scales with eight or more grades there were extremely few workers classified in the two lowest grades, which in a number of cases gave rise to egalitarianism and reduced the material incentive for workers to aspire to higher grades.[33] In 1956, for example, among workers of the 38 most numerous and typical trades in the machine-building industry only 0·01 per cent were classified in the first grade and 1·1 per cent in the second grade.[34] The number of wage scales in use has also been drastically reduced from some 2,000 to 12.[35]

It was in connection with the decision to introduce minimum-wage legislation that an element of self-contradiction appeared in official declarations on wage policy. On the one hand Mikoyan, speaking at the XX Party Congress in 1956, envisaged the 'liquidation of a certain disproportion in our economy, the liquidation of the excessive gap between the wages of the lower-paid workers and employees and those of the higher-paid category'. Mikoyan proceeded to explain:[36]

'During the period when we were carrying out industrialisation in a peasant country, this gap was natural, since it stimulated the rapid formation of cadres of highly skilled workers of whom the country was in dire need. Now, when there exists a working class which is highly skilled and has a high cultural level, and which is annually replenished by people graduating from seven- and ten-year schools, the difference, though necessarily preserved, must be reduced. This proceeds from the new level of our development and signifies a new step forward in the advance towards Communism.'

Kaganovich, on the other hand, speaking two days later, said that the wage-scale system had not been essentially changed since 1932, and that therefore the wage scale, 'owing to various accretions in the course of 20 years, contains elements of egalitarianism'.* [37]

Since May, 1955, a State Committee of the USSR Council of Ministers on Questions of Labour and Wages had been charged with 'intensifying State control over the work of Ministries and Departments and improving their work in the sphere of labour and wages'.[41] The appointment of Kaganovich, then still one of the most powerful men in the country, as Chairman of the State Committee, seemed to proclaim its importance. The Committee was empowered to draft laws and decrees on labour and wages;[42] it was also provided with its own Inspectorates to 'uncover shortcomings in the work of enterprises and Ministries in the sphere of labour organisations and wages, and help to get rid of these shortcomings'.[43] The Committee has published its own periodical, *Socialist Labour* (*Sotsialistichesky Trud*), since January, 1956.

It was, however, only after Kaganovich's resignation as Chairman in June, 1956, and his replacement by a previously unknown figure, A. P. Volkov, that the serious work of bringing order into the wage structure began. The main line taken in this was, according to Volkov, to eliminate the unjustifiable multiplicity of wage rates and wage scales and to restore to the basic wage rate its proper fundamental position in the worker's earnings.[44] According to a leading article in the Committee's

* 'Egalitarianism' is here a translation of the Russian word *uravnilovka* (literally 'levelling'), and has the pejorative sense which this word—with or without the epithets 'rotten',[38] 'petty bourgeois'[39] and so forth—has borne ever since Stalin's speech of 1931, and which it continues to bear.[40]

periodical 'particularly careful thought' had to be given to the question of the ratio of lower to higher grades:[45]

'so that the wages of workers placed in the lower grades of the scale should increase as the productivity of labour increases more quickly than those of workers in higher grades.'

The new scales had therefore to be sufficient to give workers an incentive to raise their qualifications 'without leading to unjustified gaps' between the grades.[46] The Committee attempted to meet these requirements by setting the difference between the bottom and top grades rather lower than before the war but higher than it was subsequently to become, the commonest ratio put forward being 1 : 2·8 on an eight-grade scale. Steeper scales were envisaged for 'the leading branches of industry which have the greatest need of qualified cadres'.[47] These proposals did not meet with universal approval in the enterprises. Some protested that the 1 : 2·8 ratio was too low and suggested a steeper scale of something like 1 : 3·2 or 1 : 3·4. This the Committee rejected on the grounds that it did not accord with the decisions of the XX Party Congress on the need to raise the wages of the lowest paid workers.

By 1958 these diverging views on the egalitarian element in the new wage system had evidently been resolved. According to one authority 'the gap between minimum and maximum wage will be reduced, eliminating at the same time any possibility of egalitarianism'.[48] In April, 1958, a resolution of the Central Committee, Council of Ministers and AUCCTU, introducing shorter working hours in some heavy industries,[49] also laid it down that the State Committee on Labour and Wages, jointly with other interested bodies, should put forward proposals for reorganising the wages system which would raise the wages of the lowest paid workers and 'close the gap between the maximum and minimum wage'. This policy was maintained in the 'Control Figures for the Development of the Economy of the USSR in the years 1959–65',[50] which indicated that the 'gradual bringing of order into wages will mean raising the wages of low- and average-paid workers in comparison with the higher paid groups'. (A departure from this general principle occurred in 1964 with the introduction of new rates of pay for underground workers in the coal shale industry. The scale contained seven grades instead of the more normal six, with a bottom-to-top ratio of 1 : 2·81.[51]) It was decided at the XXI

Congress that the process of reorganising the wages system would be completed by the end of 1962.[52] From 1956 to 1961 more than 40 million people, about two-thirds of the total number of factory and office workers, had been brought under the new system of payment. The rest were to be transferred by the end of 1962.[53]

The principle of improving wage rates and raising the wages of lower-paid workers has now been embodied in the directives of the XXIII CPSU Congress on the current (1966–70) Five-Year Plan. But the chief means of increasing earnings are now incentive bonuses.[54]

Soviet sources consistently deny that the new system, under which bottom-to-top ratios in wage scales have been reduced to about 1 : 2 in engineering and a number of branches of heavy industry, and 1 : 1·8 in the light and food industries,[55] is in any way egalitarian:

> 'This policy in the sphere of wages has nothing in common with the petty-bourgeois wage-levelling methods against which our Party has always fought and continues to fight; [on the contrary] it fully conforms to the objective demands of economic development in the period of the extended construction of a Communist society.'[56]

THE GRADING OF JOBS

The grade (*tarifny razryad*) of a job—and of the worker who does it—in the scale is determined according to a handbook of wage scales and qualifications (*tarifno-kvalifikatsionny spravochnik*) for the branch or group of homogeneous branches of industry concerned. First introduced with the first wage scale in 1922, and revised in 1931–2, these handbooks were compiled by the appropriate Ministries 'enlisting the assistance of the staff of the chief administrations, trade union organisations, institutes of scientific research, engineering and technical staff, and workers at the enterprise'.[57]

Changes in industry since then—notably the appearance of new trades, the 1957 reorganisation of industrial administration and the reorganisation of the wages system—have necessitated far-reaching revision of the handbooks, a task which devolved upon the State Committee for Labour and Wages. Unified handbooks for the various branches of industry, instead of the former Departments and Ministries, were drawn up. In addition a unified handbook was introduced for similar trades occurring in various industries.[58] In 1961, 60–65 per cent of all jobs in industry were covered by this handbook.[59]

The criteria for grading a job are its complexity, the accuracy demanded, and the responsibility involved. The grades themselves are defined under three headings, saying what the worker must know, what he must be able to do, and giving an example of a job. The immediate responsibility for grading a job falls on the foremen, who have the right 'to allot to workers, subject to confirmation according to the established procedure, wage scale grades in accordance with the handbook of wage scales and qualifications and with a test or trials passed by the worker'.[60] If the newly arrived worker's qualifications are not known, or if the foreman has any doubt that they are correct, he may require him to pass a test in accordance with the grade definition in the appropriate handbook. Should a worker be dissatisfied with the grade he is given, he has a right of appeal to the Trade Union Labour Disputes Commission.[61] If a worker qualifies for a certain grade, this involves the management in an obligation to give him work in that grade; but if 'owing to conditions of production' a worker is doing work of a higher or lower grade than his own, the general rule is that he be paid according to that grade.[62]

'The basic method of the organisation of the payment of the labour of workers and employees in the USSR', according to a Soviet handbook on labour and wages, 'is the State regulation of wages'. In more detail: 'At the present time all the basic regulations on the payment of labour are established by joint resolutions of the CC CPSU, the USSR Council of Ministers and the AUCCTU.'[63] The basic wage scale rates (*tarifnye stavki*) worked out in this way are included in the annual Collective Agreements concluded between the local trade union body and the management,[64] but it would be wrong to think that this implies any collective bargaining since '. . . enterprises and institutions cannot independently and of their own free will organise wages; they are obliged to observe the existing laws and regulations'.[65] After the economic reforms of September, 1965, the view that the system of fixing wage rates and scales nationally should be abolished, and enterprises permitted to do this, gained some currency. The Chairman of the State Committee for Labour and Wages rejected this view on the ground that it would lead to wide differences in earnings for exactly similar work.[66]

The wage scale establishes only the relationship between various grades of job, the higher grades being expressed as coefficients of Grade I. Once the wage rate of Grade I is known, then all others are arrived at by simple multiplication. It does not follow that Grade I (and therefore any other grade) of a given wage scale is always translated into the same wage. On the contrary, differentiation is practised here too, in accordance with definite aims of State economic policy. In most industries the rates for piece-workers are fixed about 10–16 per cent higher than those for time-workers.[67] The physical conditions of work are also taken into account: for example, rates for Grade I (and consequently all subsequent grades) for workers engaged on hot or cold jobs, or jobs with unhealthy conditions, are set higher than for similar jobs in normal conditions. Under the reorganised system of payments, underground work, for example, is paid at 20–25 per cent above the rate for similar work on the surface. For work in hot, difficult or unhealthy conditions the rate is 10–20 per cent higher and in particularly arduous conditions a further 10–20 per cent above the normal rate.[68] The State Committee for Labour and Wages and the AUCCTU have worked out a single list of jobs to be paid at these higher rates.[69]

Wage scales may be hourly, daily or monthly. The following hourly rates were in force in 1965 for Grade I in the leading branches of the machine-building industry:[*][70]

Time-workers on cold jobs	27·5 kopecks.
Time-workers on hot, heavy and unhealthy jobs, piece-workers on cold jobs	32 kopecks.
Piece-workers on hot, heavy and unhealthy jobs and time-workers on particularly heavy or unhealthy jobs	36·7 kopecks.
Piece-workers on exceptionally heavy and unhealthy jobs	39 kopecks.

Other reasons for raising the basic wage scale rate may be territorial—in industrial centres where living costs are high, or if climatic conditions create additional difficulties in the work[†][72] —or they may derive from industrial policy: to create a per-

* The rates for ordinary work in this industry are some 14 per cent lower than those for work in hot, heavy or unhealthy conditions and 21 per cent lower than for work in particularly heavy or particularly unhealthy conditions.[71]

† Other monetary inducements to work in inclement areas are mentioned on p. 68.

manent cadre of skilled workers at an enterprise the basic rates of 'leading groups and trades' have sometimes been raised by up to 15 per cent.[73]

PIECE-WORK AND NORMS

Whereas differentiated wage scales serve to further industrial progress in the long run by encouraging workers to acquire higher skills, other incentives are needed as a direct stimulus to increased output at the bench. In the Soviet Union the most important of these has been the widespread use of piece-work systems.

As early as 1918 Lenin, writing of the need to 'improve labour discipline and increase the productivity of labour', proposed the introduction of piece payment and the 'application of much that is scientific and progressive in the Taylor system'.*[74] Lenin's suggestions, in spite of some initial doubts on the part of the trade unions, were adopted in 1919 by the Second Trade Union Congress, which recommended the application of piece-rates wherever possible;[75] and the Party Congress of 1923 resolved in favour of the 'real dependence of individual wages on actual output'.[76]

Stalin's speech of 1931 was the signal for a far-reaching extension of piece-work: the Central Committee of the Miners' Trade Union and the managers of the Donets coal-mine were instructed to transfer 85 to 90 per cent of the underground staffs and 70 per cent of all other workers to piece-rates.[77] By 1937 three-quarters of the total man-hours worked were paid on piece-rates, compared with just over half before the reform.[78] At this level it remained until 1955 when 'almost three-quarters' of the workers in industry were on piece-work.[79] Since the reorganisation of the wages system, begun in 1956, the proportion of piece-workers has fallen by 15–20 per cent.[80] With the gradual extension of automated processes in industry, which largely preclude the possibility of piece-rate working, the proportion of piece-workers may be expected to fall still further. One Soviet authority has estimated that by 1970 the proportion of piece-workers will fall to 45–50 per cent.[81] By 1965 the proportion of piece-workers in the chemical industry had fallen to 36 per cent, in the oil extraction industry to

* So called from its originator, the American engineer F. W. Taylor (1856–1915).

12 per cent and in the electric power industry to eight per cent. In the machine-building and metal-working industries the proportion of piece-workers was signicantly higher at 57 per cent.[82]

The basic wage rate, as described above, is in the form of a time-wage (so much per hour, day, or month). This is converted into a piece-rate (*sdelnaya rastsenka*) by means of an output norm, that is a standard of output in a given period of time. (The principle is the same when a time-norm, such as 20 minutes for a given job, is used, since this is merely a different and sometimes more convenient way of expressing a standard of output.) If, for instance, the hourly wage rate for the sixth grade is 50 kopecks, a norm of two items per hour gives a piece-rate of 25 kopeks.

The commonest and simplest form of piece-work is 'direct, individual piece-work', on which over half of all piece-workers were paid in 1954.[83] (By 1961 only 19·5 per cent of workers were paid under this system alone, the majority of piece-workers [68 per cent] being also involved in schemes paying bonuses for fulfilment of production plans.)[84] Although now less widespread, it remains the most common single piece-work system; in 1965, 83 per cent of all piece-workers in one economic region of the Soviet Union were paid under this system.[85] In this form of payment the piece-rate is the same for each unit of product produced by a given worker. If he exactly fulfils his norm, his earnings will be equal to his wage rate; if he exceeds the norm, they will be more than his wage rate; if he fails to reach the norm, they will fall short of his wage rate. If his failure to achieve his norm is adjudged to be his own fault, he is paid at his piece-rate according to the amount and quality of what he has produced, 'without a guarantee of any minimum wage whatsoever'.[86] If the worker is exonerated from blame for failure to achieve the norm, he is usually paid a minimum of two-thirds of his wage rate.

If direct piece-work gives the worker a straightforward incentive to produce as much as he can, sometimes at the expense of quality of output[87] 'progressive piece-work' is designed to spur him to even greater efforts. As a Soviet author has put it:[88]

> 'To increase the stimulating rôle of wages in raising the productivity of labour and in the struggle for the fulfilment and overfulfilment of norms, the progressive piece-work system of wages is applied at enterprises.'

In particular it is applied in 'leading sectors' of production—sectors on which the enterprise's or shop's plan-fulfilment depends; it may be brought into play 'if it is necessary to increase production without installing additional equipment or taking on additional labour'; and it may be used to deal with 'bottlenecks which cannot be eliminated by organisational and technical measures'.[89] The application of the progressive piece-work system has, during recent years, been 'steadily dropping'.[90]

The essence of the progressive piece-work system is that once the norm is fulfilled, the rate of payment per unit of product goes up. Many variations on this theme are possible. In some cases the increase in piece-rate is, so to speak, retrospective, and covers production within the norm as well as above it. Sometimes the percentage increase in the piece-rate itself increases with the percentage over-fulfilment of the norm; occasionally the last 10 or 20 per cent below the norm are made eligible for progressive rates. The system is highly flexible, and discrimination may be freely exercised: 'leading trades' and men working in severe conditions, or looking after more than the average amount of equipment (e.g. looms in the textile industry) may be specially favoured,[91] so as to provide additional incentives for various purposes. Current practice is to calculate the percentage over-fulfilment from the worker's monthly (not daily) output; this ensures that his efforts to exceed the norm are continuous.[92]

Piece-rates may be combined with bonuses for specific achievements, such as good-quality work, fuel economy and so forth. In this system, known as the 'piece-work-bonus system', bonuses are paid as percentages of the worker's earnings on the basic piece-rate,[93] thus accentuating the difference between grades. This system has, however, led to abuses through a multiplicity of accretions to the basic wage rate, which has been known, as a result, to constitute as little as a quarter of the worker's total earnings.[94] This problem was tackled by the State Committee for Labour and Wages and by 1962 the average proportion of the basic wage rate in workers' earnings had increased to 70–80 per cent.[95] The piece-work-bonus system is now the most common form of piece-work employed in the leading branches of industry[96] and now covers about a quarter of all piece-workers.[97]

Three more forms of piece-work may be mentioned briefly.[98] The 'brigade piece-work system' is used where reckoning for the individual workman is impossible, for instance where a group or 'brigade' of men are assembling machines. Here a norm is set for the brigade as a whole, and brigade piece-rates paid accordingly; these are then divided among the members of the brigade according to their grades and the number of hours each has worked. Secondly, a similar system, known as the 'agreement system' (*akkordnaya sistema*), where a definite payment is set for a given job (e.g. pumping out a flooded shaft) is usually applied to a group of workers. It is in wide use in the building industry.[99] The job is assessed and a time-norm set; then if the group get it done before time, they qualify for a progressive increment to the original sum named. The following comment, from the same Soviet author, is perhaps revealing:[100]

'Under the agreement system, control of the quality of the work being done requires particularly accurate organisation. In the event of unsatisfactory quality, the brigade is obliged to do the work again without any additional remuneration.'

Lastly, there are various types of 'indirect piece-work system', which are used to promote efficiency in ancillary workers whose work has an effect on the productivity of the productive workers' labour, and which all consist essentially in gearing the ancillary workers' earnings to the output of the basic workers served by them.[101]

NORM-SETTING AND REVISION

Originally, according to the Labour Codex of 1922, output norms were fixed by agreement between the management of the enterprise or department and the trade union concerned,[102] and approved in the Rates and Conflicts Commission (*RKK*), on which both workers and management were represented.[*] [103] Here too, however, the transition from NEP to planning had its effect. In 1932 a Party conference recommended that the responsibility for norm-setting at enterprises should be laid upon 'directors, technical directors, and shop engineering and technical staff'.[104] The hint was taken by the AUCCTU, whose Presidium resolved in 1933 to leave norm-setting entirely to the discretion of the management, a resolution which was repeated in formal terms by the AUCCTU Plenum in December,

* *See* p. 180.

1935.[105] The local trade union was thus left with no duty but to give its formal approval to the new norms. Regulation of norms and rates was strictly centralised. In 1938 the USSR *SovNarKom* approved a decision that its Economic Council must give permission before People's Commissariats and central establishments of the USSR and also republican *SovNarKoms* could issue orders on wage questions, including substantive revision of output norms and rates'.[106] Even minor variations in norms were taken out of the hands of the sector heads to whom they had been entrusted in coal-mines; henceforward they were to be sanctioned only by the directors of trusts.[107]

At the enterprises, according to a Labour Law textbook of 1949,[108]

'the output norms are approved by the manager on the recommendation of the heads of shops. Immediately after approval, the new norms become obligatory and the workers are notified.'

Occasionally norms have been determined directly by the Government;[109] but in general, as can be seen from the procedure just described, the quantitative determination of norms is left to the managerial authority on the spot. The extent to which the local trade union can assume a bargaining rôle in norm setting, previously minimal, was increased, at least in theory, in 1958. An edict of the Presidium of the USSR Supreme Soviet increasing the rights of local factory trade union committees laid down that factory administrations had to secure the agreement of the trade union committees before setting new norms or revising existing ones.[110]

The way in which the norm-setting authority arrives at a figure has varied at different times in the USSR, and continues to be the subject of repeated injunctions by the Party. In the early period, before the pace of industrialisation grew really hot, a method known as 'summary norm-setting' (*summarnoe normirovanie*) was tolerated. According to this method, the norm was determined either by the rate-fixer or foreman 'by eye', or else by taking the average of the actual past output of workers on analogous jobs, or by a combination of the two. This type of norm-setting came to be known as 'norm-setting by experience and statistics' (*opytno-statisticheskoe normirovanie*).[111] Already in 1924, however, another type of norm had been defined when the Plenum of the Party Central Committee resolved that it was necessary 'to increase output norms wherever they have not reached the technically possible norms, reckoning with the machines' maximum load and the use of the whole working day'.[112] This second type of norm-setting, known variously as 'calculated' (*raschëtnoe*), 'analytical', 'technical', or 'technically-based' (*tekhnicheski obosnovannoe*) norm-setting,[113] and approximating to the methods of Time-and-Motion study, soon became a regularly repeated item of policy. The Party conference of 1932 resolved that 'technical norm-setting should be made the basis of the correct organisation of labour and intra-plant planning'.[114] The Stakhanov movement gave a fresh fillip to the campaign, and led at least one Party enthusiast to go beyond even technical norms in his ambitions for the workers' output. Pyakatov, then Commissar for Heavy Industry, addressing a conference of Stakhanovites in the autumn of 1935, said:[115]

'The essence of the Stakhanov movement lies in the fact that the Stakhanovite . . . overthrows all so-called technical work norms. . . . Technically-based norms represent a phantom that served to intimidate us, a brake that held us back. . . . We will smash the devil himself and attain unheard of production results of which no one has ever dreamed. . . . One must simply shout: "The devil take it!"'

But Stalin, in his address to the same conference, denied that technical norms could be thus summarily thrown overboard:[116]

'That is not true, Comrades. More, it is stupid. Without technical [norms] planned economy is impossible. Technical [norms] are, moreover, necessary to help the masses who have fallen behind to catch up with the more advanced. . . . We therefore need technical [norms]; not those, however, that now exist, but higher ones. . . . We need technical [norms] somewhere between the present technical [norms] and those achieved by people like Stakhanov and Busygin.'

The two main points on which the authorities could concentrate, therefore, were the drive for transition from 'experience-and-statistics' to 'technical' norms, and the upward revision of the technical norms themselves. The Party Central Committee Plenum in December, 1935, in a statement still quoted as authoritative many years later,[117] emphasised both these points:[118]

'It is necessary to replace the present obsolete technical norms with higher norms. . . . The predominance in norm-setting practice of so-called 'experience-and-statistics' norms, the tendency to fall into line with the output of a worker who has a poor grasp of the technique of his production, the absence in the process of setting output norms of a genuine analysis of the growth of the enterprise's and shop's productive capacities, of the growth of power-supply per worker, and of the growth of the worker's technical and cultural level—all this makes the existing practice of norm-setting a brake on the further growth of labour productivity and worker's earnings.'

These two themes have continued to form the *leitmotiv* of official policy on norms. In 1939 the Economic Council endorsed an order of the USSR *SovNarKom's* Committee for Construction Affairs raising output norms on average by 4·3 per cent.[119] The legislation enacted at the approach of war in 1940, extending the working day and the working week,* automatically entailed an upward revision of daily and monthly output norms; and piece-rates were lowered at the same time so as to hold earnings down.[120] Stalin's idea that norms should be somewhere between the existing technical norms and the standards reached by Stakhanovites was later translated into a regular practice of upward revision. 'State Plans', we read in the USSR Council of Ministers' decree on the State Plan for 1947, '... must be calculated not on average-arithmetic norms, achieved in production, but on *average-progressive norms,* i.e. *in emulation of advanced workers*'.† [121]

'Progressive norms', it soon became clear, also meant norms liable to early revision. 'Newly-established norms', said a Labour Law textbook in 1949, 'are valid for one year'.[122] Annual revision became a regular feature.[123] 'General orders' for norm-revision were issued by the appropriate People's Commissar (Minister), together with the Secretary of the AUCCTU.[124] In August, 1956, however, this centralised procedure, described as 'mass simultaneous norm-revision', was abolished on the grounds that it did not 'create real technical and organisational conditions for a consistent rise in the productivity of labour throughout the year'. It was replaced by a less centralised system of piecemeal revision, under which 'calendar plans' for revision are worked out at enterprises 'on the basis of tasks for raising the productivity of labour, the planned level of average wages, and the plan for lowering the cost of production'.[125] The amount of the upward revision was

* *See* pp. 119f., 123. † Italics added.

to be decided by the management 'by agreement with' the Trade Union Factory Committee.

It is not only improvements in technique that are taken into account in raising norms: demands are also made on the worker. As a Soviet monograph on wages under Socialism put it:[126]

'Our technical norms used to be set up as quantities given once and for all. They were compiled on the basis of the 'limiting' technical characteristics of the apparatus and machine-assemblies, without taking into account the rôle of the worker, who has a decisive influence on the use of equipment. . . . The cultural and technical growth of the workers has demonstrated the full bankruptcy of 'limiting' norms. Innovators in production have shown in practice that more can be got out of equipment than limiting technical norms envisage, and that the establishment of such norms is a brake on the further growth of the productivity of labour.'

Or again, more succinctly:[127]

'As the technique of production is perfected, [as] the organisation of labour improves, and [as] the workers' qualifications grow, the norm changes accordingly, and *in this lies its progressive character.*'*

Indeed the norm itself is to be a spur to improvements:[128]

'The progressive norm is an enormous organising force for the broad masses in the struggle for the undeviating growth and perfection of Socialist production.'

Parallel with this, the campaign to replace 'experience-and-statistics' norms by technical norms regained momentum after the war. The Fourth Five-Year Plan stipulated that 'suitably technically calculated output norms shall be more widely introduced in industry, due account being taken of up-to-date technological methods and the increased mechanisation of labour'.[129] Nevertheless Malenkov complained to the XIX Party Congress in 1952 that, although technical norm-setting had a great significance in raising the productivity of labour, there were very many 'experience-and-statistics' norms in operation: 'The proportion of experience-and-statistics norms is very high and at many enterprises amounts to more than 50 per cent of all current output norms'.[130]

The reorganisation of the wages system, begun in 1956, facilitated the spread of technically based norms. Prior to this,

* Italics added.

the general pattern throughout industry had been for large numbers of workers to exceed the norm by as much as one-and-a-half times. The introduction of the technically based norms understandably met with resistance from the workers, who suffered a reduction of earnings in many cases.[131]

With the reorganisation of the wages system the proportion of technical norms has increased at the expense of 'experience-and-statistics' norms. In the main branches of industry technical norms account for 70–80 per cent of all norms.[132] For example, in the coal industry the proportion is now about 80 per cent, in the cement industry 76 per cent and in the food industry 70 per cent.[133] At the Karacharovsky plastics factory between 1958 and 1959, the proportion of technical norms rose from 19 per cent to 60 per cent, while that of 'experience-and-statistics' norms fell from 71 to 40 per cent.[134]

Following the introduction of the new wages structure in the chemical industry, for example, the overall average of workers fulfilling the norm by 150 per cent fell from 47·5 to 5·4 per cent; and by 120–150 per cent from 26·5 to 18·4 per cent. On the other hand the proportion of workers fulfilling the norm by 100–110 per cent rose from 9·3 to 40·2 per cent.[135]

The new system of wages and norms still permits serious anomalies. In October, 1961, Volkov complained[136] of 'serious faults in the establishment of work norms in a number of engineering and ferro-concrete enterprises and oil refineries, and particularly in the auxiliary departments of iron and steel, light and other industries', where wages were frequently higher than in the main shops. In April, 1962,[137] Volkov further condemned the practice, increasingly common in conditions of shortage of particular kinds of labour, of managements 'fiddling' work norms to guarantee unjustified bonuses whenever this seemed necessary to attract more labour into certain types of jobs. A recent Soviet handbook on wages and norms complained that technically based norms are often disregarded or incorrectly set, enabling workers to overfulfil them to an excessive degree.[138]

BONUSES

Two temptations are obviously attendant on the position of the piece-rate worker: to achieve a high quantitative output (and therefore high earnings) at the cost either of the extravagant use of power and materials or of the quality of his product, or both. These tendencies, particularly poor-quality production, were serious problems in the USSR,[139] and steps had to be taken to offset them. Apart from systems of control and inspection, bonuses are paid 'for economies in fuel and electric power beyond the Plan, for cost-cutting beyond the Plan, and for other qualitative and quantitative indices'.[140] Bonuses are also given for the quick assimilation of new line of production, although 'basically all indices for bonuses are reducible to rewards for the achievement of high-quality production and for cutting its costs'.[141] In spite of this, bonuses for piece-workers became exceedingly complicated. The introduction of the new wages system, however, simplified matters: in most industries piece-work and bonuses or time and bonus systems were introduced at the same time as part of the new wages structure, forming the basic method of payment. By 1961 from 60 to 90 per cent of all workers were included in these considerably improved bonus systems.[142]

Bonuses are particularly widely used in connection with time-rates. The rôle of time-rates, which 'correspond less [than piece-rates] to the Socialist principle of payment according to labour',[143] and do not 'ensure the personal material interest of the worker in raising the productivity of his labour',[144] has been gradually reduced to a minimum by the Soviet Government, and they are applied only where piece-rates are wholly impracticable. The proportion of workers paid by 'simple time-rates' (i.e. with no bonus system) fell from 15·1 per cent in 1940 to 9 per cent in 1954 and to some 6 per cent in 1961. At the Urals Heavy Engineering Works in 1965 this proportion was as low as 4 per cent.[145] Wherever possible, time-rates are supplemented by some sort of bonus system.

The reorganised bonus system has eliminated the practice of awarding bonuses which in fact duplicated each other, enabling workers to receive several bonuses for the same piece of work. Time- and piece-workers are now mainly awarded bonuses for fulfilment and over-fulfilment of production plans, improving the quality of goods produced, strictly adhering to the technical regulations, economising in raw materials, electricity, etc. Depending on the economic importance of the particular branch or sector of industry, the bonus for fulfilling monthly output plans ranges from 10 to 20 per cent, and for each one per cent by which the plan is over-fulfilled, the worker's monthly earnings or wage rate is increased by a further 1 or 2 per cent. Bonuses for attaining a high quality of production may be as high as 30 per cent of the monthly wage rate. Economy in raw materials, etc., is rewarded by a bonus directly proportional to the economy effected but not exceeding 40 per cent of this economy.[146] Major changes were made in 1959 in the system of paying bonuses to leading engineering workers and technologists.[147] These changes were intended to stimulate the material incentive of leading workers to improve the quality of output, and to eliminate the excessive award of bonuses to some groups of workers. The chief reform was that bonuses were to be paid for fulfilling and over-fulfilling the plan for the reduction of unit-costs and for effecting economies. In some industries where output is not limited by availability of raw materials (coal, oil) additional bonuses are payable for over-fulfilling production plans.

In general payment of bonuses for fulfilling or over-fulfilling the plan to reduce production costs is conditional upon the fufilment by the enterprise of the general output plan, the labour productivity plan, the plan for deliveries to enterprises in other economic regions and so on.[148]

Apart from these standard bonuses for quality production, cost-cutting and fulfilling and over-fulfilling production plans, there are a number of others, awarded singly for special purposes. Some of these come from the 'Enterprise Fund', which is a development of the 'Director's Fund' introduced in 1936 with the aim of encouraging managers to run their enterprises at a profit.[149] This aim is served, now as then, by feeding the fund solely from enterprise profits; if there are no profits (or if the enterprise does not fulfil the output or cost reduction plans), there will be no Enterprise Fund. Otherwise the fund is financed from between one per cent and six per cent of the planned profit, plus between 30 per cent and 60 per cent of profit accruing above the planned figure; the exact percentages within these limits vary according to the branch of industry, heavy industry being given preference over consumer goods production. The fund must not exceed 5·5 per cent (or up to seven per cent in some branches of heavy industry) of the annual wages fund for the productive industrial personnel of the enterprise, adjusted to the actual volume of goods produced for sale. Not less than 20 per cent of the fund so formed is devoted to introducing new techniques, modernising equipment and expanding production; not less than 40 per cent goes to building and repairing enterprise housing and other amenities such as clubs, crèches and nurseries, sports facilities, etc.; the remaining 40 per cent is devoted to awarding individual bonuses, free passes to rest houses, and grants-in-aid to workers. Disposal of the fund is decided jointly by the director and the factory trade union committee.[150]

Since the introduction of the economic reforms the Enterprise Fund regulations must be considered to be in the melting pot. In his report on the reforms to the CPSU Central Committee in September, 1965, Kosygin said that material incentives for production collectives and individual workers had proved 'completely inadequate'. Opportunities for enterprises to set up extra sources of income were extremely limited:

> 'About half the industrial enterprises do not have their own fund formed out of profit, and where there is an enterprise fund it is extremely small and the incentive money distributed from it is insignificant. Almost all types of bonuses and other incentives are paid not out of profit but from the wages fund. Success achieved by the enterprise in increasing profit and raising the profitability of production has no direct effect upon the earnings of the workers of the enterprise.'[151]

Under the economic reforms, enterprises (of which about 700 had gone over to the new system by the end of 1966) are to be allowed to keep a greater proportion of their profits and payments into bonus and welfare funds considerably stepped up. The precise amount to be paid into these funds is to be fixed by the appropriate ministries, in consultation with other interested government departments and the Trade Unions.[152] It is envisaged that the proportion of take-home pay deriving from bonuses will increase.[153]

Another form of bonus paid from funds created within the individual enterprise is that awarded at the discretion of foremen to workers under them. This bonus, which was introduced in 1940 as one of a number of measures designed to enhance the status of foremen in the heavy machine-building industry, originally amounted to up to 2 per cent of the wages fund of the workers subordinate to the foreman concerned; in 1955, when the same thing was done for foremen in a large number of other industries, this figure was raised to 3 per cent.[154] Already in 1940 foremen had been distinguished from the rank-and-file workers by being given a share in bonuses for high output when production in their department was in excess of the planned quota.[155]

Since 1942 bonuses or rewards have been paid to the authors of inventions, technical improvements or proposals for the rationalisation of production. Under revised regulations issued in 1959[156] authors of inventions who are awarded diplomas by the State Committee for Inventions and Discoveries of the USSR Council of Ministers may be paid a lump sum of up to 5,000 roubles (new currency). Where diplomas are awarded to a group of people or in the name of an enterprise, similar sums are payable and are divided amongst those responsible for the invention. Persons responsible for introducing their own inventions into production are paid bonuses according to the amount of economy achieved. These range from 25 per cent of an annual economy of up to 100 roubles (in new currency) but not less than 20 roubles, to 2 per cent plus 2,100 roubles, but not more than 20,000 roubles for an annual saving of over 100,000 roubles. Authors of rationalisation schemes are rewarded on a similar basis, bonuses ranging from 13·75 per cent (not less than 10 roubles) of an annual economy of up to 100 roubles, to 0·5 per cent plus 860 roubles (not more than 5,000 roubles) of an annual economy of over 100,000 roubles. People who adapt schemes introduced in other factories may also receive a bonus not exceeding half their wage rate.

Another form of bonus is the payment of extraordinary grants at the end of the year to workers with long service in underground, laborious, unhealthy or dangerous jobs. The longer the uninterrupted service the larger the bonus. The minimum length of uninterrupted service entitling a worker to such a bonus is two years for underground workers and three years for others. Sums paid range from 0·8 per cent of the monthly wage rate or salary for 2–3 years' service to 2·0 per cent for over 15 years' service.[157] At the end of 1965 Volkov, Chairman of the State Committee for Labour and Wages, stated that bonuses were to be paid for long service at a particular enterprise.[158] The purpose seemed to be to encourage workers to stay in their jobs and not seek better pay elsewhere.

The last source of single-bonus payments, 'Socialist competition', is treated separately.*

* *See* pp. 73–84.

OVERTIME AND OTHER EXTRA PAYMENTS; REDUCTIONS OF WAGES

In accordance with the Labour Codex of 1922, time-workers are paid at a minimum of time-and-a-half for the first two hours of overtime, and at double time for each hour after two. Piece-workers are paid their piece-rates, plus 50 per cent of the hourly wage-rate of their grade for the first two hours of overtime, and 100 per cent for each hour after two. Payment for work on annual national holidays is at double time-rates or double piece-rates; but, if the workers agree, an alternative holiday may be given instead of extra payment. If work on weekly holidays (normally Sundays) is not compensated by an extra day off, double rates are paid. Some of these payments are on a reduced scale in the building and timber industries.[159]

Night work (between 10 p.m. and 6 a.m.) is normally paid at eight-sevenths or seven-sixths of the day rate; piece-workers get their piece-rate plus one-seventh, one-sixth, or one-fifth of the hourly day rate for their grade.[160]

Workers doing the work of more than one trade, or minding extra lathes, are paid full piece-rates, unless the enterprise has had to install special equipment; in this case the payment may be reduced to 60 per cent of the rate for work on the basic lathes.

Workers doing work of different qualifications are paid the rate for the higher qualification.

Workers who conclude agreements to work in the Far North of Russia, including members of the local population, are paid an increment of 10 per cent of their basic monthly wages for every six months' service in the North, up to a maximum of 80 per cent. Similar privileges are granted to workers in certain other remote areas except that 10 per cent increments are paid for every year's service after the first two years, up to 50 per cent of their basic monthly wages.[161]

Annual leave is paid at the rate of the worker's average wages over the previous year. Time spent at major congresses and conferences of State, Party, trade union, *Komsomol* and co-operative organisations is paid on the average over the quarter or month previous. Time spent as an assessor or witness in a People's Court, or answering a summons from the military authorities, is similarly paid; during periods of military training the worker retains half his average wages for the previous quarter.[162]

As against these extra payments, there are various occasions for the reduction of wages. The temptation inherent in a system of production plans and piece-work—to achieve quantity at the expense of quality—has made sub-standard quality goods a recurrent problem in Soviet industry. 'The intensification of the struggle against rejects'[163] as it was called in a resolution of the XIX Party Congress, has long motivated legislation on this point:[164]

> 'The current rules about rejected products have as their aim the stimulation of workers in an active struggle for the necessary quality of goods produced and the elimination of the causes which give rise to sub-standard production. Being an active participant in the collective body of a Socialist enterprise, every worker has, through social organisations, production conferences, etc., the opportunity to expose the cause of rejects and to help in eliminating these causes.'

A campaign to raise the quality of goods to the best world standards was started shortly after Khrushchev's removal. In December, 1964, Kosygin stressed:

> 'The improvement of the quality of production is becoming one of the chief, one of the most important economic tasks. This is dictated by the whole course of the development of our economy. It is one of the main sources of raising the productivity of socially useful labour and an indispensable condition for meeting the growing demands of the population for consumer goods.'[165]

Besides the 'opportunity', therefore, the worker is also given considerable material incentive to avoid sub-standard production. The carrot of a bonus for good-quality work is supplemented by the stick of a pay stoppage for defective output. For sub-standard work, where the worker is held to blame, he is not paid at all. For work which is partially sub-standard the guilty worker is paid at a reduced rate; the rate is established by the management according to how much use the product is, but cannot in any case be more than half the normal time-rate for the appropriate grade. Where the worker is not to blame, completely sub-standard work is paid at two-thirds of the corresponding time-rate; partial rejects are paid at a reduced rate assessed by the management down to a minimum of two-thirds of the corresponding time-rate. Only in a few instances—notably during the assimilation of new techniques—is a blameless worker paid full time-rates for sub-standard production.[166]

Idle-standing, where the worker is to blame, is not paid for at all. Where the worker is not to blame, it is paid for at half the corresponding time-rate, except in the metallurgical, mining and coke industries, where it is paid for at two-thirds, and during periods of assimilation of new techniques, when it is paid for at the full time-rate.[167]

It would appear that loss of earnings through idle-standing is not inconsiderable. Addressing a Plenum of the AUCCTU in November, 1961, Grishin complained:

'At many enterprises idle-standing is frequently caused by shortcomings in the organisation of production and unsatisfactory material and technical supplies. In 1960 in enterprises of the Councils of National Economy of the Russian Federation and Ukraine alone over 11 million working days were lost through idle-standing for whole days or during shifts.'[168]

Two years later Grishin said that, 'in 1962, in industry subordinated to the Councils of National Economy, recorded idle-standing alone exceeded 14 million working days'.[169] Losses of working time since then have been stated to have fallen 'insignificantly'. Idle-standing during shifts causes a loss of 10–12 per cent of working time.[170] In September, 1966, *Pravda* reported that a survey of 2,000 factories conducted by the Central Statistical Administration had revealed losses in working time of 254,000 man-hours in one three-shift day, the equivalent of 36,000 people not turning up for work.[171]

Present Soviet fiscal policy is to rely for the most part on indirect taxes to meet budgetary needs, despite Lenin's dictum that indirect taxation is unjust because it puts a disproportionate burden on the lowest paid.[172]

As part of the process of whittling away direct taxes the tax-free level of worker's earnings and the incidence of tax were lowered under a decree of March 23, 1957,[173] and the number of people affected by the bachelor or childless tax was cut under decrees of September, 1956,[174] and December, 1957.[175] Contributions and stoppage of pay for State loans were discontinued in 1958.[176]

A further law of May 7, 1960,[177] provided for the complete abolition of income tax and bachelor tax over the period 1960–5 by annual stages. On October 1, 1960, all tax was abolished on basic salaries of up to 50 roubles a month, and tax on salaries of from 50 to 60 roubles was to be reduced by

40 per cent. From October 1, 1961, the tax-free ceiling was raised to salaries of 60 roubles with a 40 per cent reduction on salaries of 61 to 70 roubles a month. This progression was to be maintained annually until tax was completely abolished on salaries of up to 100 roubles on October 1, 1965. From that date those earning under 100 roubles a month were to receive their full pay; those earning from 100 to 200 roubles were to have their pay scales reduced by part (i.e., between 21 per cent and 90 per cent) of the tax they would no longer be paying. Workers and employees earning over 200 roubles would scarcely benefit, since their salaries were to be cut by the full amount gained through abolition of income tax. As from October 1, 1965, the bachelor or childless tax, hitherto amounting to 6 per cent of gross salary, was to have been completely abolished.

In arguing for the abolition of income tax at the XXI Party Congress, Khrushchev had pointed out that it already represented only a minor contribution to the State revenue. The statistical evidence is that whereas direct taxes amounted to only 7·5 per cent of State revenue in 1960 indirect taxes (the turnover and profits taxes) amounted to 64·9 of the revenue.[178] Looked at another way, whereas the highest level of income tax in that year was 13 per cent, indirect taxes added some 70 per cent to the level of retail prices.[179] Furthermore the incidence of these indirect taxes is heavier on foodstuffs and essentials than on such luxury goods as refrigerators and cars. To quote *Izvestiya* of July 8, 1960, on the burden of taxation in the United States, 'indirect taxes are the most unfair, as they make the deepest hole in the pockets of the plain people'.

In September, 1962, however, the Presidium of the USSR Supreme Soviet issued a decree postponing 'temporarily, pending a special announcement', the progressive reduction of direct taxation provided for by the law of May, 1960.[180] Those due to be released from direct taxes or have their income tax reduced by 40 per cent from October 1, 1962 (i.e. those earning up to 70 and from 71 to 80 roubles a month respectively), and also those with higher earnings, will have to wait until the progressive reduction in direct taxation is resumed at an unspecified date.

The decree cited as reasons for this retrograde step the important measures being undertaken for the upsurge of agriculture and industry, the increase in consumer goods production and house-building and also 'the intensification of the aggressive machinations of imperialism and the need to strengthen the defence capability of the Soviet Union'.

There is a 30 per cent tax reduction for workers and employees with more than four dependants.[181] Lenin (formerly Stalin) Prizes, and the first 1,000 roubles of each bonus for an invention, technical improvement or rationalisation proposal are tax free.[182]

Fines, which are intended 'to assist [the] inculcation in workers of a careful attitude to State Socialist property'[183] were instituted in the First Five-Year Plan period.[184] and the RSFSR Labour Codex was amended accordingly.[185] According to current legislation, a worker is 'materially responsible' for materials and manufactured articles, and also factory property (instruments, special clothing, etc.) issued for his use, within limits fixed 'in agreement with the AUCCTU' by an Instruction of the *NKT*.[186] This Instruction, originally issued in 1932, and reprinted with amendments in 1961, lays down: for theft or deliberate destruction or spoiling—a fine of five times the value of the damage; for loss or spoiling through carelessness (except careless spoiling of materials and manufactured articles)—up to five times the value; for careless spoiling of materials and manufactured articles—the full value up to two-thirds of the culprit's average monthly wage.

These fines are imposed and recovered from wages, etc., by the management, the worker having the right to appeal to the Labour Disputes Commission.[187] If a worker spoils, destroys or loses through carelessness 'instruments of production' (machines and appliances), he is fined the value of the damage 'up to one-third of his wage rate'; the fine is imposed and recovered by the management, subject to the worker's right of appeal to the Labour Disputes Commission or to the courts.[188] If his actions 'bear the mark of acts liable to criminal prosecution', however, or if full responsibility is specially envisaged by the law,[189] or by contract, or if the damage was caused otherwise than in the performance of his duties—in these cases the worker is liable to be fined the full value of the damage. Such fines, if disputed, are imposed by order of a court, which is obliged to take account of the worker's material position. The proportion of a worker's wages deducted by the management on any pay-day must not exceed a total of 50 per cent.[190]

Apart from bearing 'material responsibility' a worker is

criminally liable for 'petty theft of State or public property', which carries a penalty of a year's 'deprivation of freedom' or corrective labour; and for 'malicious destruction or damage to State or public property', punishable by a fine of a year's corrective labour, or in more severe cases, such as arson, ten years' deprivation of freedom.[191]

The issue of compulsory State Loans, which before and especially since the war were a regular and often considerable burden on the Soviet wage-earner—the 1956 State Loan, for instance, was expected to absorb as much as three or four weeks' earnings[192]—was terminated from 1958. While this doubtless gave some relief, the millions of bondholders are to forgo or at least postpone all prospect of winnings, interest or redemption of their bonds, since a 20-year moratorium on all State payments on loans was declared in the decree announcing the abolition of future loans. Repayment of debts on State Loans is to be resumed in 1977 and spread equally over 20 years; that is to say, a bondholder *may* not see his savings back until 1997. The only exception to this moratorium (apart from the 1957 loan) is the 1947–57 3 per cent Internal Convertible State Lottery Loan, redemption of which is in any case not due to start until 1967.[193]

SOCIALIST COMPETITION, SHOCK-WORK AND STAKHANOVISM

It is customary for Soviet authorities and those who have followed them[194] to trace the origin of 'Socialist competition' to the *subbotniki*, or 'voluntary Saturdays' of extra unpaid work, which began when 'Communists of the Moscow–Kazan railway sorting depot organised the first Communist *subbotnik*' in April, 1919.[195] Lenin described the event as a 'victory over personal inertia, lack of discipline, petty-bourgeois egoism, over all those habits which accursed capitalism has bequeathed to us'.[196] It is perhaps this idea that the *subbotniki* represented a pure altruistic contribution to the common good which has made it convenient for Soviet writers to derive Socialist competition from them; but it is doubtful whether the derivation is really justified in the sense intended. Lenin, at any rate, did not connect the two: in none of the nine passages where he refers to the need to organise 'competition',[197] or 'Communist competition' as he once called it,[198] is there any reference to *sub-*

botniki. Yet he had been filled with such enthusiasm by the first *subbotnik* in April, 1919, that he had called it the '*actual* beginning of Communism'.[199] It is hard to believe that if there had been any connection between the *subbotniki* and the sort of 'competition between communes, communities, producers' and consumers' societies and fellowships'[200] which Lenin had in mind, he would not have used it to point a moral.

In the same way the IX Party Congress in April, 1920, distinguished quite clearly between the *subbotniki* and competition. *Subbotniki* were to 'fructify everyday work with new initiative and fresh enthusiasm',[201] relying, it appeared, mainly on high-minded motives; competition, on the other hand, was set beside 'agitational-ideological pressure' and the 'repression of known idlers, parasites and disorganisers', as a 'mighty force for raising the productivity of labour'. And in the same section the Congress remarked that the bonus system 'must become a powerful means of stirring up competition'.[202]

In fact, the *subbotniki* reached a 'short-lived apogee'[203] in the spring of 1920 and soon died out. (Nor does it appear that the principles on which they were run were quite so voluntary as was made out: at least there was a considerable degree of Party direction of the *subbotniki,* including the issue of rules and regulations, with conditions of exemption from this supposedly voluntary work.)[204] The first 'Socialist competition pact' was signed only in March, 1929, when the workers of the *Krasny Vyborzhets* factory 'addressed to every factory in the country a challenge to develop Socialist competition and shock-work'.[205] The Party conference in March, 1929, referred back to the IX Congress of 1920 to find a text to support the idea of competition. It appealed to the workers and 'labouring peasants' to[206]

> 'organise competition in all spheres of construction, organise competition between plants, factories, mines, railways, State farms, collective farms, Soviet establishments, schools and hospitals.'

From this point Socialist competition became a part of official policy, and has since found a regular niche in Party resolutions,[207] and a mention in the Party Statutes of 1961.[208] It has also achieved the doubtful dignity of a portmanteau word, *sotssorevnovanie.*

As may be gathered from the quotation above, particularly the reference to hospitals, competition in Soviet parlance is intended to mean something quite different from normal understanding of the word. Indeed, official Soviet translations into English use the euphemistic 'emulation' to render *sorevnovanie*, reserving 'competition' for the word *konkurentsiya*, which Lenin used, in contradistinction to *sorevnovanie*, to describe competition 'under capitalism'.[209] In theory, at least, Socialist competition differs from competition under capitalism in that it does not 'violate solidarity', but merely 'raises the sum total of the products of labour'. So said the IX Party Congress of 1920.[210] In this spirit, too, the Party Conference of 1929 set the fashion of recalling the *subbotniki* in the same breath as Socialist competition, noting also that the 'principles of a Communist attitude to labour . . . [were] beginning to strike ever deeper roots in production'.[211] There was, indeed, to be some system of 'encouragement', but the rewards were to be chiefly of a moral or social type, such as widespread publicity for the best workers and factories; so far as material inducements were concerned, Lenin was quoted to imply that they would go to collective bodies rather than individuals.[212] In May, 1929, Stalin argued again that solidarity would not be impaired:[213]

'The principle of Socialist emulation is: comradely *assistance* by the foremost to the laggards, so as to achieve an advance of all . . . Socialist emulation says: . . . *catch up with the best* and secure the *advance of all.*'

Had such motives of social altruism been sufficient, solidarity might indeed have survived inviolate; but within a few months of the Party Conference's appeal for the widespread development of competition, material inducements not only for groups but for individual workers were introduced and solidarity was shattered for ever. In September, 1929, the USSR *SovNarKom*, considering it necessary that 'enterprises, groups and individual workers evincing the greatest labour upsurge and giving the best results in fulfilling Government plan tasks should be encouraged by all means', decreed that there should be 'prizes to workers and employees for improvements achieved by Socialist competition'.[214]

The weaknesses of solidarity were quickly apparent: in fact Socialist competition was not introduced without considerable opposition. In a factory in the Ivanovo-Vosnesensk *oblast*, according to a letter in *Trud* in July, 1929, 800 workers refused to take part in Socialist competition, claiming that the working day was filled to the limit anyway. The author of the letter, a metal-worker named Goshev, went on.[215]

'Present-day working conditions are called "sweating" anyway; and now Socialist competition. . . . Who are these record workers? Young Communists, youths full of strength and zeal. With that, of course, you can move mountains. And their example is imitated by reckless oldsters who may once in a while succeed in a record performance. But how long can they last? One month, two months, maybe six months. . . . But we are just ordinary workers and have to work for years to come.'

Opposition was also found in the trade unions among what were later condemned as 'Right-Trotskyite renegades and traitors' and 'politically degenerate trade unionist elements'.[216]

It is not surprising, therefore, that in these conditions the drive for Socialist competition acquired a new edge. In 1929 the Party Conference had mentioned the 'strengthening of labour discipline' among the aims of competition.[217] In November of the same year Stalin spoke no more of 'comradely assistance' but of the 'fight—by means of *Socialist emulation*—against the labour-shirkers and disrupters of proletarian labour discipline';[218] and the XVI Party Congress in the summer of 1930 instructed the trade unions not only to give 'advanced workers every kind of encouragement and prizes', but also to organise 'comrades' courts from among the best shock-workers, so as to bring pressure to bear on persons who infringe labour discipline and undermine Socialist competition'.[219]

The combination of moral pressure, enhanced social status, and material reward in cash or kind, which was used to stimulate Socialist competition from the first, is exemplified in two of its special forms—shock-work (*udarnichestvo*) and Stakhanovism. Shock-work, indeed, appears to have preceded Socialist competition in its organised form, although it was later christened its 'child';[220] for the first shock brigade was organised in 1928 at the instance of the Leningrad *Ravenstvo* factory *Komsomols*, who undertook to fulfil the plan for the output of yarn, to set an example in labour discipline, not to miss any working day, and so forth.[221] In shock-work, as in Socialist competition in general, a mixture of motives was to be found: pride in achievement, various manifestations of public esteem, and the chance of a State medal such as the Order of the Red Labour Banner were substantially buttressed by material perquisites. In factories special canteens or separate dining-rooms were opened for shock-workers, 'sometimes with flowers on the table, electro-plated spoons and forks, and special dainties'; they also got the 'best chance of receiving theatre tickets or being sent on holiday excursions'.[222] In October, 1930, the Party Central Committee ordered priority for shock-workers and participants in Socialist competition in obtaining living quarters, facilities for education and rest, and supplies of scarce consumer goods.[223] In 1931 prize funds for achievements in Socialist competition and shock-work equivalent to 0·5 per cent of the annual wage fund were established in individual enterprises.[224]

Fulfilment of the First Five-Year Plan, according to an official account, was possible only thanks to the wide development of Socialist competition and shock-work.[225] Under the Second Plan (1933–7) competition is said to have reached a 'new, higher stage' in Stakhanovism.[226] The grain of reality behind this formula lies in a distinction drawn between shock-work and Stakhanovism, which was valid at least in the early stages of the latter. Whereas in shock-work the emphasis was simply on a more intensive application of labour to existing techniques, Stakhanovism—the answer, says the official version, to Stalin's slogan of the decisive importance of 'cadres who had mastered techniques'.[227]—involved a rationalisation of the production process.[228]

In Aleksey Stakhanov's record-breaking shift at a Donbass coal-mine in August, 1935, the rationalisation consisted in assuring his pneumatic pick a constant supply of compressed air throughout the shift, attaching two timberers exclusively to him to do the pit-propping as soon as he had finished cutting, and lengthening the ledges so that one miner did not get in the way of another.[229] By this method, which amounted essentially to specialising the functions of timberer and cutter,[230] Stakhanov cut 102 tons of coal in the shift; by disregarding his assistants' contribution and ascribing the output entirely to him, the record was allowed to seem more impressive than in fact it was, but even allowing for this, the output per man was well above the average of about seven tons.[231] Stalin's estimate, given in November, 1935, was 'five or six times'[232] the average per man. Stakhanov's achievement gave rise to an immediate fever of record-breaking: within a month his own record had been beaten three times, and he had regained it at

227 tons; this continued, and a year later a miner called Puzanov is said to have cut 660 tons.[233] At the same time the idea was spread to other industries where similar individual achievements were recorded.

The official version of these events gives a picture of an initial spark of spontaneous initiative, fanned into a flame by the Communist Party. Another suggestion has been made, that the idea was not Stakhanov's own, but that he was selected, as a good representative of the proletariat, to demonstrate it.[234] While facts for conclusive proof or disproof of this theory are lacking, there is no doubt that the Party seized on the idea with promptitude and energy as a means of raising productivity: the probable ulterior purpose—to create a system of privilege among the workers and so prevent the development of working-class solidarity—was naturally not proclaimed publicly. The Party 'from the very start calculated correctly that the Stakhanovite movement could not develop spontaneously, and that it needed leadership and assistance'.[235] In November, 1935, less than three months after Stakhanov's original effort, the First All-Union Conference of Stakhanovites was convened in the Kremlin, blessed with the chairmanship of Stalin himself.

Stalin's speech at this conference is noteworthy for the attention paid to the opposition to Stakhanovism, particularly from managements. Stalin did indeed mention that Stakhanov had to 'defend himself . . . against certain workers, who jeered and hounded him because of his "new-fangled ideas"'; but as one of the main themes of the speech was that the movement 'began somehow of itself, almost spontaneously, from below', Stalin naturally represented the opposition as coming mainly from the 'administrators of our enterprises', the 'conservatism of certain of our engineers and technicians', 'professors, engineers and experts', and so forth.[236] The task now, he said, was to 'curb' these elements: the Party 'must take a hand in the matter and help the Stakhanovites to consummate the movement'.[237]

At the end of the conference a number of Stakhanovites were recommended for the Order of Lenin.[238] But Stakhanovites, like shock-workers, got more tangible perquisites than medals: among these were free holidays in trade-union rest homes and sanatoria, free home tuition for their children, free medical service at home, and others, which, added to their vastly increased piece-work earnings, raised their standard of living far above that of the ordinary worker.[239]

These privileges alone would have been sufficient to make Stakhanovites unpopular among their fellow-workers, as well as with managements, on the basis of envy alone; but there were better reasons too. At the November conference Stalin envisaged higher norms of output as an outcome of the Stakhanovite movement. In December, 1935, the Party Central Committee considered 'questions of industry and transport in connection with the Stakhanovite movement', and ordered the raising of all norms.[240] This was the real centre of the Soviet worker's opposition to Stakhanovism.

Such opposition was not universal, but it was widespread and began to show itself early. Already in October Krivonos, the Stakhanovite engine-driver, had been shunned by his fellows;[241] other Stakhanovites met ironic comments[242] or practical jokes[243] of the type that schoolboys sometimes play on the 'swot'; in a Donbass pit matters went beyond this, when a Stakhanovite miner was beaten up by two others, one of whom had remarked: 'because of you they will raise our norm'.[244] *Izvestiya* of August 23, 1935, and *Pravda* of October 29, 1935, both contain accounts of the murder of 'leading shock-workers', the first by a fitter and the second by 'two *kulak* agents'.

These were not the only instances of Stakhanovites meeting physical violence,[245] and the Party was soon roused to action. In late September, for example, the Donbass *oblast* Party Committee issued a decree on 'sabotage of Stakhanovite methods of work', ordering 'severe punishment for the guilty'.[246] Reports of trials began to come in at the end of October, when sentences of two, three and four years' 'deprivation of liberty' were imposed on 'saboteurs of the Stakhanovite movement'.[247] 'The Party', said Zhdanov in mid-November, 'will not shrink from any measures that will help to sweep away all opponents from the victorious path of the Stakhanovite movement.'[248]

When norms were raised in 1936,[249] and pressure was continued, some bad effects became apparent. There were 'gross violations of the labour laws',[250] and equipment became badly run down.[251] Many Stakhanovites fell by the wayside, and now failed to fulfil their norms.[252] But elsewhere record-hunting went on, and new figures of output per shift were reached. It was at least partly true, therefore, that 'by the end of 1936 the increased norms were being over-fulfilled'—a fact which prompted a further increase in norms for 1937.[253] Then failures were reported even from the cradles of Stakhanovism itself: Stakhanov's own mine, it became known, was no longer fulfilling the Plan, and many other famous Donbass mines were lagging.[254] The Press and Party continued to whip up the flagging mechanism: a directive signed by Stalin and Molotov in April, 1937, scolded trade unions and even Party Committees for failure to expose 'wreckers'.[255] Opposition was not finally broken until Zhdanov's threat was carried out in the purges of 1937–8.

Thereafter Stakhanovism, 'that mixture of progressive rationalisation and old-time sweated labour' as an informed observer has put it,[256] passed out of its heroic heyday, and was more or less accepted as the peculiarly Soviet style of labour. The principle and practice of Stakhanovism were continued: the order 'Hero of Socialist Labour', instituted in 1938 for 'particularly distinguished activity in introducing innovations' in industry and other branches of economic and cultural life, represents the culminating honour that can be won by individuals in the industrial field, and 'furthered the growth of the Stakhanovite movement'.[257] But the coming of the war provided new incentives; and although the movement continued to be promoted, it gradually lost its identity and even its name. To take an example, the Trade Union Statute of 1949 provided for the 'organisation of Stakhanovite schools',[258] whereas the Statute of 1954 calls them 'schools of advanced methods of labour'.[259] The less official names of 'innovator' (*novator*, from which the abstract noun *novatorstvo*), or 'advanced workers' (*peredovik*) have tended to replace 'Stakhanovite'; and the movement itself has been re-absorbed into Socialist competition. In its new guise, however, Stakhanovism is still unpopular, as it was in the past: where rationalisation results in the raising of a norm, the worker proposing it has six months' grace during which he is paid at the old piece-rate, that is, more for the same work than his fellows in the shop. In the words of a fitter in a Leningrad motor repair works, writing in June, 1956: 'This naturally causes hostility to the innovator'.[260]

During and since the 1939–45 war Socialist competition has been further encouraged and developed. In 1942 'All-Union' (i.e. nation-wide) competition between enterprises was inaugurated by the metal-workers of Kuznetsk to improve supplies to the front.[261] New rewards, and particularly new aims and new occasions for Socialist competition, were devised. On the analogy of challenge cups, 'challenge Red Banners' are awarded to victorious enterprises by the USSR Council of Ministers, the AUCCTU, Ministries, or Republican bodies according to the level on which the competition is engaged. 'Rolls of Honour', 'Books of Honour', 'Certificates of Merit', titles such as 'Best Steel-Founder', 'Best Mechanic' or 'Best Turner', badges bearing the legend 'Excellent Participant in Socialist Competition'—these were some of the honorific awards instituted for success in Socialist competitions of various kinds and at various levels.[262] New regulations on the award of prizes for successes in Socialist competition were issued by the USSR Council of Ministers and the AUCCTU in December, 1959.[263] They pointed out that honorific and monetary awards had in the past been issued to factories producing outmoded or substandard products, and excesses had occurred in the payment of bonuses to heads of enterprises. The regulations stipulate that where the sum allotted to factories for prizes does not exceed 20,000 (old) roubles, up to 100 per cent of this sum may be used for monetary awards to outstanding workers and technical personnel. Where this sum is over 20,000 roubles, 60 to 70 per cent may be used for individual prizes, the remainder being utilised for cultural-welfare facilities. Individual prizes paid to workers and technical personnel must correspond to their earnings as a proportion of the total wages fund of the enterprise.

The aims of competition have been defined as occasion demanded: 'output of excellent quality', 'excellent execution of every operation of production', 'optimal use of equipment', 'high-speed methods of work', 'reduction of labour expenditure' and 'lowering production costs in every operation' are typical of the targets set up for competition in past years.[264] Permanent, everyday competition was supplemented by regular 'pre-May' and 'pre-October' competitions, starting in March and September respectively.[265] Competition 'in honour of' the elections to the Supreme Soviet and lesser bodies was started, beginning some two months before the date of the elections.[266] Competition 'in honour of Party Congresses' superseded all others: competition before the XIX Congress in 1952 could go on only for the seven weeks between the announcement of the Congress and its inception,[267] but when the XX Congress was announced some seven months ahead in July, 1955, competition was started within ten days,[268] as it was following the announcement nine months ahead in January, 1961, of the XXII Congress.[269] Competition started within a week of the announcement six months ahead of the XXIII Congress, in September, 1965.[270]

Socialist competition continues to be fostered by the Party. Shortcomings, such as failure to give adequate publicity to competition results, or the inertia of Trade Union Central Committees, have attracted comment from senior Party figures[271] or in the trade unions' official journal,[272] and steps are taken to eliminate them: since these criticisms were made, early in 1956, an 'AUCCTU Scroll of Honour' has been instituted, and Trade Union Central Committees have been brought in on the procedure of calculating competition results.[273] In some factories now *daily* competition results are kept, and the winning brigade and shift are rewarded with pennants.[274] The Party Central Committee Plenum of December, 1956, called for an even wider development of Socialist competition. Shortly afterwards the 'collectives' of leading enterprises in Moscow[275]

"summoned all workers in industry and transport in the capital to deploy Socialist competition for the fulfilment of the State Plan for 1957 before time, to mark the 40th anniversary of Great October with new successes in the struggle for technical progress . . .'.

Competition between Moscow and Leningrad in honour of the 50th anniversary of the October Revolution in November, 1967, began 14 months before the event.[276]

The Competition of Brigades and Shock-workers of Communist Labour, the most recent offspring of Socialist competition, was adumbrated by Khrushchev in his theses preceding the XXI Party Congress of January, 1959. Described as a further development of Socialist competition on a new, historical stage, the prime purpose of the Competition was to inspire in workers the *élan* necessary for the fulfilment of the 1959–65 plan for economic development. In November, 1958, the Bureau of the All-Union *Komsomol* Central Committee examined the question of a new patriotic movement of *Komsomol* members and youth for competition between 'Communist Labour Brigades'. The right to bear this title, to be awarded by *Komsomol* committees, would be based on performance in the 'all-round increase in labour productivity achieved through the introduction of technical equipment, mechanisation and automatic production'. The movement, as that of the *subbotniki,* to which it was specifically related, was said to have been voluntarily initiated by the Moscow Sortirovochnaya marshalling yards.

A feature of this movement is that its purview transcends the purely economic field. Members are not only called upon to improve their technical knowledge by spare-time study but are to become educational and cultural prototypes of the 'new Soviet man', and take an active part in useful social activities.[277]

The title 'Communist Labour Brigades' was taken literally by some enthusiasts. Cases were reported where earnings were shared out equally among members of brigades.[278] It was later stated that this new form of competition should really be called 'Socialist' and not 'Communist'.[279] Khrushchev ruled that 'one brigade, one works, one collective farm . . . could not reach Communism singly'.[280]

A more discriminatory trend was also observable. Insufficiently active people, the aged and young mothers were excluded from brigades, since their presence lessened the brigade's chance of gaining a title and financial awards.[281]

At the first All-Union Conference of Competitors for the title of 'Collectives of Communist Labour' on May 27–30, 1960, the movement was said to embrace 5 million workers or over 400,000 brigades, 40,000 of which had been awarded the title. Over 100,000 workers had been awarded the title of Shock-worker of Communist Labour. A plenum of the AUCCTU in July, 1960, resolved that: 'everything achieved by these leading workers should be adopted everywhere and their successes and methods of work should become available to the broad masses'. It was recommended that whole factories should join the competition. By mid-1964 nearly 30 million people were taking part in the Movement for Communist Labour and 85 per cent of all workers and employers were involved in this or in Socialist Competition. Nearly 4,000 factories and enterprises, 83,000 workshops and nearly 500,000 brigades had won the title 'Collective of Communist Labour' and there were 9,783,000 Shock-workers and members of Brigades of Communist Labour.[282]

A resolution passed by the AUCCTU Presidium in September, 1966, put these figures in more realistic perspective.[283] The issuing of awards was said to have become formalised to the extent that they no longer provided the necessary moral stimulus to increase production. Many individuals and collectives had received awards they did not merit; Socialist

Competition was often poorly organised, and managements frequently paid it scant regard. The resolution specified new methods of allocating the awards.

An integral and novel part of the movement was provided by the initiative of Valentina Gaganova, a textile hand from Vyshni Volochek, who at some temporary loss to her pay-packet voluntarily transferred from her own highly efficient brigade to help a backward one. This help-your-neighbour example has been taken up as a model for all workers. Mutual assistance and the mastering of more than one technique are encouraged.

Shock-work, Stakhanovism and Socialist Competition all have one feature in common: they produce privileged strata in the Soviet working class. The unpopularity of the members of this labour élite—sufficient, on past occasion, to provoke even murder—has already been pointed out. The system has also had political consequences. Working-class solidarity, which might be a threat to the régime if it could develop, tends to be broken up by the very method against which the Soviet authorities rail so insistently when they purport to find it in the free world: the creation of a relatively conservative labour aristocracy. The difference is that in the Soviet Union the stratification has been deliberately fostered.

THE INDUSTRIAL WORKER'S WAGES

One of the more striking developments in Soviet wages policy was the introduction, in September, 1956, of a decree establishing minimum wage levels for all Soviet workers except collective farmers and certain co-operative and individual craftsmen. The decree,[284] which took effect from the beginning of 1957, was introduced as a provisional step 'until such time as measures are taken to effect a general reform of the wages of workers and employees'. It laid down a minimum wage of 30–35 roubles a month for workers and employees directly employed in industrial enterprises, building sites, transport and communications; and 30 roubles a month (or 27 in country districts) for all other workers and for certain junior staff and watchmen in the industries mentioned. These figures relate to the basic wage rate: bonuses, overtime, increments, etc., were paid in addition. The minimum tax-free allowance was raised at the same time. Under the 1959–65 plan for economic development, minimum levels were established at 40–45 roubles a month in the period 1959–62; this was to be followed by a further increase to 50–60 roubles a month in the period 1963–1965.[285] These plans, however, were not realised. A universal minimum wage of 40–45 roubles a month was not achieved until 1965.[286] The present target is a minimum wage of 60 roubles a month by the end of the 1966–70 Five-Year Plan.[287]

From the early 1930s until recently, meaningful statistical data on wages were not published. The most that was revealed in Soviet statistics was percentage increase in real incomes over previous years. The only sources of information on cash wages were scattered, infrequent and indirect reference in the Soviet Press. The official silence on this subject was broken at the end of 1965 with the publication of statistical returns for 1964.[288] These gave an average cash wage for all workers and employees of 90 roubles a month in 1964, and a real income (including social service benefits of all kinds) of 121 roubles. Cash wages of industrial workers totalled 99 roubles (real income 134 roubles), though for industrial workers and employees together the figure was 90·1 roubles (compared with 33·1 roubles in 1940). This figure has since been stated to have risen to 95 roubles in 1965.[289] (This compares with 77·8 roubles in 1958; 80·1 in 1960 and 87·6 roubles in 1963.)

These figures should, however, be treated with caution. They conceal wide variations both above and below the average. Workers in manufacturing industry, for example, averaged 98·7 roubles in 1964, construction workers 103 roubles and water transport workers 131·6 roubles. But wages in the service industries are generally much lower (e.g. 65·7 roubles in trade, public catering and supplies).[290] Wages in certain industries are, however, claimed to be much higher. In July, 1961, they were said to average 217 roubles in ferrous metallurgy and 140·5 in non-ferrous metallurgy.[291] These high wages help to raise the average and conceal the numbers earning much less than the norm. An indication of how many workers earn these high wages was provided in 1960 when Khrushchev estimated that about 90 per cent of the forecast labour force would still be earning less than 100 roubles a month at the beginning of 1966. About 10 per cent would be earning between 100 and 200 roubles, and the rest (400,000 or 0·6 per cent) over 200 roubles a month.[292] During the current Five-Year Plan average wages of workers and employees are to rise to not less than 115 roubles a month.[293]

Consumption data from Soviet sources, once extremely rare, are now a little more common. A survey of budgets of 100 workers' families whose heads were employed in the steel, engineering and textile industries of Moscow, Gorky and Ivanovo[294] revealed that the average size of family was 3·6 persons, with an average total income of 176 roubles a month. The survey also revealed changes in the diet of workers' families over the period 1951–61. Each member was said to eat 39·4 per cent more meat, 73·3 per cent more butter, 81·2 per cent more sweets, 50 per cent more sugar and 100 per cent more meat and fish. Fresh fruit consumption had increased almost 4·7 times. In the absence of absolute consumption figures, however, these data must be treated with reserve, particularly in view of the reported shortages of meat and animal produce at that time. The survey also reported a 9·4 per cent reduction in consumption of potatoes, and a 36·8 per cent drop in rye bread consumption. The number of radio sets had increased from 15 to 59 and there were now 36 television sets where there were none in 1951.

Another example of a family budget, published in 1960,[295] gave a total monthly income of 396 roubles for a family of five adults, a 16-year-old schoolboy and a small child. The head of the family had a monthly pension of 81 roubles, his son earned 130 roubles, his wife 55 roubles, daughter 55 roubles, and his son-in-law 80 roubles. When his daughter-in-law decided to stay at home to look after her child, the income fell to 346 roubles, leaving an average of just under 50 roubles for each member of the family.

A more recent example, published in 1966,[296] gave the average annual income of a family of four in the Proletarsky district of Moscow at 2,552 roubles. This was made up of the wages of the head of the family, 1,297 roubles, and of the second member (usually the wife), 857 roubles; allowances and grants of 170 roubles; and social services to the value of 60 roubles [*sic*]. This gives an average monthly income from all sources of about 213 roubles. Thirty-five per cent of expenditure was on food, 4 per cent on rent and 3·6 per cent on transport. Of every 100 families in the district, 73 had television sets, 59 had radios and 25 had refrigerators. The report then quoted the budget of the Fichkovsky family. In 1958, Boris worked as a fitter, and Maria, his wife, as a checker in a factory; their two children were at school. In 1965, Boris, then 47, was a foreman, and Maria a senior checker; the children were finishing secondary school. The incomes of husband and wife increased from 1,488 and 1,097 roubles respectively in 1958 to 1,949 and 1,445 roubles in 1965. Including grants, allowances and social service benefits, the family income rose from 2,792 to 3,500 roubles. The family's expenditure on food had risen from 968 roubles 'a few years ago' to 1,413 roubles. In 1958, spending on household necessities and furniture totalled 119 roubles; it had since fallen. But nearly twice as much was spent on fabrics, clothes, linen and footwear (674 roubles). Expenditure on the cinema, theatre and other cultural and educational activities had increased two-and-a-half times.

One lesson of these published budgets is plain. More than one member of the family must go out to work to maintain a reasonable standard of living at home. This is the pattern imposed by the Five-Year Plan: whereas in 1928 little more than a quarter of all wage-earners were women, today they constitute 49 per cent.[297] Conversely, the number of dependants declined from 2·5 per wage-earner in 1928 to 1·5 in 1937. The reliability of such data on 'average' families must also be questioned. According to official statistics, only 1·6 members of each worker's family work, and average monthly income, including bonuses and social service benefits, amounted in 1964 to 194 roubles per family. Moreover, one Soviet planning official has characterised the findings of budget studies of a number of families, carried out by the Central Statistical Administration, as 'unable to claim complete or, moreover, scientific authenticity'.[298]

A Western observer has calculated on the basis of Soviet price and wage data[299] that in 1959 the Soviet worker had to work about 8 per cent longer than in 1928, in order to buy for his family the same average weekly supply of seven essential foods—bread, potatoes, beef, butter, eggs, milk and sugar. In particular he had to work about 18 per cent longer for sugar and 190 per cent longer for eggs. Beef was just as 'cheap', relatively, and potatoes and butter slightly less expensive. Indications are that prices of other consumer goods, especially clothing, rose at a higher rate than income.

An Amalgamated Engineering Union delegation which visited the Soviet Union in 1961 produced a comparative list of the length of time skilled engineering workers in the USSR and Great Britain had to work to earn sufficient to buy specified quantities of foods and particular goods. It showed convincingly that the Soviet engineer had to work much longer to buy most kinds of goods than his British counterpart.[300]

The conclusion to be drawn is that Soviet workers have to toil to fulfil their norms for relatively little reward, but their families have to take up jobs so as to safeguard a standard of living which is below that in Western Europe and, on balance, seems unlikely to be greatly better than it was in 1928, before the industrialisation drive started.

SOURCES

N.B.—Undated citations of works of which more than one edition is listed in the bibliography refer to the most recent edition there listed; earlier editions are cited with the date in brackets.

1. Lenin, Vol. 24, p. 5.
2. Dewar, pp. 26f., 162.
3. Lenin, Vol. 27, pp. 220ff.
4. See Dewar, p. 30.
5. Bergson, p. 182.
6. *K.P.S.S. v Rezolyutsiakh*, Vol. I, pp. 506f.
7. *Ibid.*, p. 545.
8. *B.S.E.*, 1st edn., Vol. on USSR, col. 1116; Bergson, p. 185; Dewar, p. 134.
9. *K.P.S.S. v Rezolyutsiakh*, Vol. II, pp. 309ff.
10. *Sedmoy Sezd Professionalnykh Soyuzov*, SSSR, quoted by Bergson, p. 187.
11. Dewar, p. 136.
12. *Loc. cit.*
13. Dobb, p. 444.
14. Hubbard, p. 93.
15. Stalin, *Problems of Leninism*, p. 463.
16. *Loc. cit.*
17. *Ibid.*, p. 464.
18. *Loc. cit.*
19. Stalin, *Works*, Vol. 13, pp.102f.
20. Kapustin, p. 4.
21. Dewar, p. 136; Bergson, pp. 154f.
22. Schwarz, pp. 148f; Baykov, p. 228.
23. Schwarz, p. 147.
24. Lozovsky, p. 50.
25. Kuznetsova, p. 17.
26. Kostin, p. 27.
27. Chigvintsev, p. 55.
28. Kuznetsova, p. 19.
29. Kostin, pp. 29f.
30. Kuznetsova, pp. 19f.
31. Kapustin, p. 23.
32. Kostin, pp. 29f.
33. Kapustin, p. 28.
34. Kostin, p. 28.
35. Kapustin, p. 26.
36. *XX Sezd K.P.S.S.*, Vol. 1, p. 307.
37. *Ibid.*, pp. 527f.
38. *K.P.S.S. v Rezolyutsiakh*, Vol. III, p. 432.
39. Chigvintsev, p. 34.
40. See, for instance, *Voprosy Ekonomiki*, 1961, No. 9, p. 145; Kapustin, p. 28.

41. *Pravda*, May 25, 1955.
42. *Sotsialistichesky Trud*, 1956, No. 1, p. 5.
43. *Loc. cit.*
44. *Sotsialistichesky Trud*, 1957, No. 1, p. 4.
45. *Sotsialistichesky Trud*, 1956, No. 9, p. 5.
46. *Loc. cit.*
47. *Sotsialistichesky, Trud*, 1957, No. 1. p. 5.
48. E. Kapustin, in *V Pomoshch Politicheskomu Samoobrazovaniyu*, 1958, No. 6, p. 98.
49. *Pravda*, April 22, 1958.
50. *Vneocherednoy XXI Sezd K.P.S.S.*, Vol. II, p. 525.
51. *Ekonomicheskaya Gazeta*, February 22, 1964.
52. Kapustin, p. 17.
53. Volkov, *Pravda*, October 6, 1961.
54. *Pravda*, February 20, 1966.
55. *Voprosy Ekonomiki*, 1961, No. 9, p. 146.
56. *Ibid.*, p. 145.
57. Kuznetsova, p. 13.
58. Kostin, p. 30.
59. Kapustin, p. 27.
60. Kuznetsova, p. 15, quoting a decree of the USSR Council of Ministers of September 20, 1955.
61. *Ibid.*, p. 15.
62. Aleksandrov, Kiselev and Stavtseva, p. 87.
63. *Spravochnye Materialy po Trudu i Zarabotnoy Plate*, p. 89.
64. *Spravochnik Profsoyuznogo Rabotnika*, p. 38.
65. Kostin, p. 12.
66. Volkov, *Pravda*, November 14, 1965.
67. Kostin, p. 26.
68. *Loc. cit.*
69. Kapustin, p. 28.
70. Remizov, p. 27.
71. Kotov, pp. 172f.
72. Aleksandrov, p. 250.
73. Kuznetsova, p. 26.
74. Lenin, Vol. 27, p. 284.
75. Dewar, pp. 39, 63.
76. *K.P.S.S. v Rezolyutsiakh*, Vol. I, p. 698.
77. VKP (*b*) *o Profsoyuzakh*, pp. 580ff.
78. *B.S.E.*, 1st edn., Vol. on USSR, col. 1117.
79. Kuznetsova, p. 26.
80. Kapustin, p. 96.
81. *Ibid.*, p. 98.
82. Kunelsky and Begidzhanov, p. 76.
83. Kuznetsova, p. 33.
84. Kapustin, p. 147.
85. Kunelsky and Begidzhanov, p. 82.
86. Kuznetsova, p. 30.
87. Kapustin, pp. 110f.
88. Kuznetsova, p. 33.
89. *Loc. cit.*
90. Kunelsky and Begidzhanov, p. 99.
91. Kuznetsova, pp. 33–6.
92. *Ibid.*, p. 37.
93. *Ibid.*, pp. 44f.
94. *Ibid.*, p. 45.
95. Volkov, *Pravda*, April 4, 1962.
96. *Spravochnye Materialy po Trudu i Zarabotnoy Plate*, p. 97.
97. Kunelsky and Begidzhanov, p. 85.
98. Kuznetsova, pp. 45ff.
99. Mutsinov, p. 38.
100. Kuznetsova, p. 51.
101. *Ibid.*, p. 51f.
102. Aleksandrov and Moskalenko, p. 94.
103. Kulski, p. 408.
104. *K.P.S.S. v Rezolyutsiakh*, Vol. III, p. 687.

105. Kulski, p. 408.
106. USSR Laws, 1938, 27; 178.
107. USSR Laws, 1938, 52: 297.
108. Quoted by Kulski, pp. 408f.
109. *Loc. cit.*, Aleksandrov and Moskalenko (1944), p. 95.
110. *Sbornik*, p. 206.
111. *B.S.E.*, 1st edn., Vol. 42, col. 377; Konakov, p. 36.
112. *K.P.S.S. v Rezolyutsiakh*, Vol. II, p. 98.
113. *B.S.E.*, 1st edn., Vol. 42, col. 377; B.S.E., 2nd edn., Vol. 30, p. 181; Konakov, p. 36.
114. *K.P.S.S. v Rezolyutsiakh*, Vol. III, p. 144.
115. *Za Industrializatsiyu*, October 24, 1935, quoted by Schwarz, p. 194.
116. Stalin, *Problems of Leninism*, pp. 674f.
117. Konakov, p. 37.
118. *K.P.S.S. v Rezolyutsiakh*, Vol. III, p. 270.
119. USSR Laws, 1939, 18: 119.
120. USSR Laws, 1940, 16: 386; 18: 437.
121. *Pravda*, March 1, 1947.
122. Quoted by Kulski, p. 409.
123. Konakov, p. 47.
124. USSR Laws, 1939, 7: 38; *Sbornik* (1956), p. 158.
125. *Sotsialistichesky Trud*, 1956, No. 9, p. 55.
126. Chigvintsev, pp. 59f.
127. Goloshchapov, pp. 16f.
128. Chigvintsev, p. 60.
129. *Five-Year Plan, 1946–50*, pp. 54f.
130. *Pravda,* October 6, 1952, p. 6.
131. Grishin, in *Pravda*, March 24, 1959.
132. Volkov, in *Pravda*, October 6, 1961.
133. Kunelsky and Begidzhanov, p. 171.
134. *Shkurko*, p. 101.
135. *Ibid.*, p. 102.
136. *Pravda*, October 6, 1961.
137. *Pravda*, April 4, 1962.
138. Kunelsky and Begidzhanov, p. 175.
139. Baykov, p. 133.
140. Konakov, p. 20.
141. Chigvintsev, p. 73.
142. Kapustin, p. 35.
143. *B.S.E.*, 2nd edn., Vol. 16, p. 458.
144. Kuznetsova, p. 53.
145. Kunelsky and Begidzhanov, p. 103.
146. Kapustin, pp. 35f.
147. *Ibid.*, p. 37; *Sbornik*, pp. 233–5.
148. Kapustin, p. 37.
149. Baykov, p. 297.
150. *Sbornik*, pp. 208–10.
151. *Pravda*, September 28, 1965.
152. *Izvestiya*, January 29, 1966.
153. *Pravda*, February 20, 1966.
154. *Spravochnik Profsoyuznogo Rabotnika* (1949), p. 32; *Sbornik*, p. 49.
155. Dobb, p. 428.
156. *Sbornik*, pp. 282–6.
157. Kostin, pp. 47f.
158. *Pravda*, November 14, 1965.
159. *Spravochnik Profsoyuznogo Rabotnika*, pp. 96f; *Sbornik*, p. 483.
160. *Sbornik*, p. 156.
161. *Ibid.*, pp. 495f.

162. *Ibid.*, pp. 297f.
163. *K.P.S.S. v Rezolyutsiakh*, Vol. III, p. 577.
164. Aleksandrov, p. 253.
165. Report to USSR Supreme Soviet. *Pravda*, December 10, 1964.
166. *Spravochnik Profsoyuznogo Rabotnika*, pp. 100f; *KZoT*, art. 68^1; in *Sbornik*, p. 189.
167. *KZoT*, arts. 68, 68^2, in *Sbornik*, pp. 189f.
168. *Pravda*, November 25, 1961.
169. *Trud*, October 29, 1963.
170. V. Patrushev in *Ekonomicheskaya Gazeta*, May 12, 1965.
171. *Pravda*, September 14, 1966.
172. Lenin, Vol. 6, p. 364.
173. *Vedomosti Verkhovnogo Soveta SSSR*, 1957, No. 7.
174. *Vedomosti Verkhovnogo Soveta SSSR*, 1956, No. 18.
175. *Vedomosti Verkhovnogo Soveta SSSR*, 1957, No. 28.
176. *Postanovlenie Tsentralnogo Komiteta K.P.S.S. i Soveta Ministrov* of April 19, 1957; *O gosudarstvennykh zaymakh, razmeshchaemykh po podpiske sredi trudyashchikhsya Sovetskogo Soyuza,Pravda*, April 20, 1957; *Spravochnik rayonnogo Finansovogo Rabotnika*, Vol. II, pp. 194–6.
177. *Vedomosti Verkhovnogo Soveta SSSR*, 1960, No. 18.
178. *Narodnoe Khozyaistvo SSSR v 1960 godu*, p. 845.
179. *Ibid.*, pp. 673, 845.
180. *Izvestiya*, September 25, 1962.
181. *Spravochnik Nalogovogo Rabotnika*, pp. 91f.
182. *Ibid.*, p. 83.
183. Aleksandrov, p. 300.
184. USSR Laws, 1929, 42: 367; 1931, 51: 334; 1932, 40: 242.
185. RSFSR Laws, 1930, 7: 83; 1932, 72: 324.
186. USSR Laws, 1932, 40: 242, art. 3; KZoT, art. 83^4 in *Sbornik*, p. 439; *Spravochnik Profsoyuznogo Rabotnika*, pp. 88f.
187. *Ibid.*, pp. 91f.
188. USSR Laws, 1929, 42: 367, arts. 1, 4, and KZoT, arts. 83 and 83^2 in *Sbornik*, pp. 438f.; *Spravochnik Profsoyuznogo Rabotnika*, pp. 87f.
189. *See*, for instance, RSFSR Laws, 1930, 42: 521.
190. USSR Laws, 1929, 42: 367, arts. 2, 6 and 7; KZoT, arts. 83^1, 83^2 and 83^6 in *Sbornik*, pp. 438f.; *Spravochnik Profsoyuz nogo Rabotnika*, pp. 87f.
191. RSFSR Criminal Codex, arts. 96, 98.
192. *Zverev* (USSR Minister of Finance) on Moscow Radio, May 14, 1956.
193. *Postanovlenie Tsentralnogo Komiteta K.P.S.S. i Soveta Ministrov* of April 19, 1957; *O gosudarstvennykh zaymakh, razmeshchaemykh po podpiske sredi trudyashchikhsya Sovetskogo Soyuza, Pravda*, April 20, 1957; *Spravochnik rayonnogo Finansovogo Rabotnika,* Vol. II, pp. 194–6.
194. *B.S.E.*, 1st edn., Vol. on *USSR*, col. 1103; Webbs,

Vol. II, p. 752; Dewar, p. 61.
195. *B.S.E.*, 1st edn. Vol. on USSR, col. 1103.
196. Lenin, Vol. 29, p. 379.
197. Lenin, Vol. 26, pp. 367–76; Vol. 27, pp. 132, 179–82, 230–3, 284; Vol. 28, p. 429; Vol. 31, p. 349; Vol. 35, p. 399.
198. Lenin, Vol. 31, p. 274.
199. Lenin, Vol. 29, p. 379.
200. Lenin, Vol. 26, p. 376.
201. *K.P.S.S. v Rezolyutsiakh*, Vol. I, p. 488.
202. *Ibid.*, p. 480.
203. Dewar, p. 61.
204. *Ibid.*, p. 62.
205. *B.S.E.*, 1st edn., Vol. 52, col. 280.
206. *K.P.S.S. v. Rezolyutsiakh*, Vol. II, p. 617.
207. *K.P.S.S. v Rezolyutsiakh*, Vol. III, pp. 65, 77, 81, 87, 221, 339.
208. *Pravda*, November 6, 1961
209. Lenin, Vol. 26, p. 367
210. *K.P.S.S. v Rezolyutsiakh*, Vol. I, p. 480.
211. *K.P.S.S. v Rezolyutsiakh*, Vol. II, p. 616–18.
212. *Ibid.*, p. 618.
213. Stalin, *Works*, Vol. 12, p. 116.
214. USSR Laws, 1929, 58: 541.
215. *Trud*, July 3, 1929, quoted by Schwarz, p. 192.
216. *B.S.E.*, 1st edn., Vol. 52, col. 280.
217. *K.P.S.S. v. Rezolyutsiakh*, Vol. II, p. 617.
218. Stalin, *Works*, Vol. 12, p. 125.
219. *K.P.S.S. v Rezolyutsiakh*, Vol. III, p. 65.
220. *Loc. cit.*
221. *B.S.E.*, 1st edn., Vol. 52, col. 280; Baykov, p. 221.
222. Webbs, Vol. II, p. 749.
223. VKP (*b*) *o Profsoyuzakh*, pp. 564f.
224. USSR Laws, 1931, 52: 337, 338.
225. *B.S.E.*, 1st edn., Vol. 52, col. 281.
226. *B.S.E.*, 1st edn., Vol. on USSR, col. 1106.
227. *Loc. cit.*
228. Baykov, p. 337.
229. Lozovsky, p. 32.
230. *B.S.E.*, 1st edn., Vol. 52, col. 790.
231. Pasquier, pp. 28f.; Hubbard, p. 77.
232. Stalin, *Problems of Leninism*, p. 671.
233. Lozovsky, p. 32; B.S.E., 1st edn., Vol. 52, cols. 788f.
234. Hubbard, p. 77.
235. *B.S.E.*, 1st edn., Vol. on USSR, col. 1107.
236. Stalin, *op. cit.*, pp. 668, 675, 676f.
237. *Ibid.*, p. 676.
238. *Ibid.*, p. 678.
239. *Trud*, November 1 and 2, 1935, quoted by Deutscher, pp. 113f.
240. *K.P.S.S. v Rezolyutsiakh*, Vol. III, p. 271.
241. *Pravda*, October 16, 1935, quoted by Schwarz, p. 195.
242. *Trud*, October 25, 1935, quoted by Schwarz, p. 196.
243. *Trud*, November 1, 1935, quoted by Schwarz, p. 196.
244 *Za Industrializatsiyu*, October 3, 1935.
245. *Za Industrializatsiyu*, October 15, 1935.
246. *Za Industrializatsiyu*, October 3, 1935.
247. *Trud*, October 23, 1935.
248. *Pravda*, November 13, 1935.

249. *B.S.E.*, 1st edn., Vol. 52, col. 792.
250. *Trud*, March 14, 1936, quoted by Schwarz, p. 197.
251. *Trud*, September 9, 1936, quoted by Schwarz, p. 197.
252. *Trud*, August 5, 1936; *Bolshevik*, 1936, No. 17, pp. 17f., quoted by Schwarz, p. 198.
253. *B.S.E.*, 1st edn., Vol. 52, col. 792.
254. *Pravda*, April 10, 1939; *Za Industrializatsiyu*, March 9, 1937; quoted by Schwarz, p. 198.
255. *Deutscher*, p. 116.
256. *Loc. cit.*
257. *B.S.E.*, 2nd edn., Vol. II, p. 142.
258. *Ustav Professionalnykh Soyuzov SSSR* (1949) art. 34(d), in *Trud*, May 11, 1949.
259. *Ustav Professionalnykh Soyuzov SSSR* (1954), art. 38(f), in *Spravochnik Profsoyuznogo Rabotnika* (1956), p. 178.
260. A. Demeshko in *Sotsialistichesky Trud*, 1956, No. 6, p. 51.
261. *B.S.E.*, 1st edn., Vol. on USSR, cols. 1108f.
262. *Spravochnik Profsoyuznogo Rabotnika* (1949), pp. 18f.
263. *Spravochnik Profsoyuznogo Rabotnika*, pp. 34f.
264. Rumyantsev, pp. 45–53.
265. *See*, for instance, *Trud*, March 27, 1952, March 24 and October 3, 1953, March 26 and September 14, 1954, and March 18, 1955.
266. *Trud*, January 12, October 7, and December 27, 1950; January 13, 1954, and January 20, 1955.
267. *Pravda*, August 20, 1952; *Trud*, August 22 and October 5, 1952.
268. *Pravda*, July 13, 1955; *Trud*, July 23, 1955.
269. *Pravda*, January 11, 1961; *Trud*, January 17, 1961.
270. *Pravda*, October 5, 1965.
271. *XX Sezd K.P.S.S.*, Vol. I, p. 525.
272. *Sovetskie Profsoyuzy*, 1956, No. 3, p. 10.
273. *Spravochnik Profsoyuznogo Rabotnika* (1956), p. 39; *Pravda*, September 13, 1956.
274. *Sovetskie Profsoyuzy*, 1956, No. 11, pp. 51f.
275. *Sovetskie Profsoyuzy*, 1957, No. 2, p. 1.
276. *Pravda*, September 13, 1966.
277. *Pravda*, November 22, 1958.
278. *Molodoy Kommunist*, No. 3, 1959, p. 25.
279. *Kommunist*, No. 8, 1960, pp. 57–8.
280. *Pravda*, May 29, 1960.
281. *Molodoy Kommunist*, No. 3, 1959, p. 25.
282. *Spravochnik Profsoyuznogo Rabotnika*, pp. 9–11.
283. *Trud*, September 27, 1966.
284. *Sbornik*, pp. 194f.
285. *Pravda*, February 8, 1959.
286. *Zakon o Gosudarstvennom Plane Razvitiya Narodnogo Khozyaistva na 1965 god*, *Pravda*, December 12, 1964.
287. *Direktivy XXIII Sezda KPSS po pyatiletnomu planu razvitiya narodnogo khozyaistva SSSR na 1966–70*, *Pravda*, April 10, 1966.

288. *Narodnoe Khozyaistvo SSSR v 1964 godu*, p. 554f.
289. *Pravda*, February 3, 1966.
290. *Narodnoe Khozyaistvo SSSR v 1964 godu*, p. 555.
291. Moscow Radio home service, July 15, 1961.
292. *Pravda*, May 6, 1960.
293. A. N. Kosygin, Report to XXIII CPSU Congress, April 5, 1966, *Pravda*, April 6, 1966.
294. *Tass* in English, December 27, 1961.
295. *Leninskoye Znamya*, May 12, 1960.
296. *Moskovskaya Pravda*, March 17, 1966; *Moscow News*, March 26, 1966.
297. *Narodnoe Khozyaistvo SSSR v 1965 godu*, p. 564.
298. *Izvestiya*, November 14, 1964.
299. Edmund Nash in *Monthly Labor Review*, April 1960, No. 4.
300. *AEU Journal*, February, 1962.

III
Labour Discipline

THE AFTERMATH OF REVOLUTION

The Soviet Communists' ideas of Labour Discipline at the time of the Revolution were characteristically idealistic, but here, as elsewhere, they had hard lessons to learn when faced with the problem of governing a backward peasant country racked by civil war.

Lenin quickly recognised the need for discipline, the need to consolidate what the Bolsheviks had won 'in solid forms of *daily labour discipline*'. They must learn, he wrote in April, 1918, 'to combine . . . the democratism of the working masses with iron discipline at work'.[1] But it was to be discipline of a new type—'discipline that is conscious and voluntary'.[2] Reasoning on these lines led Lenin to acclaim the *subbotniki*,* which gave him such high hopes of the workers' social altruism, as a 'conscious and voluntary initiative of the workers' in going over to a 'new labour discipline'.[3]

Some sixteen months later the stress of civil war and economic dislocation—notably a fuel crisis—led Lenin to express himself very differently. The year 1919 saw the introduction of a Disciplinary Code into the Red Army, which included a system of 'Comrade's Courts' (*Tovarishcheskie Sudy*) for judging minor offences;[4] it is perhaps significant that Lenin had the military example in mind. 'We have raised discipline in the forces', he wrote in a Party Central Committee circular in November, 1919. 'We must raise labour discipline.' Labour service† was the order of the day at the time, and Lenin demanded that 'those who, in spite of repeated injunctions, demands and orders, continue to avoid work [should be] punished with merciless severity'. 'Any indulgence, any weakness' was to be treated as a 'crime against the Revolution'.[5]

The day after this circular was published, 'Workers' (Com-

* *See* p. 73. † *See* p. 32.

rades') Disciplinary Courts' were set up in all enterprises and establishments so as to 'raise labour discipline and productivity to the utmost'. The courts were composed of one delegate each from the management, trade union and general workers' meeting, and were to try publicly all violators of discipline. The penalties at their disposal included: public reprimand; up to six months' suspension of trade union electoral rights; up to one month's demotion with reduced pay; direction to 'hard, socially useful labour' with 'appropriate' pay. Particularly obstructive workers would be sent to concentration camps, and criminal cases would go to higher courts.[6]

By April, 1920, when the IX Party Congress met, Lenin was prepared to justify coercion publicly:[7]

> 'We are introducing labour service and are uniting the working people without in any way fearing to use coercion, since no revolution was ever made without coercion, and the proletariat has the right to use coercion so as to hold its own at any cost. . . . Now the task is to apply to the peaceful tasks of economic construction . . . everything that can concentrate the proletariat, its absolute unity. Here iron discipline is necessary.'

The Congress resolved that the trade unions should 'introduce a spirit of the strictest efficiency and discipline'; the first function of Trade Union Factory Committees was to 'raise labour discipline by all means, including Comrades' Disciplinary Courts'. The military influence that had affected Lenin some months previously was again apparent in the Congress's resolution on labour turnover—a problem that has continued to plague the Soviet economy. In an early attempt to grasp this particular nettle firmly, the Congress denounced workers who 'wilfully leave enterprises and travel from place to place . . . seeking better living conditions' as 'labour deserters'; it ordered Soviets and trade unions to wage a 'planned, systematic, persistent, severe struggle against labour desertion'; deserters, it said, should be blacklisted, formed into 'penal worker gangs' or imprisoned in concentration camps.[8]

Closely related to high labour turnover was the problem of absenteeism, which the Soviet Government attempted to solve with equal severity a few weeks after the IX Congress. A decree of the *SovNarKom* at the end of April, 1920, ordered that absentees must forfeit pay and work off absence in overtime or on holidays, on pain of imprisonment in a concentration camp; moreover, those absent for more than three days in one month must be tried in the Workers' (Comrades') Disciplinary Courts for sabotage.[9]

Nevertheless indiscipline continued. A year later, in April, 1921, the Comrades' Courts were reorganised, 'to improve discipline and raise productivity'. The effect of the reorganisation was to make them considerably more official and less democratic. They were now to be set up, and their chairmen and vice-chairmen appointed by the AUCCTU; their activity was to be guided by the AUCCTU and the Commissariat of Justice; their members were to be elected by factory managements, and their alternate members by general factory meetings of trade unionists. A string of petty offences within the Comrades' Courts' competence was enumerated, ranging from lateness at work to abetting indiscipline. The penalties the courts might impose were not substantially altered, merely defined rather more closely: the maximum sentence was six months in a concentration camp. More serious offences were dealt with by the People's Courts.[10] Expectant mothers and mothers of young children were exempt from imprisonment for labour desertion and other violations of labour discipline.[11]

RECOVERY

By November, 1922, when the new Labour Codex was promulgated, the Civil War had been over for more than two years, and NEP had been functioning for 18 months; at the same time the reflux of workers from the villages created urban unemployment,[12] which doubtless had its effect on the workers' attitude to their employers. The Labour Codex of 1922, therefore, reflected a decreased anxiety on the part of the Government over the problems of absenteeism and turnover which had given concern hitherto. Whereas hitherto a worker who wished to leave his job had to give reasons, which had to be scrutinised by the factory committee,[13] he might now demand termination of a contract of indefinite duration at any time on giving one day's notice if he was paid weekly, or seven days' notice if paid fortnightly or monthly. Grounds were laid down on which he might demand the termination of a contract of definite duration before expiry—if his wages were not paid on time, if his employer neglected his obligations under the contract or the labour laws, if he was badly treated by the employer, by representatives of the management or members of their families, or if the sanitary conditions of his work deteriorated. On the other hand, he could be sacked without notice if he was absent for three consecutive days, or six days in any one month.[14]

The 1922 Codex replaced the Comrades' Disciplinary Courts by a new system of enforcing labour discipline in enterprises.[15] *Rules of Internal Order*, or as they came to be known more commonly *Rules of Internal Labour Order* (*Pravila Vnutrennego Trudovogo Rasporyadka*), were to be introduced in all enterprises and establishments employing more than four persons. The Rules were to contain 'clear, exact, and, so far as possible, exhaustive indications of the general and special duties of workers and management, and the limits and nature of responsibility for their violation'. For guidance, *Model Rules* (*Tipovye Pravila*) would be issued by the *NKT* in agreement with the AUCCTU and the *VSNKh*,* and would apply in enterprises until specific rules had been worked out locally and confirmed by *NKT* inspectors.[16] Model rules were, in fact, confirmed by the *NKT* in September, 1924,[17] and by the Presidium of the AUCCTU a year later.[18] At the same time, a 'table of penalties' was established for dealing with three types of minor offence—coming late or going early without valid reason, 'wilful temporary absence' and 'illegal refusal to work'. The penalties—reprimand, public reprimand and dismissal—were to be imposed by the management, not by a court; but public reprimand and dismissal could be imposed only for repeated offences, and dismissal had to be effected through the Rates and Conflicts Commission (*RKK*), on which workers and management were equally represented.†[19]

THE INDUSTRIALISATION DRIVE

By 1926 *Gosplan* had been instructed to work out a Five-Year Perspective Plan for the industrialisation of the country.[20] The need to find funds for investment from home resources brought to the fore the whole issue of efficiency and productivity. In April, 1926, Stalin spoke on economic policy to a Party Central Committee Plenum,[21] which then decreed 'decisive measures to raise productivity' by rationalisation and by 'fully using the working day, strengthening labour discipline, struggling against

* The Supreme Council of National Economy (abolished in 1932).
† *See* p. 180.

absenteeism, etc.'.[22] 'It is necessary', Stalin told Leningrad Party members a few days later, 'to conduct a campaign to put a stop to absenteeism at the mills and factories, to raise the productivity of labour, and to strengthen labour discipline in our enterprises. Tens and hundreds of thousands of man-days are lost to industry owing to absenteeism . . . '.[23]

In August, 1927, following a Party Central Committee directive in March,[24] the relevant article of the Labour Codex was revised to make sanctions against absenteeism more stringent: three days' absence without good reason in any one month (instead of three consecutive days or six days in one month) became punishable by dismissal without notice.[25] This proved inadequate: absenteeism remained high, reaching a figure of 5·96 days per man in 1931 and 1932.[26] In November, 1932, therefore, the Government took really drastic steps: henceforward for even one day's non-appearance for work without good reason the worker could be dismissed, deprived of his right to use ration cards issued to him as a worker in a particular factory, and evicted from any housing allotted to him by the enterprise.[27] The *NKT* soon afterwards explained that evictions must be carried out 'instantly', without regard to the worker's lack of other accommodation, 'at any time of year', and 'without provision of transport facilities'.[28] Absenteeism fell immediately to 0·93 days per man in 1933, to 0·67 in 1934 and 0·76 in 1935.[29]

At the same time measures to 'strengthen labour discipline' in general were adopted.[30] By a decree of March, 1929, which deemed it 'necessary for economic organs and trade unions to concentrate exceptional attention at present on questions of labour discipline', and complained that managements had been 'very feeble' in using their rights, managements were empowered to impose the full 'table of penalties' independently; the rôle of the Rates and Conflicts Commissions in this matter was reduced to deciding appeals from dissatisfied workers.[31] Soon afterwards the *VSNKh* was ordered to 'strengthen the responsibility of managements' for factory discipline, and 'not to hesitate to remove personnel who tolerate violators of labour discipline'.[32]

Parallel with this, Comrades' Courts, which had been reintroduced in a very limited sphere since 1928, with a maximum sentence of public censure or a fine up to ten roubles, were set up in all enterprises with 100 or more employees, renamed 'production-comradely' and given more militant functions: maintaining 'firm production discipline', 'applying measures of a preventive and disciplinary character to persons who violate labour discipline . . . [or] who have a negligent attitude' to enterprise property, and finally, 'struggling against survivals of the old life . . . which disrupt labour discipline . . . [such as] drunkenness, brawling, insults, hooliganism'. The chairman, deputy chairman and members of the courts were elected annually from among shock-workers and employees, but were subject to recall by general workers' meetings. Their competence extended over the usual run of petty offences—lateness, absenteeism, neglect of property (machines, materials, etc.), insults, minor assault, petty theft, hooliganism—but also included 'transfer from one enterprise to another without valid reason'. The maximum fine the courts could impose was still only ten roubles, but they could now 'raise with managements' the question of a worker's dismissal, or propose to his trade union that he be suspended from membership. Courts were to be guided by the AUCCTU and by the local organs of the Commissariat of Justice.[33] These courts, however, never 'achieved the scope they should have' and gradually died out without formal abolition. Only since 1951 has a form of Comrades' Courts been revived, with powers to award reprimands, to raise with managements the question of dismissal or of handing the case over to the judicial authorities.[*][34]

Against labour turnover, however, these courts were at that time hardly likely to be effective, since the most severe penalty they could hope to award was dismissal—itself a stimulus to further turnover. In 1930 the rate of labour turnover reached its highest point: in industry as a whole hirings of labour were over 176 per cent and discharges over 152 per cent of the average number of workers employed that year. In coal and iron mining the average employment period fell in 1930 to some four months, or less than half what it was in 1928.[35] The fundamental causes of this disturbing phenomenon were such that they could not be removed quickly; only the growth of an industrial tradition in the labour force, with better living conditions, was likely to bring the problem under control. Meanwhile, it could be dealt with only as a disease may be treated, symptomatically. Various forms of moral and economic pres-

* *See* pp. 108ff.

sure were therefore applied to induce workers to stay longer at their jobs. 'Courts of Honour' in workshops and the displaying of 'floaters'' names on notice-boards were among the milder measures applied;[36] trade unions used the threat of expulsion against members who might be inclined to leave their jobs after short periods without express permission,[37] and the Mid-Volga *oblast* Committee of the *Komsomol* forbade members to change jobs without valid reason and the sanction of the local *Komsomol* organisation.[38] Workers were 'encouraged' to sign a pledge that they would stay at their jobs till the Five-Year Plan was completed.[39] At the Petrovsky Works in Dnepropetrovsk, those who refused to sign were branded as 'traitors to the cause of industrialisation and the Five-Year Plan': only 'immediate signature of the voluntary pledge', it was said, 'can expiate this crime'.[40]

Positive advantages were offered to those who stuck to their jobs. In the autumn of 1930 a 'lengthy period [of work] at the same enterprise' was made one of the conditions for priority in housing, free entrance to higher education, rest homes and sanatoria, preferential rations of scarce goods, and so forth; in certain vital industries those who did two or more years' work at the same enterprise became eligible for three days' extra paid annual leave.[41] In January, 1931, even sickness benefit was brought into play: the full amount of benefit was made available only to those who were union members and who had been employed for more than three years altogether, with more than two in their present job.[42]

At the same time the penalties against 'floating' were stiffened. 'Persistent floaters' now became liable to lose their workers' (i.e. preferential) ration cards.[43] 'Deserters' and 'floaters' were barred from work in industry or transportation for six months.[44] A new label—'disorganisers of production'—came into use after a decree of the *NKT* in January, 1931, and was mainly applied to people who left their jobs, either without giving due notice or more than once in twelve months (even with notice).[45] The original provisions of the Labour Codex, which guaranteed the worker freedom to change his job, were thus undermined.

The last of the measures enacted at this period attempted to control labour turnover by registration of the worker's movements from job to job in a document carried always with him. A proposal to introduce Labour Books was discussed for some months in the winter of 1930–1, and preliminary legislative steps were taken;[46] but the whole plan was soon shelved, a substitute being found in the Internal Passport. One of the provisions of the law on passports was that every worker must show his passport on applying for work, and have his place of work entered in it.[47] *Pravda* explained that passports would help to purge construction projects and State enterprises of 'floaters' and 'money-grabbers'.[48]

All these expedients had some effect; by 1935 the turnover rate had fallen to rather more than half the figure for 1930.[49] Even this, which implies an average stay at one job of less than a year and a half, is high enough; but no further steps were taken to combat labour turnover and absenteeism until 1938.

THE WAR

The years 1938–40 are marked in the USSR by two developments; the relaxation of the purges which had terrorised the population since 1936, and the increasing tension of the international scene. Both these factors may be supposed to have had some influence on the Government's labour policy in those years. On the one hand, the relaxation of the purge may well have encouraged people to lift their heads and move around again instead of 'staying put'; no figures for labour turnover were published after 1935, but 1938 is the year that it reappears as a subject of discussion and concern in the economic Press.[50] On the other hand, the danger of war demanded an increase in investment in defence industry, and thus subjected the economy to new strains;[51] more than ever, an efficient, disciplined labour force would be needed.

The first step was taken on December 20, 1938, with the introduction of Labour Books. The decree on the introduction of Labour Books, still in force today,* provides that the books should be uniform throughout the USSR, and printed in Russian and in the language of the Union or Autonomous Republic concerned.[52] Managements are obliged to enter the

* At the beginning of 1964 it was proposed to introduce a new document, the Labour Passport, which would combine the Internal Passport and the Labour Book. The idea was strongly supported by Khrushchev. After an enthusiastic but short-lived Press campaign in favour of the Labour Passport, the proposal was tacitly dropped and has not been heard of since.

following information in the Labour Book: the holder's full name, age, education, trade, 'information about his work', transfers from one enterprise or establishment to another (with reasons), and details of 'encouragements and awards'.[53] Punishments are not to be entered;[54] however, as the *Large Soviet Encyclopaedia* points out, the fact that the books contain 'notes of change of place of work, and of encouragements and awards . . . makes it possible to distinguish the conscientious worker from the floater'.[55] Managements may engage workers and employees (other than those entering employment for the first time) only on presentation of their Labour Books,[56] which the management then keeps until the worker is discharged.[57] Managements, however, are frequently lax in fulfilling their obligations concerning Labour Books.[58]

Further measures to tighten labour discipline were not long delayed. A decree of December 28, 1938, restated the problem:[59]

'The overwhelming majority of workers and employees [said the preamble to the decree] work . . . honestly and conscientiously . . . affording examples of shock-work and labour heroism, strengthening the might and defensive capacity of the Motherland. But . . . there are still individual unconscious, backward or unconscientious persons—floaters, idlers, absentees, and money-grabbers—[who] by their unconscientious work, absenteeism, lateness for work, aimless wandering about the plant in working hours and other violations of the Rules of Internal Labour Order, and also by wilful transfers from one enterprise to another, subvert labour discipline and do great harm to industry, transport and the whole national economy.'

These people 'strive to give the State as little work as possible and to get as much money as possible'; they 'abuse Soviet labour laws and rules, using them in their own selfish interests'.[60] To deal with this situation, the decree obliged managements and trade unions 'to wage a decisive struggle . . . against all who have a dishonest attitude to their work'. Punishments for lateness, going early to dinner or coming back late, leaving early or idling in working hours—each of which was now said to constitute a 'gross violation of labour discipline'—were enumerated: warnings, reprimands, and reprimands with warning of dismissal, transfer to lower-paid work for up to three months, or demotion to a lower post. Moreover, three such violations of labour discipline in one month, or four in two consecutive months, became punishable by dismissal.[61] 'Floating' or 'wilful departure' was the object of three new provisions. First, the notice required for terminating a labour contract of indefinite duration was lengthened to one month.[62] It appears, however, that this provision was short-lived, since it is omitted from the text of the decree given in a Labour Law Handbook of 1941.[63] Secondly, the period of work at one enterprise required in qualification for a worker's first annual leave was doubled.[*][64] Finally, a system was introduced whereby rights to social insurance were related to the length of employment in one enterprise.[65] Workers dismissed for a breach of labour discipline, or for committing a crime, or leaving at their own request, not only lost some of their social insurance rights but were liable to eviction from housing provided by the enterprise 'within ten days . . . without provision of dwelling space'.[66]

Possibly the most striking innovation arising from this decree was the definition given to 'absenteeism'. On January 8, 1939, a 'clarifying decision' of the Party Central Committee, USSR *SovNarKom* and the AUCCTU laid down that absenteeism could consist of being 'more than twenty minutes late'.[67] Already, under the decree of November, 1932, this meant that anything over 20 minutes' lateness on a single occasion was punishable by dismissal; in conjunction with later legislation, which increased the penalties for absenteeism still further, it provided one of the harshest points in Soviet legislation on labour during the war and for some years after it.

The Government evidently realised that managers might be unwilling to apply measures of such unusual severity to the workers under them. On December 31, three days after the decree, the USSR Procurator-General ordered his subordinates to prosecute managers who failed to carry out the provisions.[68] The first sentence was soon announced—eight months' deprivation of freedom for a departmental head at the Karl Liebknecht Works in Dnepropetrovsk for not sacking three absentees.[69] Dismissals for absenteeism rose sharply; in January, 1939, alone there were 129 at the *Krasny Proletary* Works in Moscow, and 500 at the Petrovsky works, Dnepropetrovsk.[70]

Further steps were taken in 1940. On June 26 of that year the AUCCTU declared that there were three or four per cent of workers, young people who had recently entered employment, who 'abuse the patience of the Soviet State [and] by

* *See* p. 127.

running from plant to plant subvert the cause of discipline . . .'[71] The same day the Presidium of the USSR Supreme Soviet issued a new edict on this recurrent subject. The edict, which also extended the working day and the working week,* prohibited workers from leaving enterprises and establishments except by permission of the management.[72] In certain cases—old-age pensioners, or workers declared unfit by the medical-labour commission or enrolling in a higher or special secondary educational establishment—the management had to give permission.[73] Workers leaving 'wilfully' (i.e. without permission) were to be 'prosecuted and subjected, by sentence of a People's Court, to imprisonment for two to four months'. For 'absenteeism without good reason' the current punishment of dismissal was abolished: instead, absentees were to be 'prosecuted and punished, by sentence of a People's Court, with corrective labour at their place of work for up to six months, with a 25 per cent stoppage of pay.'[74] The edict ended with a new threat of prosecution for managers who failed to hand over to the courts absentees or persons guilty of 'wilful departure'.[75]

The definition of 'absenteeism' as anything more than 20 minutes' lateness was soon specifically confirmed in connection with the edict of June 26,[76] and even extended. Not only late arrival at work, but more than 20 minutes' lateness after the lunch break, or earliness in going for lunch or at the end of the day, or idling on the job, were all held to constitute absenteeism.[77] Those who qualified as absentees by virtue of three violations of labour discipline in one month or four in two months were equally liable to the new penalties.[78] From October, 1940, engineers, skilled workers, etc., who refused transfer orders† became liable to prosecution under the edict.[79]

A further tightening of labour discipline at this time was provided by the removal of certain minor offences—petty theft and hooliganism—from the jurisdiction of the 'production-comradely courts'. These offences now fell within the competence of the People's Courts, and were punishable by one year's imprisonment, 'unless by their character they entail a more severe penalty under the law'.[80]

The XVIII Party Conference in February, 1941, found that the edict of June 26 had 'considerably improved the state of labour discipline in enterprises'. Nevertheless, the conference

* *See* pp. 119, 123.

† *See* pp. 30 f.

declared, absenteeism and wilful departure 'have still not nearly ceased in many factories. . . . It is essential *to eliminate absenteeism completely* . . . and to strengthen labour discipline in industry and transport. . . .'[81] By the outbreak of war in June, 1941, therefore, the Soviet State had acquired legal powers to keep workers hard at their jobs on pain of four months' imprisonment or six months' forced labour; yet absenteeism and turnover continued. The war gave occasion for a steep increase in the penalties for wilful departure. An edict of the Supreme Soviet of the USSR of December 26, 1941, declared all workers and employees in 'enterprises of war industry' mobilised for the duration of the war and 'tied to the enterprises employing them'. Since 'war industry' covered also 'industrial establishments co-operating in supplying war industry', the scope of the edict was extremely wide; and an edict of September, 1942, widened it still further to cover workers and employees in all State enterprises and establishments 'located close to the front'. Persons leaving their jobs without permission were deemed to be 'deserters', to be tried by military tribunals; they could be sentenced to five to eight years' imprisonment. By a further edict of April, 1943, all railways, and subsequently river and marine transport, were put under martial law.[82]

POST-WAR DEVELOPMENTS

The successful prosecution of the war led to the reappearance of 'floating' and 'wilful departure' in new forms. Workers in factories evacuated eastwards began to drift back to their home areas in 1944, and *Pravda* published an editorial on the subject under the headline 'Fight Floating!'[83] Returning to the subject some days later, *Pravda* diagnosed another cause of floating—the recent intake into industry of 'millions of new young workers who have not yet acquired factory habits, and in whom the spirit of consciously applied Socialist discipline has not been adequately inculcated'.[84] Post-war experience confirms that labour turnover is still a matter of concern to the Soviet authorities. At a Plenum of the Party Central Committee in July, 1955, Bulganin described the elimination of labour turnover as an 'urgent task'. According to a recent Soviet source: 'It can hardly be denied that fluidity of cadres does great harm to the economy, which is expressed in most varied forms:

labour productivity falls, quality of production, labour and technological discipline gets worse, and the growth of the technical and economic standard of the workers slows down. As a result, the national economy loses milliards of roubles every year.'[85] One of the main causes of turnover, according to Bulganin, was the poor housing and living conditions which managements provided for their workers.[86] Plainly, the removal of a cause like this would take time, and in fact has not yet been eliminated. Its effect is particularly marked in the developing eastern regions where housing conditions are especially acute. In 1959–63, for example, over a quarter of a million more people left Siberia than migrated there.[87] Inadequate housing and other amenities were among the chief causes.[88] The results of an inquiry published in a Soviet specialist periodical indicate that in some widely-separated regions the number of workers changing their jobs in 1960 was about 36 per cent of the average number of persons on the employment rolls and in one was as high as 60 per cent.[89] More recent comparable figures are not available but data on labour turnover in selected coal-mines in the Kuzbass, quoted in 1965, indicated a turnover of between 12·8 and 23·2 per cent of the labour force.[90] The publication in 1965 of a booklet on means of overcoming fluidity of labour,[91] and numerous Press references to the difficulties it poses, testify to the persistent seriousness of the problem.

In recent years several investigations have been conducted into the causes of labour turnover. An inquiry conducted among 11,000 Leningrad workers (41·6 per cent of whom were married women) published at the end of 1964[92] cited the following main reasons for changing jobs: dissatisfaction with the nature of the work—37·4 per cent; a desire to secure better or more conveniently situated housing—29·9 per cent; higher wages—23·5 per cent. However, of the 11,000, 4,545 received more money in their new jobs, 4,242 the same amount and 2,839 less pay. The proportion of those seeking higher pay by changing jobs was greater among lower-paid workers, most of whom improved their wages in so doing.

Absenteeism and wilful departure from work survived as criminal offences for over 10 years after the end of the Second World War. It is only since April, 1956, that they have ceased to be criminal offences and that dismissal has been reinstated as a punishment for absenteeism. A worker may now as a rule leave his job on giving two weeks' notice to the management.[93] Until 1960, however, if he did so 'at his own wish', he lost his record of uninterrupted service (*nepreryvny stazh*), which affects the scale of his social insurance benefits; further, he lost for six months the right to temporary disability benefits. Since January, 1960, however, a worker who voluntarily leaves his job does not lose his record of uninterrupted work if he gets another job within one month, nor does he forfeit his temporary disability benefit. Equally, a worker who leaves his job voluntarily does not lose his record of uninterrupted service if he: leaves because of illness or transfers to a pension; enrols at a higher educational establishment; leaves because the wife or husband has moved to another area. Pregnant women or mothers with children under one year who are transferred to work in another area are similarly treated.[94] Workers who are transferred by managements to other jobs retain their record of uninterrupted service.[95]

The years 1957–60 witnessed the increasing involvement of the public in maintaining public order in general and labour discipline in particular. The passing of anti-parasite laws and the parallel revival of the Comrades' Courts are two main examples of this. In 1957 draft laws 'On intensifying the struggle against anti-social, parasitic elements' were put out in all Republics directed against persons making a living by supplying the public with much-needed consumer goods or services in a manner not approved by the authorities. That of the RSFSR[96] read, in part:

> 'Adult, able-bodied citizens who lead an anti-social, parasitic life and wilfully shun socially useful work, as well as those living on unearned incomes, may be subjected to measures of public coercion in the form of banishment for a term of two to five years with compulsory labour at the place of banishment.'

Backsliding citizens were to be tried by 'a general meeting of citizens convened in towns and urban settlements by street committees or house administration commissions for maintenance of public order and, in rural localities, by the village Soviet of workers' deputies'. Sentences passed by such general meetings were to be submitted for confirmation to the executive committees of the district or urban Soviet. Although about half of the Union Republics passed anti-parasite laws in the next eighteen months, the RSFSR did not do so until May, 1961, when the remaining Republics followed suit.

The Comrades' Courts were revitalised in October, 1959, 'in conformity with the decisions of the XXI Congress', and a draft Model Statute of Comrades' Courts was published.[97] These were finally approved in the RSFSR in July, 1961,[98] though with some modification. Other Republics followed suit. In October, 1963, the powers of the Comrades' Courts in the RSFSR were extended and some of the original (1959) provisions restored.[99] Other Republics, once again, introduced similar amendments. The chief effect of the 1963 amendments was to enable the Courts to deal with minor criminal offences previously dealt with by the People's Courts. Their powers of punishment were further increased in January, 1965.[100] The Comrades' Courts are now empowered to deal with cases of:

> 'violations of labour discipline, including: absenteeism without valid reason; lateness at work or leaving early; poor-quality work or the direct consequences of a worker's unconscientious attitude to his duties; failure to observe safety regulations or other labour protection rules, excluding cases involving criminal liability; the destruction, loss or damage of equipment, instruments, materials and other State or public property resulting from a person's unconscientious attitude to his duties, and which do not cause substantial damage'.

Similarly, the Comrades' Courts deal with cases of the use without permission of equipment or transport belonging to enterprises, where no substantial damage is caused. They may also deal with first offences of petty hooliganism, speculation, misappropriation of State or public property, and the theft of articles of small value from fellow-workers. Other cases within their competence include: drunkenness in public or at work, hooch-distilling on a small scale for personal consumption; unworthy conduct towards wife, parents or children; slander of a member of the same 'collective'; causing slight bodily injuries (first offences); using foul language; minor cases of damage to trees, plants and public buildings; the non-observance of fire precautions; housing disputes of various kinds; minor property quarrels and other anti-social acts.

Cases may be submitted to Comrades' Courts through the factory trade union committee, people's squads, street, house, sector or district committees and other public organisations, or meetings of citizens; through local Soviets, State organs, directors of enterprises, institutions, etc. Comrades' Courts also examine cases transferred to them from the militia, people's courts or public prosecutor's office, cases raised through 'statements by citizens' and also investigate cases on their own initiative. Punishment ranges from public apology by the accused, public reprimand or a fine of up to 50 roubles, to a representation to the management that a worker be dismissed, put on paid but unskilled labour for up to 15 days or transferred to lower-paid work or a lower post for an unspecified period. The decision of a Comrades' Court is final though a trade union committee or local Soviet may suggest a re-hearing. This provision has caused misgivings in Soviet legal circles. Because the Comrades' Courts often tend to make illegal decisions, a People's Judge has advocated allowing appeal against their decisions through the People's Courts. Public prosecutors, too, should be allowed to challenge such decisions, he said.[101]

The Courts appear to have been acting as a poor man's court. According to the deputy Minister of Justice of the RSFSR, 'in an absolute majority of instances they examine the cases of workers and employees and very seldom the cases of engineering, technical and administration personnel'.[102] After the 1963 regulations the Comrades' Courts began to pay less attention to questions of labour discipline, concentrating mainly on cases of anti-social acts sent to them by the militia, the public prosecutor or the Courts. Managements sent to the Courts few cases of infringement of labour discipline.[103] Since Khrushchev's downfall, the Comrades' Courts have attracted a good deal of criticism for their inactivity as well as their proneness to illegal decisions. There has, however, been no sign that they are to be abolished.

The campaign against parasites appeared to lapse temporarily after the first drive of 1957, partly because the legal profession was opposed to such large powers being placed in the hands of public meetings. It was conducted with resumed violence after the Conference of the Movement of Communist Labour in May, 1960, which resolved[104]:

'It is essential . . . to become more intolerant . . . towards drones, hooligans and wreckers.'

Throughout the rest of the summer there was a full-throated campaign in the Soviet Press against idleness, parasitism, speculation in motor-cars, flats and *dachas*, and the conversion of communal gardens into private plots. The RSFSR Law on anti-social parasites in the Soviet body politic of May 4, 1961, again placed parasites under the jurisdiction of the Courts of law in addition to 'workers' collectives'. Those Republics which had not adopted the anti-parasites law now did so: others amended their legislation to bring it into line with the RSFSR decree. Subsequent legislation removed parasites from the jurisdiction of the 'workers' collective', transferring responsibility for compelling idlers to work to the Soviet executive committees and the People's Courts.[105]

THE MODEL RULES OF INTERNAL LABOUR ORDER

The model *Rules of Internal Labour Order* form the basis on which individual industries, 'by agreement with the Trade Union Central Committees', compile rules appropriate to their own special conditions. Supplements to suit the needs of individual enterprises can be introduced by the managements by agreement with the Trade Union Committee of the enterprise.[106] The model Rules currently in force are those drawn up in January, 1957. After reminding workers of their constitutional duty to observe labour discipline, the Rules declare their aim of 'ensuring the strengthening of Socialist labour discipline, the correct organisation and safety of working conditions, full and rational use of working time, the raising of labour productivity and the output of good-quality products'.[107]

They then proceed to their subject under five headings: hiring and dismissal of workers, 'basic obligations of managements and workers'; working time and its utilisation; incentives; and penalties.

When engaging a worker the management must demand (*a*) his Labour Book or certificate of previous occupation, and (*b*) his passport.[108] In practice managements began to demand numerous other documents from workers. This illegal custom was the subject of a Party Central Committee and Council of Ministers resolution in February, 1960.[109] They must then instruct him in work procedures and the use of equipment, and in the *Rules of Internal Labour Order* and safety, sanitary and fire regulations.[110] They must issue him with a Pay Book* within five days.[111] On his departure the management must give

* *See* p. 18.

him his Labour Book, after entering the reason for his dismissal or departure 'in strict accord with the formulations of current labour legislation or in the form of a reference to an article (point) of current legislation'.[112]

The obligations of managements are:[113]

(*a*) to organise correctly the labour of workers and employees so that each may work according to his speciality and skill;
(*b*) to issue work orders punctually and to supply workers with instruments, materials and spare parts;
(*c*) to secure to each worker and employee a particular work-place, lathe, machine, etc.;
(*d*) to ensure maintenance of machines, lathes, and other equipment;
(*e*) to create conditions for the all-round growth of labour productivity, the development of the movement of innovators, for the broad dissemination of the experience of advanced workers, the combination of professions; introduce technically based norms, new techniques and technology, modernise existing equipment, mechanise heavy and labour-consuming jobs;
(*f*) to strengthen labour and production discipline;
(*g*) to observe the laws and rules on labour protection, including the strict maintenance of the established working day, the measures for safety and production sanitation (instruct workers in safe modes of work, provide workers and employees with drinking water, install wash-rooms and cloak-rooms, issue special clothing, precautionary devices, etc.);
(*h*) to issue pay at the established times;
(*i*) to secure the systematic raising of production and professional qualifications of workers and employers;
(*j*) to take measures to improve housing and everyday conditions of workers and employees and pay attention to their needs and requirements;

Workers, for their part, are obliged:[114]

(*a*) to work honestly and conscientiously;
(*b*) to observe labour discipline and carry out the *Rules of Internal Labour Order*; arrive at work on time; to observe strictly and without any infractions the established length of the working day; utilise all working time exclusively for production work and official duties; to execute punctually and accurately orders by the management;
(*c*) to carry out punctually and carefully work on orders and tasks; fulfil output norms and strive to over-fulfil them; strictly observe technological discipline, to eliminate waste and strive for high quality indices;

(*d*) to exercise care for Socialist property: machines, lathes, instruments, material, special clothing, etc.;

(*e*) to fully observe the safety, production and sanitary requirements and to use special clothing and precautionary devices issued;

(*f*) to keep their work-places clean and in order, maintain cleanliness in the workshop and on factory premises and to hand over their work-places to workers in the next shift in a clean and tidy condition.

Socialist competition is not mentioned among the workers' duties. This, presumably, is because, in the words of a Soviet authority on labour law, 'for workers and employees, participation in Socialist competition is a moral, not a juridical obligation'; for management, on the other hand, furtherance of Socialist competition is a juridical as well as a moral duty (though not under the *Rules of Internal Labour Order*).[115]

The model Rules specify that the shift rota shall be changed regularly, as a rule once a week.[116] They lay down the procedure for clocking in and out, workers on continuous production being forbidden to leave until relieved.[117] They forbid the following during working hours: calling workers or employees away from their work to fulfil 'social duties', convening assemblies, conferences or meetings 'relative to public matters'.* [118]

The Rules provide for incentives to good work, fulfilment of norms and duties, innovations, inventions and rationalisation proposals, continuous and irreproachable work in one enterprise, etc.... [120] These may take the form of an expression of gratitude to the worker; the award of a certificate; inscription of the worker's name in the book or scroll of honour; award of the title of the best worker of a particular profession; cash bonuses or a valuable gift. All awards are made by the management in consultation with the factory trade union committee and are entered in the worker's Labour Book.[121] The Rules prescribe that any violation of labour discipline entails a disciplinary penalty.[122] These are (*a*) reproof, (*b*) reprimand, (*c*) severe reprimand and (*d*) transfer to other lower-paid work for up three months (demotion to a lower post in the case of employees).[123] Absenteeism, defined as absence from work for a whole day without good reason, is specifically mentioned as

* In 1963 the AUCCTU Presidium issued a resolution criticising the growing practice of union committees holding meetings and conferences during working hours.[119]

an offence to be covered by these penalties.[124] Absenteeism may also be punished by a reduction of up to 25 per cent of single long-service awards, or withdrawal of long-service increments for a period of up to three months, or dismissal with a note in the worker's Labour Book of the reason for dismissal. Drunkenness at work is treated as absenteeism. Instead of imposing disciplinary penalties managements may hand over materials concerning infractions of labour discipline to a Comrades' Court.[125] Managements must act immediately once an offence is discovered and must hear the offender's explanations. No penalties may be imposed after the expiry of one month from the date the offence was discovered and 'disciplinary penalties' may not be imposed after six months have elapsed since the offence was committed.[126] Reproofs and reprimands are lifted if a year passes without the commission of another offence; for good work and behaviour and at managerial discretion this period may be reduced.[127]

SOURCES

N.B.—Undated citations of works of which more than one edition is listed in the bibliography refer to the most recent edition there listed; earlier editions are cited with the date in brackets.

1. Lenin, Vol. 27, p. 241.
2. *Ibid.*, p. 240.
3. Lenin, Vol. 29, p. 391.
4. Fedotoff White, pp. 110–14.
5. Lenin, Vol. 29, p. 120.
6. RSFSR Laws, 1919, 56: 537.
7. Lenin, Vol. 30, pp. 423f.
8. *K.P.S.S. v Rezolyutsiakh*, Vol. 1, pp. 488, 492f.
9. RSFSR Laws, 1920, 36:172.
10. RSFSR Laws, 1921, 23/34: 142.
11. RSFSR Laws, 1921, 14:86.
12. Carr, pp. 322, 323n.
13. *KZoT* (1918), art. 51.
14. *KZoT* (1922), arts. 46–8.
15. *B.S.E.*, 2nd edn., Vol. 14, p. 490.
16. *KZoT* (1922), arts 50–5.
17. *Trudovoe Zakonodatelstvo SSSR*, p. 243.
18. *Spravochnik Profsoyuznogo Rabotnika* (1926), p. 637.
19. *Loc. cit.*
20. Dobb, p. 231.
21. Stalin, *Works*, Vol. 8, p. 380, note 51.
22. *K.P.S.S. v Rezolyutsiakh*, Vol. II, p. 267.
23. Stalin, *Works*, Vol. 8, p. 144.
24. *VKP (b) o Profsoyuzakh*, p. 338.
25. RSFSR Laws, 1927, 87: 577.
26. *Sotsialisticheskoe Stroitelstvo SSSR*, p. 530.
27. USSR Laws, 1932, 78:475.

28. Ya. Kiselev and S. Malkin, quoted by Schwarz, p. 99.
29. *Sotsialisticheskoe Stroitelstvo SSSR*, p. 530.
30. Aleksandrov (1949), p. 95.
31. USSR Laws, 1929, 19:167.
32. *Ibid.*, 46:400, art. 5a.
33. RSFSR Laws, 1928, 114: 707; 1930, 4:52; 1931, 14:160.
34. Dvornikov, Kaftanovskaya and Nikitinsky, pp. 9f., 24.
35. *Sotsialisticheskoe Stroitelstvo SSSR*, p. 531.
36. I. Zaromsky in *Voprosy Truda*, September, 1930, quoted by Schwarz, p. 90.
37. *Loc. cit.*
38. Z. Mokhov in *Voprosy Truda*, March-April, 1931, quoted by Schwarz, p. 90.
39. *Pravda*, September 3, 1930, quoted by Schwarz, p. 91.
40. *VKP (b) o Profsoyuzakh*, p. 564; *Za Industrializatsiyu*, September 16, 1930, quoted by Schwarz, p. 92.
41. *VKP (b) o Profsoyuzakh*, p. 565; USSR Laws, 1930, 60:641.
42. *Pravda*, February 6, 1931, quoted by Schwarz, pp. 312f.
43. *Izvestiya NarKomTruda*, 1930, No. 26–7, quoted by Schwarz, p. 94.
44. *VKP (b) o Profsoyuzakh* p. 565.
45. *Izvestiya*, January 19, 1931, quoted by Schwarz, pp. 95f.
46. RSFSR Laws, 1930, 44: 530, art. 13e.
47. USSR Laws, 1932, 84:517.
48. *Pravda*, December 28, 1932, quoted by Schwarz, p. 97.
49. *Sotsialisticheskoe Stroitelstvo SSSR*, p. 531.
50. Dobb, p. 445.
51. *Ibid.*, pp. 290f.
52. USSR Laws, 1938, 58: 329, art. 1.
53. *Ibid.*, arts. 2, 5, 10.
54. *Ibid.*, art. 10.
55. *B.S.E.*, 2nd edn., Vol. 14, p. 487.
56. USSR Laws, 1938, 58: 329, art. 6.
57. *Ibid.*, art. 9.
58. See, for example, *Pravda*, February 10, 1960, *Sotsialisticheskaya Zakonnost*, 1960, No. 8, p. 98.
59. USSR Laws, 1939, 1:1, preamble.
60. *Loc. cit.*
61. *Ibid.*, art. 1.
62. *Ibid.*, art. 3.
63. *Trudovoe Zakonodatelstvo SSSR*, p. 13.
64. USSR Laws, 1939, 1:1, art. 13.
65. *Ibid.*, arts. 5–10.
66. *Ibid.*, arts. 11, 12.
67. *Izvestiya*, January 9, 1939.
68. *Sovetskaya Zakonnost*, 1939, No. 1, quoted by Schwarz, p. 104.
69. *Pravda*, January 26, 1939, quoted by Schwarz, p. 104.
70. *Trud*, February 2, 1939, *Industriya*, February 2, 1939, both quoted by Schwarz, p. 105.
71. *Pravda*, June 26, 1940.
72. *Ukaz Prezidiuma Verkhovnogo Soveta SSSR* of June 26, 1940: *O perekhode na vosmichasovoy rabochy den, na semidnevnuyu rabochuyu nedelyu i o zapreshchenii samovolnogo ukhoda rabochikh i sluzhashchikh s predpriyatiy*

i uchrezhdeniy, in *Vedomosti Verkhovnogo Soveta SSSR*, 1940, No. 20 (83), art. 3.

73. *Ibid.*, art. 4.
74. *Ibid.*, art. 5.
75. *Ibid.*, art. 6.
76. *Prikaz NKYu SSSR i Prokurora SSSR* of July 22, 1940, No. 84/133, in *Trudovoe Zakonodatelstvo SSSR*, p. 237.
77. *Trudovoe Zakonodatelstvo SSSR*, p. 238; *Sovetskaya Zakonnost*, December 1940, p. 7, quoted by Schwarz, p. 108.
78. *Postanovlenie Plenuma Verkhovnogo Suda SSSR* of August 15, 1940, No. 29/15/U, art. 2, in *Trudovoe Zakonodatelstvo SSSR*, p. 237.
79. *Ukaz Prezidiuma Verkhovnogo Soveta SSSR*, of October 19, 1940, No. 42 (105), art. 5.
80. *Vedomosti Verkhovnogo Soveta SSSR*, 1940, No. 28 (91); *B.S.E.*, 1st edn., Vol. 47, col. 169.
81. *K.P.S.S. v Rezolyutsiakh*, Vol. 111, p. 432.
82. *Izvestiya*, December 27, 1941; Aleksandrov (1949), p. 111.
83. *Pravda*, September 9, 1944, quoted by Schwarz, p. 125.
84. *Pravda*, September 24, 1944, quoted by Schwarz, pp. 125f.
85. Yagodkin, p. 4.
86. *Pravda*, July 17, 1955.
87. *Literaturnaya Gazeta*, March 10, 1966.
88. *Ibid.*, September 4, 1965; Yagodkin, pp. 97, 121.
89. *Trud i Zarabotnaya Plata*, 1961, No. 4, p. 33.
90. Yagodkin, p. 94.
91. *Op. cit.*
92. *Trud*, December 2, 1964.
93. *Vedomosti Verkhovnogo Soveta SSSR*, 1956, No. 10 (852): 203, art. 5.
94. *Sbornik*, p. 106.
95. *Spravochnik Profsoynuznogo Rabotnika*, p. 300.
96. *Sovetskaya Rossiya*, August 21, 1957.
97. *Izvestiya*, October 24, 1959.
98. *Vedomosti Verkhovnogo Soveta RSFSR*, 1961, No. 26.
99. *Ukaz Prezidiuma Verkhovnogo Soveta RSFSR*, October 23, 1963, in *Vedomosti Verkhovnogo Soveta RSFSR*, 1963, No. 43.
100. *Ukaz Prezidiuma Verkhovnogo Soveta RSFSR*, January 16, 1965, in *Vedomosti Verkhovnogo Soveta RSFSR*, 1965, No. 4.
101. *Izvestiya*, September 12, 1965.
102. N. Prusakov, *Trud*, January 7, 1961.
103. See, for example, *Postanovlenie Prezidiuma VTsSPS* of June 5, 1964, in *Sbornik Postanovleniy VTsSPS*, April-June, 1964, pp. 80f.
104. *Pravda*, May 31, 1960.
105. *Ukaz Prezidiuma Verkhovnogo Soveta RSFSR*, September 20, 1965, in *Vedomosti Verkhovnogo Soveta RSFSR*, 1965, No. 38.

106. *Sbnorik*, p. 422n.
107. *Tipovye Pravila Vnutrennogo Trudovogo Rasporyadka dlya rabochikh i sluzhaschikh gosudarstvennykh, kooperativnikh i obshchestvennykh predpriyatiyakh,* art. 2, in *Sbnornik*, pp. 423–7.
108. *Ibid.*, art. 3.
109. *Sbornik*, pp. 71–3.
110. *Tipovye Pravila . . .*, art. 4.
111. *Ibid.*, art. 5.
112. *Ibid.*, art. 8.
113. *Ibid.*, art. 9.
114. *Ibid.*, art. 10.
115. Aleksandrov, p. 291.
116. *Tipovye Pravila . . .*, art. 12.
117. *Ibid.*, arts. 14–16.
118. *Ibid.*, art. 18.
119. *Postanovlenie Prezidiuma VTsSPS*, April 19, 1963, in *Spravochnik Profsoyuznogo Rabotnika*, pp. 41–42.
120. *Tipovye Pravila . . .*, art. 19.
121. *Ibid.*, art. 20.
122. *Ibid.*, art. 21.
123. *Ibid.*, art. 22.
124. *Ibid.*, art. 23.
125. *Ibid.*, art. 24.
126. *Ibid.*, art. 25.
127. *Ibid.*, art. 28.

IV
Working Hours, Leave and Labour Protection

THE WORKING DAY

The eight-hour working day, which had figured as one of the demands in the Russian Social-Democratic (later Communist) Party's first programme of 1903,[1] was introduced in the RSFSR by a decree of November, 1917.[2] The VIII Party Congress in 1919, already conscious of the need for a higher standard of skills among the workers, wrote into the Party Programme the task of establishing:[3]

> 'in the future, with the general increase in the productivity of labour, a six-hour maximum working day without loss of remuneration for work, but with an obligation for workers to devote an additional two hours, without special remuneration, to the theory of their trade and production and to practical training in the technique of State administration and in the military art'.

This proposal, however, remained 'in the future': the Labour Codex of 1922 retained the eight-hour day as a full *working* day, though it provided for a shorter day for juveniles, office workers, and workers underground and in unhealthy trades listed by the *NKT*.[4] At the same time the Codex laid down that hours of work on the day before the rest day must not exceed six, wages being paid as for a full working day.[5]

The next step was the introduction of a seven-hour day in 1927. The *Manifesto* announcing this remarked that, in contrast to capitalist countries, the 'proletarian State has as its aim the improvement of the standard of living of the mass of the workers and peasants'.[6] Other reasons, of a more specific and utilitarian character, have also been suggested. The introduction of a seven-hour day made it possible to work more multiple shifts, and thus to absorb some of the unemployed labour which was a serious problem at the time;[7] and in fact the 28 enterprises, with 126,588 workers, which were transferred to the seven-hour day in 1927–8, were simultaneously turned over to three-shift working.[8] Three-shift working equally implied a fuller use of machinery and equipment: the introduction of the seven-hour day was not only to be carried out gradually 'in accordance with the progress made in reorganising the plants and increasing efficiency and production',[9] but was expected to increase production, and not necessarily to improve the workers' lot. As the People's Commissar of Labour told the AUCCTU: 'The introduction of the seven-hour day must increase production. But our task is to keep the resulting burden from being placed exclusively on the workers' shoulders.'[10]

In the event, three-shift working ran into difficulties. There were not enough skilled workers and technical and supervisory staff; the supply of raw materials sometimes could not be expanded to meet the new demand.[11] The effect on workers' living conditions was bad. As a Soviet newspaper report of the time described it: 'The three-shift schedule has completely upset the usual pattern of life in the factory barracks. Day and night the barracks buzz. In the extremely crowded conditions . . . there is no chance for a worker to get normal rest.'[12] As a result there was later a 'reversion in many cases to two-shift working'.[13]

Nevertheless, the seven-hour day was maintained. By 1930, according to Stalin, it was in force for over 830,000 industrial workers,[14] and by 1934 'in all surface industries'.[15] The eight-hour day was retained only for a few categories of workers, mainly those engaged in building and on the State farms; and quite large numbers—20·2 per cent in the coal industry, 28·6 per cent in non-ferrous metallurgy, 38·8 per cent in the aniline dyes industry—were on a six-hour day.[16] In 1936 the seven-hour day, 'for the overwhelming majority of workers', was enshrined in the Soviet Constitution.[17]

All this was altered by the legislation of June 26, 1940.* The AUCCTU statement of that date declared that, '. . . to strengthen further the defensive might of the Motherland the working class of the USSR must make the necessary sacrifices'.[18] As with the introduction of the seven-hour day, a contrast was drawn with the capitalist countries, though the conclusion was different:[19]

'If in capitalist countries the worker is compelled to work 10–12

* *See* pp. 104ff.

hours for the bourgeoisie, then our Soviet worker can and must work longer than at present, at least eight hours, since he works for himself, for his Socialist State, for the good of the people.'

The edict of June 26 restored the eight-hour day in all enterprises with a seven-hour day, for employees in establishments (who had had a six-hour day), and for juvenile workers over the age of 16; workers who had been on a six-hour day were now to work seven hours, except for those in trades or jobs with harmful conditions of work according to lists confirmed by the *SovNarKom* of the USSR.[20] The first such list was confirmed on July 1, and was later supplemented by various directives and decrees;[21] certain jobs for radiologists and in mercury-production were limited to a five- and four-hour day respectively.[22] Provision was also made for People's Commissariats, by agreement with the AUCCTU, to re-establish a normal (i.e. longer) working day, if the harmfulness of a job was diminished.[23]

At their introduction these changes were evidently considered as temporary, for the Soviet Constitution was not at first amended to accord with them. It might have been thought that the end of the war would be the occasion for a return to the seven-hour day; but this was to be much delayed. The Fourth Five-Year Plan for 1946–50 declared one of its principal aims to be 'to raise the productivity of labour by making the utmost of the eight-hour working day'.[24] Then, in February, 1947, the USSR Supreme Soviet amended Article 119 of the Constitution to include the eight-hour instead of the seven-hour day.[25] A volume of the *Large Soviet Encyclopaedia* published in 1951 was thus reduced to the cautious boast that the USSR 'is the only country in which the eight-hour working day has been consistently realised'.[26]

The question of shorter working hours was raised again in 1952 by Stalin himself. One of the conditions for a 'real transition to Communism', he wrote then, was a 'substantial advance in the cultural standard of the members of society', to achieve which it was necessary 'to shorten the working day at least to six, and subsequently to five hours'.[27] What was offered, in fact, was a distant prospect, rather than a practical proposition; and the prospect itself was dependent on the increased productivity of labour. 'During the period of gradual transition to Communism', it was stated in 1955, the working day 'will be systematically shortened according to the growth of labour productivity'.[28]

It was only at the XX Party Congress in 1956 that the subject was raised again on a serious level, when Khrushchev recalled the VIII Congress's Programme.[29] Evidently Khrushchev preferred to go back some way into history for his text, rather than take it from Stalin's pronouncement of 1952, although to do so he had to omit all mention of the VIII Congress's reference to two hours' study after work. The war, Khrushchev argued, had interrupted the process of shortening the working day. It was now within the country's capacity to resume it; the Central Committee had decided that all workers and employees should go over to a seven-hour day during the Sixth Five-Year Plan. The process began in 1956 with the transfer of miners in the Donets and Lvov-Volynsk coalfields to a six-hour day.[30] In 1957 workers and employees of enterprises in the mining and coal-tar industries were transferred to the shorter working day[31] and the following year it was introduced in the coal, chemical and metallurgical industries[32] and in the defence, aviation, shipbuilding, radio-technical and oil and gas industries.[33] The Control Figures for the 1959–65 Seven-Year Plan, published in February, 1959, laid down that, in accordance with the decisions of the XX Party Congress, by the end of 1960 all workers and employees would be transferred to a seven-hour day and underground workers to a six-hour day. In September, 1959, a statement by the CPSU Central Committee, USSR Council of Ministers and AUCCTU[34] confirmed that by the end of 1960 all workers and employees would work a seven-hour day with underground workers of 'leading trades' working a six-hour day (which does not include travel to and from the coal face or place of work). The statement laid down schedules for the introduction of shorter hours in various industries and geographical regions. In May, 1960, a USSR law confirmed the plans to reduce hours laid down in the Control Figures. According to Grishin, the transfer of all workers and employees to the seven- and six-hour working day was completed in 1960.[35] The remaining 43 million would be switched in stages by the end of the year. Average daily hours worked were 6·94 at the end of 1960, according to another source.[36] It is unlikely they have changed significantly since then, for the length of the working week has remained stable.

In August, 1961, at the height of the Berlin 'crisis', the

AUCCTU sent a proposal to the Party Central Committee offering to introduce an eight-hour day in certain factories of the defence industry.[37] There is no evidence of this proposal having been implemented even on a temporary basis.

None of the reductions of hours mentioned above applies to workers with an 'unstandardised working day', who are obliged, where circumstances warrant it, to carry out their duties beyond normal hours without extra payment. These workers—mainly administrative, technical and directing personnel—may be compensated for heavy or extra work by extra leave, up to 12 working days a year.[38]

THE WORKING WEEK

An uninterrupted weekly rest period of not less than 42 hours—as it might be, from noon on Saturday to 6 a.m. the following Monday—was demanded by the Party Programme of 1903 and enacted in the Labour Codex of 1922.[39]

The first encroachment of the 42-hour weekly break came in 1929, with the beginning of a number of experiments in altering the length and nature of the working week. In August of that year the *SovNarKom* of the USSR decreed the 'systematic conversion' of enterprises and establishments to 'continuous production';[40] rest days, in fact, were to be staggered so that the machinery did not have an idle day. Most enterprises and establishments on continuous production were shortly afterwards transferred to a 'five-day week'—meaning that each worker had four days' work followed by one day's rest and that on any one day one-fifth of the workers were off duty. There were to be more weekly rest periods during the year ('not less than 72') but of shorter duration ('not less than 39 hours'); and working hours on the eve of the rest day were to be those of a full day.[41] During the next few years a number of variations in this experiment were introduced. In the mid-'thirties there were four types of working week in operation: the five-day 'uninterrupted' (as just described); a six-day 'uninterrupted'; a six-day 'interrupted' (the same five days on and one day off for all workers); and the old-style seven-day 'interrupted' week.[42]

The experiment with the uninterrupted week was both unpopular and unsuccessful: families complained that they could not spend their rest days together—'What do we have families for?' wrote a group of Moscow workers to *Pravda* in October,

1929[43]—and the complex shift system involved led to what was known as 'depersonalisation' (*obezlichka*), that is, a lack of personal responsibility by the worker for his job. Stalin, it is true, said in 1931 that depersonalisation was due not to the uninterrupted week *per se*, but to its over-hasty introduction; he therefore approved the reconversion of the Stalingrad tractor works to an interrupted week 'temporarily', with the prospect of an 'eventual return to the uninterrupted week, but not to lack of personal responsibility'.[44] In the event, however, the 'thirties saw a substantial reconversion to the 'interrupted six-day week' with rest days on the 6th, 12th, 18th, 24th and 30th of each month (March 1 instead of February 30). The fact that these arrangements clashed with the 'old labour regimen connected with religious holidays' was, of course, regarded as an advantage.[45]

Here, as elsewhere, June, 1940, brought a change. The AUCCTU declared that the 'existing organisation of work . . . on the basis of the six-day week reduces output' and that its introduction had 'made a breach between the working people of the town and of the country', where the seven-day week persisted.[46] The seven-day week, with the rest day on Sunday, as is normal in most other countries, was therefore restored in the USSR; and there has been no further recurrence of exotic experiments.

The 42-hour weekly break, however, has remained a casualty. When the seven-day week was made general again in June, 1940, the *SovNarKom* of the USSR specifically decreed that the day before holidays should be a full working day.[47] This position was left unchanged for some 16 years, until March, 1956, when it was decreed that working hours on the day before rest days and holidays should be 'two hours shorter than normal, that is six hours'.[48] Under this legislation, on the eve of a rest-day or holiday, an eight-hour day is reduced to six, a seven-hour day also reduced to six, and a six-hour or shorter day is left unchanged.[49] Time-workers are to be paid as for a full day; but piece-workers only for output, managements being enjoined to improve the organisation of labour so that monthly earnings do not decline.[50] In enterprises where work is continuous—no less than half of Soviet industrial workers are employed in such enterprises[51]—workers get an extra day off for every four 'eves-of-holidays' on which they have worked a full day.[52]

Although this is an improvement on the years 1940–56, it still does not guarantee the 42-hour break which the Party Programme and the Labour Codex originally demanded: a late shift on Saturday followed by an early shift on Monday is hardly likely to leave more than 36 hours free. It is doubtless for this reason that the relevant article of the Labour Codex is omitted from the Collection of Labour Laws passed for publication in September, 1961,[53] and from a more recent trade union workers' handbook.[54] The Party Programme, adopted by the XXII Congress of the CPSU in October, 1961, makes no mention of this point.

Under the Seven-Year-Plan the statutory working week has been reduced to 41 hours for workers and employees. Other aspects of the plan were, however, not realised. The 40-hour week promised for the end of 1962[55] has not materialised. Progress towards a five-day week of 30–35 hours, due to begin in 1964, has been slow and only partially implemented. This was to have been spread over five years and completed in 1966–8, and to have brought the allegedly shortest working week in the world. The movement towards the five-day week dates from 1958 when continuous-process factories in the machine-building, oil and gas industries were permitted to opt for an eight-hour day, five-day week where conditions permitted. Since August, 1960, a five-day week has been recommended for those working evening and night shifts in textile mills operating a three-shift system. Following the fall of Khrushchev the movement gained further impetus after pilot schemes in certain areas of the Ukraine had proved successful.[56] Five-day working at present involves no reduction in the length of the working week, the working day being adjusted to give a 41-hour week.[57] The 1966–70 Plan Directives,[58] however, provide in vague terms for the planned transition to the five-day week with no reduction in the present hours per week. They set no date for this.

By 1960 the average working week was 39·4 hours for all workers and employees, and 40 hours for industrial workers and employees. It is still the same today.[59]

PUBLIC HOLIDAYS

The Labour Codex of 1922 originally provided that no work should be done on the following general annual holidays:

January 1; January 22 (the anniversary of 'Bloody Sunday' in 1905); March 12 (the overthrow of the Tsarist autocracy in 1917); March 18 (the Paris Commune, 1871); May 1 (International Labour Day); November 7 (the October Revolution).[60] In addition local departments of the *NKT*, in agreement with Trade Union Councils, might fix not more than 10 special holidays 'to harmonise with local conditions, the composition of the population, popular festivals, etc.'[61] Lenin's death on January 21, 1924, was thereafter celebrated on January 22, together with Bloody Sunday, and therefore did not give rise to an extra holiday.[62] The total was thus 16 holidays a year.

Reduction of this number began in the late 'twenties. In 1927, when the anniversary of the October Revolution was converted into a two-day holiday—November 8 being added to November 7—the maximum number of special holidays was reduced from ten to seven.[63] The following year May 2 was similarly added to May 1, the maximum of special holidays being cut to six.[64] 'Continuous production' provided the occasion of the next curtailment: from 1929 workers in enterprises with a continuous working week had holidays only on January 22, May 1 and 2, and November 7 and 8; the celebration of other 'revolutionary events' was to be carried out 'without releasing workers and employees from work', and work was to be done as usual on New Year's Day and 'all religious festivals'.[65] This brought the total down to 11.

The reversion to the 'interrupted six-day week' in the 'thirties did not, however, bring with it a return to more public holidays. In 1935, the only public holidays were the five days of January 22, May 1 and 2 and November 7 and 8. 'This list', moreover, could not 'be altered by the local labour organs'.[66] It appears from this statement that the six special holidays had been squeezed out, at least in the towns, for no mention is made of them. One concession only was made at this time: on December 5, 1936, the Extraordinary VIII Congress of Soviets established that day as a public holiday to commemorate the adoption of the Stalin Constitution.[67] The annual total was thus brought to six.

The legislation of June, 1940, left these six days as they were, but specifically abolished the six special holidays and the revolutionary holidays of March 12 and 18, which had lingered in the countryside.[68] Moreover, in November, 1940, it was laid down that if the weekly rest day coincided with the holidays of November 7 or 8, it was not to be transferred to another working day, as had hitherto been the practice.[69] Subsequently this principle was apparently applied to all cases of coincidence; according to an authoritative textbook of 1949, 'in those cases where the weekly day of rest coincides with another non-working day (for instance, November 7) no substitute day of rest is granted'.[70] The 1954 edition of the same textbook passes over the point in discreet silence.[71]

For two years after the war May 9 was made a holiday to mark the victory over Germany, but in December, 1947, New Year's Day was substituted.[72] This brought the total to seven (unless one of them happened to fall on a weekly rest day). But in August, 1951, it was thought necessary

> 'to meet the wishes of numerous workers, and take account of representations by trade union and other public organisations which justly point out that the holding of January 21 as a non-working holiday does not accord with the character of the events to which this day is devoted—the memory of the death of V. I. Lenin, and also of January 22, 1905'.

January 22 was therefore declared a working day.[73] In 1965 two more public holidays were declared. May 9 was restored to mark the 'victory of the Soviet people in the Great Patriotic War (1941–5)',[74] and March 8, International Women's Day, was made a public holiday in honour of women's contribution during the war.[75]

There are thus eight public holidays a year in the USSR (always supposing that none of them happens to fall on a weekly rest day) instead of the 16 originally envisaged by the Labour Codex of 1922: January 1, March 8, May 1 and 2, May 9, November 7 and 8 and December 5.

ANNUAL LEAVE

The first RSFSR Labour Codex of December, 1918, set the normal duration of annual leave at one month after one year's continuous work.[76] The Party Programme of March, 1919, however, while it welcomed this enactment, noted that owing to the 'extreme destruction caused by war and the onslaught of world imperialism', the Soviet régime had had to make a number of retreats, including the 'temporary granting of two weeks' leave instead of one month'.[77] The Labour Codex of 1922 maintained the retreat. The relevant article reads: 'All persons working for hire who have worked uninterruptedly for not less than 5½ months are granted ordinary leave once a year for not less than two weeks'.[78] The 5½ months' continuity of employment was not considered broken if a worker was moved from one enterprise to another by managerial order, or if he himself moved from one State enterprise to another without stopping work.[79] Persons working in 'specially harmful and dangerous 'enterprises were to get not less than two weeks' extra leave a year.[80]

In 1930 the *NKT* confirmed leave regulations which, with amendments, remain in force today. During the war leave was cancelled altogether, and replaced by bonuses and then by allotments of Government bonds, but the pre-war regulations were re-established in 1945.[81]

The regulations of 1930 consolidated 'the retreat' of 1919; but, taking account of the different lengths of week then in operation, they replaced the words 'two weeks' leave' by '12 working days with the addition of such rest days as fall in the leave period'.[82] As before, a worker was entitled to leave after working uninterruptedly 'for the same employer' for 5½ months, 17½ months, 29½ months, etc. Work for the same 'employer' might have been held to cover work in different State enterprises, enabling workers to move at their own will without losing their entitlement to leave, as they could do in the 'twenties; but this would have clashed with the policy of combating labour turnover, and an amendment was soon issued by the *NKT* to the effect that if a worker were transferred without interruption of work 'from one enterprise or establishment to another' on the instructions of a 'labour organ' or one of its commissions, or a Party, *Komsomol* or trade union organisation, he could count time in his previous job towards his qualification for leave.[83] If he moved without being so transferred (it was implied), he had to start again from scratch.

The position as regards counting time in a previous job towards qualification for leave has not altered substantially since. Only the names of the transferring authorities are different. Today time is counted if a worker is transferred 'by order of the management or at the instance of a social organisation'[84] (i.e. Party, *Komsomol* or trade union).[85] There has, however, been one important change. When the problem of labour turnover came to the fore again in the late 'thirties, it was found that with the 5½ months' qualifying period 'drifters and slackers, by running from one enterprise to another, contrive to get two leaves during the year', and the law was altered so that workers and employees do not have the right to their annual leave until they have worked for 11 months continuously in the same enterprise.[86] The same purpose—to induce workers to stick to the same job—is served by the grant of three days' extra annual leave after two years' uninterrupted service in the same enterprise in certain industries, transport services and 'major construction projects'.[87] Where a worker is transferred to another enterprise or project where such extra holidays are granted, with the agreement of both managements or on instructions from a higher body, his record of uninterrupted work is not affected.[88]

Leave overdrawn—if a worker takes his annual leave and then moves elsewhere before the expiry of the year for which the leave is granted—is adjusted by stoppage of pay for the number of days' leave taken but not worked for. There are certain exceptions to this rule, for instance when a worker is dismissed as part of a staff reduction, or is transferred by authority.[89] If, on the other hand, some leave is left unused at the end of the period, the worker is compensated financially at the rate of one day's average wages for each month worked, or 12 days' average wages for 11 months or more.[90]

Although 12 working days is the normal duration of annual leave, there are certain cases in which more than this is granted. So-called 'lengthened leave' is granted to juveniles; and certain workers in establishments for research, education and 'cultural enlightenment' get lengthened leave of 24 to 48 days.[91] Secondly, various classes of workers qualify for 'additional leave'. Among these are men and women working in trades or jobs with dangerous or noxious working conditions. A list of such trades, which dates from 1941 with later amendments,[92] provided for additional leave of six to 12 working days for workers in a wide variety of trades in most branches of industry, and of as much as 36 days for those working with mercury and some other particularly noxious materials. A new list was drawn up in 1963.[93] To qualify for the full additional leave allowance the worker must have worked at least 5½ months of his working year—consecutively or with interruptions—in harmful conditions; where he has worked for less than this in harmful conditions he gets a *pro rata* allowance. To count for additional leave, at least half of any day must have been worked in harmful conditions.[94] Additional leave of this type must be taken as leave: financial compensation is not permitted, unless the worker is leaving his job.[95]

Additional leave is also granted to employees with an 'unstandardised' working day—up to 12 working days in compensation for long hours[96]—and to certain classes of workers studying for examinations.

Workers enjoying privileges for work in the Far North or other remote areas also have the right to additional leave: in the Far North—18 days and in other areas classified as remote areas—12 days.[97]

OVERTIME

Overtime, according to the Labour Codex of 1922, is 'as a general rule, not permitted'.[98] Officially, however, it may be allowed in the following exceptional circumstances:[99]

(*a*) on work 'necessary for the defence of the republic or for averting public disasters or dangers';
(*b*) on 'socially essential' work (water supply, sewerage, transport, lighting, post, telegraph and telephone services);
(*c*) on the 'necessary completion of work begun, which cannot be completed during working hours and will entail damage to materials or machinery if not completed';
(*d*) on repair and maintenance work, where its interruption would put a 'significant number' of workers out of work.

In these cases, overtime originally had to have the sanction of the Rates and Conflicts Commission.*[100] Nowadays, however, overtime may be worked only with the permission of the factory union committee. Trade Union Councils, *oblast*, *krai* and Republican trade union committees, exercise control of the correctness of permission for overtime granted by factory committees.[101] The Codex further provides that no worker shall do more than 120 hours' overtime in a year, and not more than four hours on two consecutive days, except on work of a seasonal character, when these limits may be exceeded 'by agreement' with the AUCCTU.[102]

A notable omission from the list of acceptable reasons for using overtime is the exigency of fulfilling the production plan on time. Yet this in fact provides the most common cause of

* *See* p. 180f.

overtime. At the XIX Party Congress in 1952, Malenkov had this to say of 'irregular output during the month':[103]

'The Party has more than once directed the attention of economic leaders to this shortcoming. But even now many enterprises work in fits and starts, and almost half the month's planned output is produced in the last ten-day period. This leads to . . . the use of overtime work.'

This phenomenon, known as 'unrhythmical working' or 'rushing' (*shturmovshchina*), is really not so much irregular as cyclical, since it takes the form of a regular pile-up of work towards the end of the month. Moreover, it has proved so persistent that it appears to be inherent in the Soviet system of plans and targets. It was apparent before the war;[104] in 1955 Bulganin, describing it as a 'major shortcoming', instanced three factories in which over 70 per cent of the monthly output was produced in the last 10-day period;[105] and it has persisted since then.[106] In a leading article in August, 1965, *Pravda*[107] cited the example of the Kremenchug Motor Works, where 'over 40 per cent' of output was produced in the last ten days of each month. *Pravda* referred to the 'mass idling of workers and machinery' at the beginning of the month at a number of factories. A principal cause of this is the 'late delivery to the factory or building site of the necessary materials, equipment and semi-manufactures'.[108] But it is not apparent why the delay in supplies should always occur in the first part of the month. If it does so, however, it implies cyclical output in the supplying enterprises, which has equally to be explained. It seems possible, therefore, that the root cause lies in the more fundamental—and less corrigible—human failing of procrastination. In support of this, it may be noted that the last months of the year, as well as the last days of the month, are sometimes characterised by a rush of work.[109]

In such circumstances the law on overtime is widely disregarded in practice. In November, 1961, for instance, Grishin complained at an AUCCTU Plenum that 'some economic directors . . . employ overtime and change and cancel rest days'. In the second quarter of 1961, he reported, overtime in the RSFSR had increased by 'almost 4 million man-hours' over the first quarter.[110] Since payment of overtime is costly and tends to lead managers to over-expenditure of their Wages Fund, they frequently avoid paying the proper rate for the overtime worked. An article in *Trud* in March, 1961,[111] stated that in 1960, 165,000 hours of overtime were worked at one Riga factory* and 96,000 at another:

'. . . But this is only what is officially reckoned. How many more so-called hidden hours of overtime are there not reckoned up by anyone and for which, moreover, the worker is not paid as the law requires. . . . Such work can be measured in thousands of hours.'

When bad organisation of production or factory planning, shortages of material and technical supplies threaten to frustrate the plan, the article states, 'the director grabs at overtime like a life-belt'. In March, 1965, the USSR Council of National Economy† complained that overtime was being worked illegally and rest days cancelled or changed chiefly because of 'organisational difficulties and hold-ups in material and technical supplies'. At the Moscow *Krasnaya Presnya* foundry equipment works 28,000 hours of overtime were worked in the first half of 1964.[112] The Leningrad public prosecutor has stated that in 1965 almost 12,000 hours of overtime were worked at the *Egorov* factory in Leningrad without the agreement of the factory trade union committee. At another factory the director had cancelled three rest days in a drive to complete the quarterly plan. Overtime working in the city was on the increase.[113] According to another source, instances of the infringement of the procedure for arranging overtime work have 'become a mass feature at many Leningrad factories'.[114]

Sometimes managements apply pressure and bullying tactics to compel rest-day working. This was graphically illustrated in a letter from a Donbass miner published in *Pravda Ukrainy* of August 3, 1966:

'From the office of the mine's deputy chief engineer . . . resounds some choice invective. It is interrogation time for the "criminals"—those who decided to take their Sunday leisure. We've worked every Sunday in May. No excuses accepted. . . . And if anyone were to say that he had planned, say, to take the family on an outing to the woods on Sunday, he is answered by invective, insults and threats. With the words: "I'll have you crawling under my feet", [the deputy director] takes out of his safe a "blacklist" of those who did not work on Sunday.'

Factory managers, it will thus be seen, tend to impose over-

* According to *Kommunist Sovetsky Latvii*, No. 10, 1962 (p. 12), in 1960, 178,752 hours of overtime were worked at this factory, and 288,410 hours in 1961.

† Since abolished.

time and rest-day working without consulting the trade unions. The unions frequently take no action to prevent excessive overtime or readily acquiesce in managements' instructions on overtime.[115]

The trade unions' position as implementers of Government and Party decisions frequently leads them to connive at these abuses which have, for the reasons cited, become essential to the fulfilment of production plans. But it would not be surprising to learn that many Soviet workers in fact welcome the opportunity to supplement their frequently meagre wages.

NIGHT WORK

In case of night work (i.e. between 10 p.m. and 6 a.m.) one hour less is worked than in the daytime.[116] There are, however, exceptions to this provision which reduce its value to certain workers. In 'uninterrupted production' (for instance in certain hot shops, in electric power stations, etc.), the night shift is as long as the day shift.[117] The same is true when the working day is already shortened owing to harmful conditions, or when the worker is hired specifically for night work (e.g. a night watchman).[118]

SAFETY MEASURES AND PRODUCTION HYGIENE

The Labour Codex of 1922 prescribed that all enterprises and establishments must take measures to "eliminate or reduce harmful working conditions, to prevent accidents and to maintain places of work in a proper sanitary and hygienic condition . . .'.[119] This was to be done in accordance with 'general and special compulsory decrees governing individual branches of production'.[120] Originally issued by the *NKT*, general decrees applying to industry as a whole were, after 1933, issued by the AUCCTU or by individual Commissariats (later Ministries) on the basis of special authority given by the Government. Still more recently, such general regulations have usually appeared in the form of 'State All-Union Standards' (Russian initials: *GOST*) and have been promulgated by the Administration for Standardisation under the USSR Council of Ministers. Many of the *GOST* concern products and technique, and only a fraction of the standards issued by the Administration deal with safety and hygiene.[121] Special rules for individual branches of the economy are issued by Trade

Union Central Committees by agreement with interested Ministries and departments.[122] In 1959 Technical Inspectors of trade union councils were introduced and in 1963 Labour Protection Committees established in factories and enterprises to supervise the observance of safety and hygiene regulations.[123] The committees had 1,793,000 members in 1964.[124]

There is good reason to believe, however, that Soviet safety regulations do not set such high standards and are not as stringently enforced as in Britain. Mr Joe O'Hagan, a member of the British TUC delegation to the Soviet Union in September, 1966, is reported to have told the management of the Leningrad *Electrosila* works that they were neglecting industrial safety. He said he had seen a woman paint-sprayer at work without protective clothing or mask, and cutting machinery without guards.[125]

Some of the more general regulations may be briefly mentioned. The Labour Codex prescribes that in particularly harmful occupations, or those involving exposure to abnormal temperatures, humidity or dirt, or where 'considerations of public hygiene' require it, workers are to be supplied with special clothing and protective equipment (goggles, masks, etc.).[126] Lists of trades eligible for special clothing, together with specifications of the clothing, are established either by the AUCCTU in conjunction with Ministries or by the Government.[127] According to the Labour Codex, both protective clothing and protective equipment were to be issued to the worker free,[128] but by a decree of May, 1942, encroachment on this right of the worker was permitted 'in a number of Ministries', where the worker could be made to pay for his special clothing and footwear.[129]

This provision appears to have lapsed. Comprehensive instructions for the issue, preservation and utilisation of special clothing, footwear and protective devices were issued in 1960 by the State Committee on Labour and Wages and the Presidium of the AUCCTU.[130] They provide for the free issue of such clothing and equipment according to standards laid down by Union Republican councils of ministers and USSR Ministries and departments.[131] In August, 1966, the USSR Council of Ministers and AUCCTU issued a decree designed to improve the provision of special clothing, footwear and protective equipment.[132] All items issued free remain the property of the enterprise, must not be taken away or used outside working hours and must be surrendered by a worker leaving the enterprise.[133] Workers must look after special clothing and inform the management of the need for cleaning or repairing.[134] Disputes concerning the loss or damage of special clothing or equipment are referred to the Labour Disputes Commission of the enterprise.[135]

Managements are obliged to provide soap for washing hands during and after work and, in particularly dirty jobs, an extra issue of 400 grams of 'special soap' to be taken home.[136] Similarly, drinking water must be provided and, in hot shops, salted soda water.[137]

Rules for work out of doors in very cold weather provide for breaks in work for workers to get warm, or for a complete cessation of work in especially severe conditions. The respective levels of air temperature and wind force are set locally by Soviet Executive Committees, and the number, duration and organisation of the breaks for warming are decided by managements in agreement with the trade union organisation.[138]

WOMEN WORKERS

The fact that female labour is very widely used in industry in the USSR is almost too well known to require documentation. The following are official Soviet statistics:[139]

Proportion of Women among Workers and Employees by Branches of the USSR National Economy

(in percentages of total number of workers and employees)

	1929	*1940*	*1950*	*1960*	*1964*
Total in national economy	27	38	47	47	49
Industry (proper)	28	41	45	45	46
Construction	7	23	33	29	29
Transport	9	21	30	24	24
Communications	28	48	59	64	65
Trade, public catering, procurement, material and technical supplies	19	44	58	66	72

In accordance with the official view of woman as a worker first and a mother second, the Soviet State takes measures to relieve her of her maternal duties so that she may concentrate on her job. For this purpose it aims to provide crèches and kindergartens, though the scale of provision is often inadequate.

Crèches, according to a volume of the *Small Soviet Encyclopaedia* published in August, 1960,[140] are 'institutions for the protection of motherhood and childhood which assist working mothers to combine the upbringing and care of their children with production and public activity'. The majority are built by government Ministries and departments, Councils of National Economy, local Soviets and trade unions. Since 1959 crèches have been combined with the kindergartens in single establishments under the jurisdiction of Union Republican Ministries of Education, health supervision being the responsibility of Republican Ministries of Health.[141] Crèches cater for children aged two months to three years.[142] As a rule children stay in the crèche for 10–11 hours a day or more, and there is provision for them to be kept all round the clock. In summer the children may be taken out to houses in the country (*dachi*) run by the crèches.[143]

Fees are payable according to place of residence, the child's length of stay, and the parents' income—in which are included not only the parents' combined wages but also all pensions, scholarship grants, maternity grants and alimony. In 1957 the rates for one child per month were:[144]

Monthly Crèche Fees for One Child
(in roubles)*

Parents' Monthly Income	*In Towns and Workers' Settlements* — *Child's length of stay* — *9–10 hours*	*12–14 hours*	*24 hours*	*At a* Dacha
Up to 400 . .	30	38	45	60
401–600 . .	40	50	60	80
601–800 . .	50	63	75	100
801–1,200 . .	65	81	98	130
Over 1,200 . .	80	100	120	160
	In Rural Areas			
Up to 400 . .	15	19	23	30
401–600 . .	25	31	38	50
601–800 . .	35	44	53	70
801–1,200 . .	50	63	75	100
Over 1,200 . .	65	81	98	130

* Figures given in old roubles. They should be divided by ten.

This scale of fees has evidently not changed. *Trud* of October 25, 1966, gave identical figures for minimum and maximum charges for round-the-clock residence in crèches in urban and rural areas. The newspaper added that unmarried mothers earning less than 60 roubles a month, and also mothers with four or more children, gain a reduction of 50 per cent. Parents with two or three children have smaller reductions, depending on their income.

Priority of admission to crèches goes to the children of trade union members.[145] A decree of October, 1948, laid down that there should be crèches at factories with more than 500 employees, on the basis of 12 places to every 100 women.[146] In addition to factory crèches, there are also *raion* crèches, serving mothers from their place of residence,[147] which presumably cater for women employed in smaller factories. Between 1940 and 1965 crèche accommodation trebled from 781,400 to 2,419,500.[148] While this may represent a notable achievement in absolute terms, in fact the plan for crèche building has been regularly neglected. Kovrigina, the then USSR Minister of Health, said at the XX Party Congress in 1956 that the plan in the previous five years was fulfilled by less than half.[149] Under the Seven-Year Plan (1959–65) it was proposed to increase the number of places in crèches by 'over two-and-a-half times' by 1965. This target in fact was under-fulfilled by over 30 per cent.[150] Thus there is now crèche accommodation for at the most one-fifth of the 13 million or so children under three. The plan cited by *Pravda* as long ago as 1954 to 'ensure that in the next two or three years kindergartens and crèches should completely accommodate the children of all working women'[151] remains no nearer fulfilment over a decade later.

Nevertheless the intention to make the most of female labour is undiminished and labour legislation has therefore paid special attention to questions raised by the employment of women in industry. The Labour Codex of 1922 lays down that women should not be employed on 'particularly heavy and unhealthy work, or on work underground'.[152] A list of the maximum weights which women may be required to move—20 kg. (44 lb.) by hand, 50 kg. (110 lb.) by wheelbarrow, 60–115 kg. (132–253 lb.) by hand-carts, and 600 kg. (1,320 lb.) by trucks on rails—was laid down in 1932, and is still in force.[153] The current list of jobs in which women may not be employed also dates from 1932, with amendments made at various times since.

The trend of these amendments is of interest, for it has been to increase rather than decrease the number of jobs on which women may work. In 1937, for instance, restrictions on female labour in timber-floating and lumbering were cancelled;[154] in November, 1938, the ban on employing women as railway engine-drivers, stokers, assistant drivers and mechanics for running repairs to locomotives was lifted,[155] in June, 1940, the restrictions on female labour in river transport were relaxed to permit the employment of women on all jobs except as stokers in solid-fuel ships, seamen in cargo-passenger ships, and quartermasters in ships with manual steering gear.[156]

The Labour Codex's ban on women working underground was for many years a dead letter. Another law of 1940, enlarging the scope of female labour in mines, gave as a reason the 'growth of mechanisation and the improvement of safety techniques in underground work'; on this basis only a few underground trades were henceforth reserved to men, namely hewers (except for mining sand and clay), loaders, shoring workers, drillers using hand drills, pit-prop workers in steep galleries, and shot-firers in vertical workings.[157] In fact, however, this decree appears to have done little more than legalise an existing state of affairs, since, on the authority of Mr Sam Watson, Durham Area Secretary of the British National Union of Mineworkers, women were at work underground at least as early as 1936.[158] During the war the proportion of women employed in industry, including mining, rose steeply. According to a report in *Pravda* in December, 1944, 'in many pits women have become the basic, decisive force. In various coal trusts . . . the proportion of women to the total of miners is 50–60 per cent.[159]

At various times Soviet authorities have made declarations to the effect that the employment of women on heavy work is to cease—sooner or later. Mr Watson was told, first in 1936 and again in 1956, that the use of female labour in the mines was only temporary.[160] In 1947 the AUCCTU Secretariat invited Ministries to envisage the 'complete replacement in the course of 1947–8 of female labour by male labour on work connected with the moving of heavy weights'.[161] Shvernik assured a British workers' delegation in 1953 that the employment of women in heavy industry would not be a permanent feature of Soviet life,[162] and Bulganin said in 1956 that the 'employment of female labour in arduous jobs is declining all the time and should eventually be eliminated completely'.[163]

These forecasts need critical evaluation. Mr Watson found, on his visit to the USSR in 1954, that the proportion of women underground had increased, instead of decreasing as he had been led to expect in 1936.[164] In some areas at least, notably Karaganda in Kazakhstan, the number of women working in the mines was increasing as late as 1954, when the total of women employed in the coal industry grew by 8,000.[165]

A delegation of mineworkers from Nottingham, which visited the USSR in July, 1955, reported that women were working as 'banksmen, onsetters, screen-hands, underground diesel loco drivers at loading points—pushing heavy tubs around just as any man would in an English pit'. Moreover, 'no special sanitary arrangements for the women were seen'.[166] The leaders of Swedish and Danish trade union delegations visiting the USSR in the summer of 1956 also commented critically on the employment of women on heavy work in industry.[167]

Shortly after Bulganin's statement of 1956, a delegation from the British National Coal Board reported, after a visit to a number of coalfields in the USSR, that women in the Soviet Union 'are required in many cases to do work that is the hardest of manual work—to work in the pits, to do the heaviest jobs, including the handling of heavy materials and the mixing of concrete on the surface'.[168]

It is only in recent years that any serious action has been taken to relieve women of underground work. A decree of the Council of Ministers of the USSR, published in October, 1957, but issued earlier in the year, set dates by which the employment of women underground in certain jobs in mining and underground construction should cease. The dates set were: in the coal and shale industries and in transport construction—January 1, 1959; in ferrous and non-ferrous metallurgy—July 1, 1958; in the chemical and local fuel industries—April 1, 1958; in the coal enterprise construction industry—August 1, 1957; in the building materials industry—February 1, 1958; in light industry, the food industry and in enterprises of the Ministry of Geology—September 1, 1957. There are a number of exceptions from the provisions of the decree: women in responsible posts not doing physical work, women sanitary workers, cleaners, etc., women doing courses of training, and women doing jobs which involve going underground from time to time for non-physical work. These women will continue to work underground.[169] There is, however, evidence that the regulations banning the employment of women in heavy underground work have been put into practice. In the Kazakhstan mining town of Ekibastuz, for instance, there were in 1964 almost no jobs for women.[170] *Pravda* has said that 'in Kazakhstan in all the mining undertakings women were withdrawn from underground work a long time ago'. Several thousand were released in the Karaganda basin alone.[171] The chairman of the Donets *oblast* Soviet has stated that work in the region's heavy industry and mining was becoming more and more a male preserve, especially since the 'very correct decision' obliging managers of coalmines to release women from underground work.[172]

Though this represents progress from a humanitarian standpoint, it has created unemployment among women in areas of mining and heavy industry, where few alternative jobs are available. The solution to this problem is now seen in the development of light industries employing women.[173]

Apart from general and particular prohibitions on women doing heavy and dangerous work, other legal provisions make allowances for the 'physiological peculiarities of the female organism'.[174] The Labour Codex of 1922 originally laid down that women might not be employed at all on night work (except by permission of the *NKT* and the AUCCTU 'in branches of industry where it is required by special necessity').[175] In the first years of industrialisation, however, when three-shift working was introduced, this provision lapsed entirely, and has never been revived. An article forbidding night work and overtime for pregnant women and nursing mothers remains in force.[176] At the XXII Party Congress Khrushchev said the question of abolishing night work for women was 'a big problem' that would take time and the necessary conditions to solve completely. The Party and Government would do everything to solve it.[177] If need be, pregnant women may be transferred to lighter work, retaining, as a minimum, their average rate of pay for the preceding six months.[178] Expectant mothers may not be transferred to work away from their permanent place of work from the beginning of their fifth month of pregnancy, unless they give their consent.[179] Nursing mothers must be given extra paid breaks of not less than half an hour every 3½ hours' working time in order to feed their children.[180] Maternity allowances are paid in accordance with official policy; paid maternity leave has been increased, since April, 1956, to 56 calendar days before childbirth and 56 days after; in the case of abnormal or multiple births, post-natal leave may be increased to 70 days;[181] and up to three months' additional unpaid leave must be granted if the woman so wishes.[182]

These provisions are obviously inconvenient to managements employing pregnant women, and it is not altogether surprising to find them circumvented or disregarded. That there would be a tendency on the part of managers to get rid of pregnant women was early foreseen by the Soviet authorities, who laid down in 1922 that pregnant women could be dismissed from work only in exceptional circumstances, with the permission of the Labour Inspector in each case.[183] This was followed in 1936, when a number of measures were passed with the object of re-establishing the family as a basic social unit, by a decree making it a criminal offence to refuse work to a woman or to reduce her wages because of pregnancy;[184] for this offence a punishment of six months' corrective labour, or a fine of 1,000 roubles,* was instituted, with two years' deprivation of freedom for repeated offenders.[185] (The following year, however, when the campaign against labour turnover started again, these provisions were made inapplicable if the pregnant woman had worked in the same enterprise for less than a year.[186]) Under the RSFSR Criminal Codex issued in 1960 the penalty for dismissing or refusing a woman work because of pregnancy is up to one year's corrective labour, or dismissal.[187]

Nevertheless, infringements of the law take place. From time to time direct reports of them find their way into the Press: one such report, from Kirgizia in May, 1957, stated that at 17 enterprises of the Kirgiz Ministry of Light Industry, and a few other enterprises in Kirgizia, pregnant women and nursing mothers had been working on night shifts, and that elsewhere managers were conniving at the illegal dismissal of pregnant women.[188] In October, 1961, *Izvestiya* reported a case of girls having to load sacks of cement heavier than themselves.[189] But the main evidence for the existence of these malpractices is the continuing flow of exhortations against them. In 1955 Shvernik

* In old currency

warned the Trade Union Congress that trade unions 'must ... improve the protection of labour for women',[190] and the Presidium of the AUCCTU remarked in October of that year:[191]

> 'In some enterprises there are cases of violation of the legislation on the protection of labour for women, and of an inconsiderate attitude on the part of economic and trade union organisations to the complaints and needs of mothers';

concluding with an injunction to unions to supervise the observance of female labour legislation closely. In 1957 the cry was still the same: 'These laws [on female labour] are known to all. But it must be said that in some places these laws are not observed sufficiently fully, strictly or enthusiastically.'[192] In 1962 the AUCCTU Presidium instructed trade unions to call strictly to account persons violating labour legislation on women and in particular to ensure that laws on the work of pregnant women, nursing mothers and juveniles were strictly enforced.[193] In January, 1965, the Presidium reminded union committees of legislation on pregnant women and unmarried mothers with children under one year old.[194] In 1966 *Pravda* complained that many trade union organisations controlled the observance of labour legislation in a purely formal way. The newspaper added that not a single point of a resolution issued over a year previously by the Kazakhstan Trade Union Council on shortcomings in women's working conditions had been implemented.[195]

In June, 1960, a decree of the USSR Council of Ministers, to take effect on October 1, 1961, prohibited women from working in fishing, scouting and collecting-transporting vessels of fishing fleets. Women were to be replaced by men and transferred to work ashore.[196]

Meanwhile, women continue to be employed in heavy manual work. This was well illustrated in an article in *Pravda* in July, 1966.[197] Jobs women were reported to be doing include: unloading heavy cans of paint, digging trenches for the foundations of houses, 'odd jobs' on building sites, pushing trolley-loads of raw materials, semi-manufactured and wet goods in a textile factory (while men did lighter work), laying kerbstones, turning over with a shovel up to 16 tons of rye in a single shift at a brewery, and handling heavy sacks of sugar and flour in shops. This list could be greatly extended. Since Soviet industry relies so heavily on female manual labour, this state of affairs seems likely to exist for some time—until industrial methods become much more sophisticated. The problem was put in its context by Khrushchev in May, 1962:

'It is painful to see . . . women armed with crowbars packing ballast under [railway] sleepers by hand . . . At a time when we have reached the Moon we have no machine to replace the worker's crowbar and equip him. In particular, I repeat, this applies to women. Something is lacking. . . .'[198]

JUVENILES

The Labour Codex of 1922, forbidding as a general rule the employment of young people under 16, allowed juveniles not younger than 14 to be employed 'in exceptional cases' with trade union consent.[199] This rule held good for 34 years until its revision in December, 1956. The general prohibition of employment of juveniles under 16 was then reaffirmed, while the absolute minimum age for employment 'in exceptional circumstances . . . by agreement with the factory and local Trade Union Committee' was raised to 15.[200]

Juveniles under 18 are barred by the Labour Codex from 'particularly heavy or unhealthy work or work underground'.[201] As with women, however, the period of the early Five-Year Plans saw the original legislation being somewhat whittled down. The *NKT*, publishing in 1932 the list of occupations from which juveniles were excluded, removed the ban on 11 of them in respect of 17-year-olds 'undergoing instruction in an organised manner' (in *FZU* and other such schools) subject to the consent of the Labour Inspector and the medical authorities.[202] Later the list was further reduced, allegedly 'in connection with a general improvement in working conditions and the elimination of the harmful nature of a number of trades'.[203] In 1936, for instance, work underground was added to the list of occupations permitted to 17-year-olds under instruction.[204] In 1939 the ban on employing juveniles in a number of trades in the rubber and tyre industries was lifted 'in connection with the improvement of labour organisation, mechanisation and ventilation'.[205] The 1932 list was superseded in 1959 and replaced by a new one issued by the State Committee for Labour and Wages, with the agreement of the AUCCTU.[206]

Legal limits on the movement of heavy weights by juveniles are also laid down. Juveniles may not be employed exclusively to carry or move weights heavier than 4·1 kg. (9 lb.). Young people aged 16 and 17 may, however, be called upon to shift weights for not more than one-third of the working time, subject to maxima ranging from 16 kg. (36 lb.) carried by hand to 115 kg. (253 lb.) on a two-wheeled handcart and 492 kg. (1,083 lb.) on a truck on rails. Lower maxima are laid down in each case for girls, except for wheelbarrows and two-wheeled carts, which they are not allowed to use at all. Weights of half these amounts may be shifted by 15-year-olds in 'exceptional cases', but not on wheelbarrows or two-wheeled carts.[207]

The Labour Codex of 1922 originally limited the working day for 16- and 17-year-olds to six hours, and for 14- and 15-year-olds to four hours.[208] From June, 1940, when the adult working day was extended to eight hours, juveniles of 16 and 17 were treated as adults, and worked eight hours;[209] subsequently the hours for 14- and 15-year-olds were extended to six.[210] These severe measures remained in force until January, 1956, when 14- and 15-year-old trainees were limited to four hours' work a day, and 16- and 17-year-olds to seven hours[211]—a figure which was further reduced six months later to six hours.[212] When the general employment of young people under 16 was forbidden in December, 1956, 15-year-olds employed 'in exceptional cases' were limited to four hours' work a day.[213] Since managements are legally bound to pay juveniles as for a full working day, the temptation to abuse the law in one way or another is considerable.*

Overtime and night work have followed a similar pattern. Originally forbidden in the 1922 Codex to all juveniles under 18,[214] they were made legal in July, 1940, for 16- and 17-year-olds on the same basis as for adults.[215] This concession to the needs of national defence was withdrawn ten years after the end of the war, and since August, 1955, overtime and night work have again become illegal for young workers under the age of 18.[216]

Similarly with the regulations on leave for juveniles. The Labour Codex's provision,[217] for leave of 'not less than one month' in the year for persons under 18, which had been defined more closely as 'one calendar month, but not less than 24 working days' in 1930,[218] was set aside in 1940. From 1940 to 1955 16- and 17-year-olds were treated for leave on a par

* *See* p. 38.

with adults—and during the war, it will be remembered, this meant no leave at all. Only since 1955 has the pre-war allowance of one calendar month been restored.[219] The summer months are reserved preferentially to juveniles when an enterprise is making out its annual leave rota.[220]

By law, juveniles must be medically examined before employment, and re-examined at least once a year.[221]

Although legislation affords juveniles a good deal of protection, infringements of the law are not infrequent. In November, 1962, an AUCCTU resolution on strengthening trade union control over the observance of this legislation revealed a number of 'serious shortcomings'. Juveniles were 'frequently' taken on without medical examination and placed in jobs irrespective of their state of health. The resolution cited cases of juveniles working longer than the stipulated hours and on night shifts, performing heavy and arduous work and not receiving their full leave entitlements. Accidents among young workers were ascribed to inadequate supervision.[222] Similar infringements continue to be reported in the Press.[223]

SOURCES

N.B.—Undated citations of works of which more than one edition is listed in the bibliography refer to the most recent edition there listed; earlier editions are cited with the date in brackets.

1. *K.P.S.S. v Rezolyutsiakh*, Vol. I, p. 41.
2. RSFSR Laws, 1917, 1:10.
3. *K.P.S.S. v Rezolyutsiakh*, Vol. I, p. 429.
4. *KZoT* (1922), arts. 94 and 95.
5. *KZoT* (1922), art. 113.
6. USSR Laws, 1929, 61:613.
7. Dobb, p. 190.
8. Dewar, p. 155n.
9. USSR Laws, 1927, 61:613.
10. V. V. Schmidt in *Trud*, October 31, 1928, quoted by Schwarz, p. 262.
11. Dobb, pp. 190f.
12. *Komsomolskaya Pravda*, February 28, 1928, quoted by Schwarz, p. 265.
13. Dobb, p. 191n.
14. Stalin, *Works*, Vol. 13, p. 301.
15. Stalin, *Problems of Leninism*, p. 621.
16. Lozovsky, p. 71.
17. *Constitution (Fundamental Law) of the Union of Soviet Socialist Republics* (1937), art. 119.
18. *Pravda*, June 26, 1940.
19. *Loc. cit.*
20. *Vedomosti Verkhovnogo Soveta SSSR*, 1940, No. 20 (43).
21. USSR Laws, 1940, 18:436; 24:588; 25:612; 30:731; 31:767; 32:807; 1941, 1: 11; 1:22; 4:75; 7:122;

1946, 9:158; 1947, 6:119; *Spravochnik Profsoyuznogo Rabotnika* (1948), pp. 185f.

22. Aleksandrov (1949), p. 179.
23. USSR Laws, 1940, 18:436, art. 4.
24. *Five-Year Plan, 1946–50*, p. 10.
25. *Izvestiya*, February 26, 1947.
26. *B.S.E.*, 2nd edn., Vol. 9, p. 222.
27. Stalin, *Economic Problems of Socialism*, pp. 76f.
28. *Entsiklopedichesky Slovar*, Vol. III, p. 55.
29. *XX Sezd K.P.S.S.*, Vol. I, pp. 76f.
30. Kapustin, p. 15.
31. *Vestnik Statistiki*, 1961, No. 5, p. 1.
32. *Pravda*, April 22, 1958.
33. *Pravda*, November 4, 1958.
34. *Pravda*, September 20, 1959.
35. *Trud*, October 29, 1963.
36. *Vestnik Statistiki*, 1961, No. 5, p. 7.
37. *Pravda*, September 4, 1961.
38. *Sbornik*, p. 177; Yamenfeld, Pavlov and Dvinov, pp. 222f.
39. *KZoT* (1922), art. 109.
40. USSR Laws, 1929, 54:502.
41. *B.S.E.*, 1st edn., Vol. 22, col. 784.
42. *Ibid.*, col. 785.
43. *Pravda*, October 1, 1929, quoted by Schwarz, p. 273.
44. Stalin, *Problems of Leninism*, p. 468.
45. *B.S.E.*, 1st edn., Vol. 22, col. 785f.
46. *Pravda*, June 26, 1940.
47. USSR Laws, 1940, 16:385, art. 4.
48. *Ukaz Prezidiuma Verkhovnogo Soveta SSSH of March* 8, 1956, in *Sbornik*, p. 165.
49. *Postanovlenie Soveta Ministrov SSSR: O sokrashchenii prodolzhitelnosti rabochego dnya dlya rabochikh i sluzhashchikh v predvykhodnye i predprazdnichnye dni*, in *Pravda*, March 9, 1956, art. 1; *Sbornik*, p. 165.
50. *Ibid.*, art. 3.
51. *Kommunist*, 1962, No. 2, p. 36.
52. *Postanovlenie Soveta Ministrov SSSR: O sokrashchenii . . .* , art. 2.
53. *KZoT*, art. 109, omitted from *Sbornik*, p. 158.
54. *Spravochnik Profsoyuznogo Rabotnika*.
55. *Pravda*, May 8, 1960.
56. *Trud*, May 4, 1965; *Izvestiya*, May 5, 1965.
57. *Ibid.* Also Kosygin's report on the Five-Year-Plan Directives of XXIII Party Congress, *Pravda*, April 6, 1966.
58. *Pravda*, April 10, 1966.
59. *Pravda*, May 11, 1966; *Sovetskie Profsoyuzy*, 1966, No. 19; *Narodnoe Khozyaistvo SSSR v 1965 godu*, p. 593.
60. *KZoT* (1922), art. 111.
61. *Ibid.*, art. 112.
62. USSR Laws, 1924, 13:126.
63. USSR Laws, 1927, 60:608.
64. USSR Laws, 1928, 22:194.
65. USSR Laws, 1929, 63:586.
66. *B.S.E.*, 1st edn., Vol. 22, col. 785.
67. *Ibid.*, Vol. 34, p. 99.

68. USSR Laws, 1940, 16:385, art. 3.
69. USSR Laws, 1940, 30:764; *B.S.E.*, 1st edn., Vol. 22, col. 785.
70. Aleksandrov (1949), p. 189.
71. Aleksandrov, pp. 233f.
72. *Spravochnik Profsoyuznogo Rabotnika*, p. 190.
73. *Pravda*, August 14, 1951.
74. *Pravda*, April 28, 1965.
75. *Pravda*, May 9, 1965.
76. *KZoT* (1918) art. 7.
77. *K.P.S.S. v Resolyutsiakh*, Vol. I, pp. 428f.
78. *KZoT* (1922), art. 114.
79. *Loc. cit.*, n.
80. *Ibid.*, art. 115.
81. *Izvestiya*, June 27, 1941; *Vedomosti Verkhovnogo Soveta SSSR*, 1942, *No.* 13 (172); *Ibid.*, 1945, No. 37 (364).
82. *Pravila ob ocherednykh i dopolnitelnykh otpuskakh*, in *Sbornik*, pp. 175–81, art. 7.
83. *Ibid.*, art. 1.
84. Aleksandrov, p. 235.
85. *Sbornik*, p. 580.
86. *Ibid.*, p. 175.
87. USSR Laws, 1939, 1:1, art. 13.
88. *Sbornik*, p. 185.
89. *Pravila ob ocherednykh i dopolnitelnykh otpuskakh*, in *Sbornik*, pp. 175–81, art. 2.
90. *Ibid.*, arts 28, 29.
91. *Sbornik*, p. 183.
92. *Spravochnik Profsoyuznogo Rabotnika* (1949), pp. 215–76. The list given in *Sbornik* (1956) is less up to date than this.
93. *Spisok proizvodstv, tsekhov, profesii i dolzhnostei s vrednymi usloviyami truda. . . .*
94. *Sbornik*, p. 177.
95. *Postanovlenie SNK SSSR* of June 12, 1941: *Ob utverzhdenii spiska profesii s vrednymi usloviyami truda dlya kotoryk ustanavlivaetsya dopolnitelny otpusk*, in *Sbornik* (1956), p. 121, art. 4.
96. *Pravila ob ocherednykh i dopolnitelnykh otpuskakh*, art. 8.
97. *Sbornik*, p. 498, art. 2.
98. *KZoT* (1922, 1931), art. 103; cf. *Sbornik*, p. 157.
99. *KZoT* (1922, 1931), art. 104; cf. *Sbornik*, pp. 157f.
100. *KZoT* (1922, 1931), art. 104n; cf. *Sbornik* (1956), p. 88.
101. *Sbornik*, p. 171.
102. *KZoT* (1922, 1931) art. 106 and note.
103. *Pravda*, October 6, 1952.
104. D. Akul'shin in *Pravda*, January 27, 1941.
105. *Pravda*, July 17, 1955.
106. Grishin in *Pravda*, November 25, 1961; Volkov in *Pravda*, October 6, 1961; A. Pelse in *Kommunist Sovetskoy Latvii*, 1962, No. 10, p. 12.
107. *Pravda*, August 17, 1965.
108. *Ibid.*
109. *Trud*, March 28, 1956.
110. *Pravda*, November 25, 1961.
111. *Trud*, March 2, 1961.
112. *Sovetskaya Rossiya*, March 2, 1965.
113. *Pravda*, September 16, 1966.
114. *Vestnik Leningradskogo Universiteta*, 1965, No. 23.

115. *Pravda*, September 16, 1966.
116. *KZoT* (1922, 1931), art. 96; *Sbornik*, p. 156.
117. *KZoT* (1922), art. 96; *Sbornik*, p. 156.
118. Aleksandrov, Kiselev and Stavtseva, p. 58.
119. *KZoT* (1922), art. 139.
120. *Loc. cit.*
121. Aleksandrov, p. 274; *B.S.E.*, 2nd edn., Vol. 12, p. 280.
122. USSR Laws, 1933, 57:333.
123. *Spravochnik Profsoyuznogo Rabotnika*, pp. 228–33.
124. *Ibid.*, p. 179.
125. *Daily Telegraph*, September 20, 1966.
126. *KZoT*, art. 141, in *Sbornik*, p. 338.
127. Aleksandrov, p. 276.
128. *KZoT*, art. 141, in *Sbornik*, p. 338.
129. *Spravochnik Profsoyuznogo Rabotnika* (1948), p. 141n.
130. *Sbornik*, pp. 355–60.
131. *Loc. cit.*, art. 1.
132. *Trud*, September 22, 1966.
133. *Ibid.*, arts. 6, 22.
134. *Ibid.*, art. 30.
135. *Ibid.*, art. 31.
136. Artemev, pp. 95f.; Aleksandrov, p. 276; *KZoT*, art. 141 in *Sbornik*, p. 338.
137. Aleksandrov, p. 276; *Sbornik*, pp. 352f.
138. Artemev, p. 99.
139. *Narodnoe Khozyaistvo SSSR v 1960 godu*, p. 642; *Narodnoe Khozyaistvo SSSR v 1965 godu*, p. 564.
140. *M.S.E.*, 3rd edn., Vol. 10, col. 1220.
141. *Postanovlenie Tsentralnogo Komiteta KPSS i Soveta Ministrov SSSR*, in *Pravda*, May 28, 1959.
142. *M.S.E.*, 3rd edn., Vol. 10, col. 1220.
143. *B.S.E.*, 2nd edn., Vol. 14, p. 162.
144. *Vysshaya Shkola*, p. 487.
145. USSR Laws, 1931, 41; 238.
146. *B.S.E.*, 2nd edn., Vol. 14, p. 162.
147. *Ibid.*, p. 163.
148. *Narodnoe Khozyaistvo SSSR v 1965 godu*, p. 752.
149. *Pravda, February* 26, 1956.
150. *Narodnoe Khozyaistvo SSSR v 1965 godu*, p. 752.
151. *Pravda*, May 15, 1954.
152. *KZoT*, art. 129, in *Sbornik*, p. 403.
153. *Postanovlenie NKT* of August 14, 1932, in *Sbornik*, p. 413.
154. *Trudovoe Zakonodatelstvo SSSR*, p. 219.
155. USSR Laws, 1938, 50:282.
156. *Trudovoe Zakonodatelstvo SSSR*, p. 220.
157. USSR Laws, 1940, 30:730.
158. *Daily Telegraph*, October 19, 1954.
159. *Pravda*, December 6, 1944.
160. *Daily Telegraph*, October 19, 1954; *Manchester Guardian*, August 18, 1956.
161. *Spravochnik Profsoyuznogo Rabotnika* (1948), p. 144.
162. *Manchester Guardian*, May 22, 1953.
163. *Pravda*, July 12, 1956.

164. *Daily Telegraph*, October 19, 1954.
165. *Kazakhstanskaya Pravda*, January 8, 1955.
166. *Report of the Delegation which visited the USSR, July* 15–26, 1955, p. 17.
167. Moscow Radio in Swedish, August 16, 1956; Moscow Radio in Danish, July 3, 1956.
168. *Report of the Delegation to the Soviet Union*, August 7–23, 1956, p. 37.
169. *Sotsialisticheskaya Zakonnost*, 1957, No. 10, p. 91.
170. *Izvestiya*, November 14, 1964.
171. *Pravda*, July 11, 1966.
172. *Izvestiya*, July 15, 1965.
173. *See*, for example, *Izvestiya*, July 15, 1965; *Pravda*, July 11, 1966.
174. Aleksandrov (1949), p. 244.
175. *KZoT* (1922), art. 130.
176. *KZoT*, art. 131, in *Sbornik*, p. 403.
177. *Pravda*, October 29, 1961.
178. *KZoT*, art. 132, as amended by RSFSR Laws, 1937, 6:40, in *Sbornik*, p. 403.
179. *KZoT*, art. 133, in *Sbornik*, p. 403.
180. *Ibid.*, art. 134, in *Sbornik*, p. 403.
181. *Ukaz Prezidiuma Verkhovnogo Soveta SSSR* of March 26, 1956, in *Sbornik*, p. 404.
182. *Loc. cit.*, n.
183. *Postanovlenie NKT RSFSR* of August 8, 1922, in *Trudovoe Zakonodatelstvo SSSR*, p. 222.
184. USSR Laws, 1936, 34:309, art. 9.
185. USSR Laws, 1936, 51:419.
186. USSR Laws, 1937, 25:99.
187. Art. 139; cf. *Sbornik*, p. 404.
188. *Sovetskaya Kirgiziya*, May 23, 1957.
189. *Izvestiya*, October 12, 1961.
190. *Trud*, June 8, 1954.
191. *Pravda*, October 21, 1955.
192. N. Popova in *Sotsialistichesky Trud*, 1957, No. 3, p. 8.
193. *Okhrana Truda*, p. 115.
194. *Sovetskaya Yustitsiya*, No. 23, December, 1965, p. 29.
195. *Pravda*, July 11, 1966.
196. *Sbornik*, p. 411.
197. *Pravda*, July 11, 1966.
198. *Pravda*, May 11, 1962.
199. *KZoT* (1922), art. 135.
200. *Pravda*, December 14, 1956.
201. *KZoT*, art. 129, in *Sbornik*, p. 403.
202. *Postanovlenie NKT SSSR* of October 13, 1932, in *Sbornik* (1956), pp. 264ff.
203. Aleksandrov, p. 278.
204. *Postanovlenie Sekretariata VTsSPS* of January 3, 1936, mentioned in *Sbornik* (1956), p. 265.
205. *Postanovlenie Sekretariata VTsSPS* of December 16, 1939, in *Trudovoe Zakonodatelstvo SSSR*, p. 666 and note.
206. *Sbornik*, p. 416. The list of jobs now prohibited to juveniles is not included.
207. *Obyazetelnoe Postanovlenie NKT RSFSR*, of March 4, 1921, in *Sbornik*, p. 416.
208. *KZoT* (1922, 1931), arts. 95, 136.
209. *Ukaz Prezidiuma Verkhovnogo Soveta SSSR* of June 26, 1940, in *Vedomosti*

Verkhovnogo Soveta, 1940, No. 20 (83), art. 1.

210. Aleksandrov, p. 281.
211. *Ukaz Prezidiuma Verkhovnogo Soveta RSFSR* of August 15, 1955, in *Sbornik,* p. 418.
212. *Ukaz Prezidiuma Verkhovnogo Soveta SSSR* of May 26, 1956, in *Sbornik,* p. 418.
213. *Pravda,* December 14, 1956.
214. *KZoT* (1922), arts. 105 and 130.
215. USSR Laws 1940, 18:438.
216. *Postanovlenie TsK K.P.S.S. i Soveta Ministrov SSSR* of August 8, 1955, art. 3, in *Sbornik,* p. 418.
217. *KZoT* (1922), art. 114.
218. *Pravila ob ocherednykh i dopolnitelnykh otpuskakh,* in *Sbornik,* pp. 175–81, art. 9.
219. *Ukaz Prezidiuma Verkhovnogo Soveta SSSR of* August 15, 1955, in *Sbornik,* p. 418.
220. *Pravila ob ocherednykh i dopolnitelnykh otpuskakh,* in *Sbornik,* pp. 175–81, art. 13.
221. RSFSR Laws, 1922, 65: 842.
222. *Spravochnik Profsoyuznogo Rabotnika,* p. 224.
223. See, for example, *Vestnik Leningradskogo Universiteta,* 1965, No. 23.

V
The Trade Unions

HISTORY

Ever since Lenin inveighed at the close of the last century against those who 'relapse from Social Democracy into *trade unionism*'*[1] there has been a distinctive Communist view of the proper relationship of a trade union to the State. In pre-revolutionary days, the Communist aim was to make the trade unions hostile to the 'feudal' or 'bourgeois' State, which was, by Marxist definition, on the side of the bosses. With the Revolution and the establishment of the 'Dictatorship of the Proletariat', however, the relationship changes: because the State is now supposedly on the side of the workers, the trade unions are to be on the side of the State. This means, in effect, the trade unions' complete surrender of their position as independent champions of the workers' interests. As Zinoviev, speaking for the Bolsheviks, once put it: 'Why and from whom do you need independence: from your own Government?'[2]

The struggle that raged round this point, involving Trotsky and Bukharin on one side (demanding complete 'statification' of the unions) and the Workers' Opposition led by Shlyapnikov on the other (asking for the transfer to the unions of the entire economic administration) was not finally settled until 1929. At the X Party Congress in 1921 a resolution was adopted embodying the much-requoted description of the trade unions as a 'school of Communism' and reasserting Party tutelage over them. 'Syndicalism' was condemned.[3] The New Economic Policy gave occasion for a reiteration of the rôle of the Party in the trade unions. Recognising the ambiguous rôle of the trade unions as, on the one hand, the supposed defenders of the workers' interests, and on the other 'sharers in State power

* It was Lenin who established the pejorative use in Russian of the English words 'trade unionism' (in Russian transliteration *tred-yunionizm*). A Soviet trade union is known as a *Profsoyuz*.

and constructors of the national economy as a whole', and seeing that this would lead to 'conflicts, disagreements, frictions, etc.', Lenin held that a 'higher authority' was necessary to settle such differences at once. This authority was to be the Communist Party.[4]

The idea of Party direction of union activity was further elaborated by Stalin in 1926. 'The system of the dictatorship of the proletariat', he said, consisted of a 'mechanism with 'transmission belts', 'levers', and a 'directing force' (the Party). First among the 'transmission belts' were the trade unions, which, although themselves 'non-Party organisations', 'connect the masses of the workers with the vanguard of the working class'. Stalin summarily defined the unions as 'mass organisations of the proletariat, linking the Party with the class primarily in this sphere of production'.[5] In plain English: conveyors of the Party's orders to the worker at the bench.

This proved to be too much, even for Bolshevik trade union leaders. When the pressure for production grew apace as the First Five-Year Plan got under way, they came out in opposition, with Tomsky as their leader. Tomsky told the VIII Trade Union Congress in 1928 of many unofficial strikes, which were due to the unions' 'inadequate attention to the needs of the masses, their detachment from the masses, and contempt for the small matters of the workers' life'.[6] He demanded real union elections; the rank and file, he said, dared not speak their minds for fear of being labelled Mensheviks or counter-revolutionaries. The economic administrations had not observed agreements with the unions, while Party resolutions on systematic education of the workers in administering the economy had been frustrated. He agreed that the unions should press for higher productivity, but argued that the pressure 'must take civilised forms'. Supported by others, who told of disregard for the needs of the workers, Tomsky was opposed by Zhdanov, Ordzhonikidze, and other Stalinists.[7] Stalin's next step was to get Kaganovich, his strong-arm man, on to the Presidium of the AUCCTU.[8] Stalin's crucial victory in the unions was won at the XVI Party Conference in 1929, which resolved:[9]

'Bukharin, Rykov and Tomsky are most dangerously opposing the unions to the Party; they aim in fact to weaken Party leadership of the union movement, they hush up defects in union work, they defend *trade-unionist* trends and manifestations of bureaucratic ossification in part of the trade union apparatus.'

The conference ordered Tomsky to be dismissed from all his posts,[10] and a resolution in the same sense was adopted by the AUCCTU a few months later[11] after the usual meeting of the Communist Party 'fraction' in the AUCCTU.

Thereby the rôle of the trade unions as instruments of Party policy—which at that time meant, above all, the drive for industrialisation—was decided for many years. There was, to be sure, some cleaning up to do first:[12]

'The new [trade union] leadership, headed by Comrade Shvernik proceeded . . . energetically to reconstruct the unions and root out remnants of the Right-wing opportunist deviation in theory and practice, to purge the union apparatus of alien persons, bureaucrats and degenerates, and to promote new cadres.'

The purge was, in fact, not even carried out by the unions themselves, but by the Party's Central Control Commission and the Workers' and Peasants' Inspectorate; for form's sake there was a 'decision of the AUCCTU', inviting these bodies to purge the unions, which was never published and is known only from a reference in the resolution of the XVI party Congress.[13]

It was at this congress, in 1930, that the Stalinist policy for the unions was clearly defined. They were to 'turn to production'; Socialist competition and shock brigades were to become the 'basis of all their production activity'; the 'centre of gravity' was to be transferred to the 'lowest primary links—the shock brigade, group, shift, shop, enterprise'. One of the defects in the unions' cultural and educational work, according to the congress, was their 'lack of political content' (*apolitichnost*), and Party organisations and Party 'fractions' in the trade unions must therefore 'infuse Communist content into all the cultural and educative work of the unions'. Indeed, Party organisations 'must improve and strengthen their concrete direction of union organisations, penetrating into the essence of their work . . . and taking care to strengthen them systematically with cadres'; the *Komsomol*, too, was to increase its participation in the unions.[14]

By the end of the First Five-Year Plan the Stalinisation of the unions was complete, and at the IX Trade Union Congress in 1932 Kaganovich pronounced the political epitaph on the old trade union leaders:[15]

'Opposing, in a Menshevik-Trotskyist spirit, the workers' interests to the interests of Socialist industry, and the unions' defensive functions to their production work, they either kept quiet about the unions' rôle as a school of Communism, or interpreted it . . . one-sidedly as a school of association, a school of defence of one's interests. . . .'

'Statification'—the unions' incorporation into the apparatus of the State—was now effected. The first step was the abolition of the *NKT*. Superficially, it might appear that the unions' powers and status were increased, since the decree of June, 1933, spoke of 'merging' the *NKT* and all its local organs, including organs of social insurance, with the AUCCTU and the local trade union bodies, and 'imposed on the AUCCTU the execution of the duties of the *NKT* and its organs'.[16] At this date these duties consisted of administering the State social insurance and supervising the observance of labour legislation and the maintenance of labour protection and safety measures.[17] In fact, however, as the trade unions' responsibilities to the State increased, their responsibility to the workers receded. They became more and more a Government department.

In 1934 the AUCCTU acquired the right to issue 'instructions, rules and explanations on the application of current labour legislation . . . subject to confirmation or preliminary sanction by the USSR *SovNarKom*'.[18] During the same year the unions took over the factory-level functions of the Commissariat of Workers' and Peasants' Inspection (*Rabkrin*—the main governmental organ of control and verification, which operated in close co-operation with the Party Central Control Commission). The AUCCTU and the union Central Committees were charged with 'verifying the fulfilment of Party and governmental directives on questions of production and wages and on the implementation of workers' proposals'.[19]

Since then the unions have been so dependent on the State and the Party that the latter has on occasion had to remind the unions of their function as defenders of the workers' interests. The first reminder came from Stalin himself in May, 1935. Stalin, who had some hard things to say about union elections 'without genuine democracy', and about lists of candidates 'forced through against the workers' wishes', pointed out that the 'average worker realised and felt the unions' bad work, and sometimes asked: "Do we need unions at all?"'; others, 'because of their lack of political consciousness, thought, and at times even said: "Maybe the unions are no longer any use"'.

Many comrades, said Stalin, regarded union work as of second- or third-rate importance; it must be reorganised to make it more attractive. He now condemned the unions for 'duplicating the work of the economic agencies ... whereas their chief task should lie in devoting full attention to the cultural and welfare needs of the masses'.[20] Party measures to deal with the situation, including the appointment of a committee under Kaganovich,[21] proved strangely ineffective. Evidently the pressure of plan fulfilment left less room for 'democracy', 'culture', and 'welfare' than even the Party thought expedient. In April, 1937, *Pravda* declared that 'if there has been any change at all in the situation, it has been for the worse'.[22] The charges of 'flagrant violations of trade union democracy',[23] the 'complete disintegration' of union activities among the masses, lack of concern for labour protection and workers' safety,[24] and failure to cater for the cultural and welfare needs of the workers,[25] formed the theme of Party and union meetings, and of a plenum of the AUCCTU in 1937.

The trade unions did not escape the Great Purge of these years, and it is presumably the need to find an ostensible target for the purge that explains the fact that criticisms of undemocratic practice and inertia in looking after the needs of the workers could be accompanied, as they were, by denunciations of 'relics of trade unionism' (*tred-yunionizm*) and of 'Tomsky and his group', as well as by complaints of 'dilatoriness, carelessness and the blunting of political vigilance in unmasking and rooting out enemies of the people who have penetrated certain parts of the trade union apparatus'.[26]

The purge of the unions was a thorough one. Shvernik was able to report to the XVIII Party Congress in 1939 that the membership of union committees in factories and other establishments had changed to the extent of 70–80 per cent, and that of union Central Committees to the extent of 96 per cent.[27] The unions' subordination to the Party was now formally written into union law. A plenum of the AUCCTU in September, 1938, decreed that all Union Statutes must henceforth include a provision to the effect that:[28]

> 'Every union in our country exercises its activities under the leadership of the Communist Party, the only proven leader and guide of all working people of the USSR in their struggle for the consolidation and perfection of the Socialist order.'

At the same time the unions' responsibility for production, as well as for culture and welfare, was explicitly stated. The XVIII Party Congress lumped the unions together with 'Party, Soviet, and economic organisations', from all of which it demanded such things as 'concentration . . . on the daily factual verification of the performance of the tasks set by the Party and Government', and the 'development of Socialist competition and the Stakhanovite movement . . . [and] the securing . . . of firm labour discipline and high labour productivity . . . '.[29] This was the congress's only reference to the trade unions; it was to these tasks, therefore, that *Trud* referred in its headline a few weeks later: 'Let us work unrelentingly to fulfil the decisions of the XVIII Congress of the CPSU!'[30] The unions accordingly 'reinforced their attention to questions of organisation of labour, production and wages, of strengthening labour discipline, and of struggling against shortcomings in production'.[31]

In the Second World War the unions 'subordinated all their activity to the interests of the front and the task of defeating the enemy'.[32] Their direct assistance to the Armed Forces was considerable. Skiers (2 million in the first two years), machine-gunners, drivers, snipers, medical personnel, etc., for the Red Army were trained by the unions' sports societies or in special courses at their expense. Unions organised 'voluntary' collections of funds for the equipment of air squadrons and tank columns, 'dozens' of which were delivered to the front. They also collected gifts for the troops and exercised 'cultural patronage' over various units, equipping 'dozens' of bath-and-laundry trains, mobile barbers' shops and libraries. Many of their sanatoria and rest homes were converted into military hospitals; and the unions paid special attention to war invalids and Servicemen's families.[33] They also took an active part in organising universal military training and anti-aircraft defence.[34]

The unions afforded 'serious assistance to the Communist Party and the Soviet Government' in putting enterprises and establishments on a war footing, in transferring factories to the East and creating new industrial centres there, and in the mass training of a new labour force consisting largely of women and youths. They 'headed' the All-Union Socialist competition begun in 1942 'for increased output of military production for the front'.[35] They also assisted 'new forms of participation of the working people in the struggle to raise labour productivity: the youth brigade movement, the acquisition of a second skill, public reviews of labour organisation, etc.'.[36]

While 'performing ceaseless, determined and painstaking work in furthering the growth of labour productivity and affording direct assistance to the front', the unions are said to have 'strengthened during the war their attention to social insurance and labour protection', and to have 'achieved [an] improvement of medical services and a reduction of traumatism and sickness'. They initiated night sanatoria at enterprises and in 1943 reopened permanent sanatoria and rest homes for workers and employees. They were particularly active in looking after workers' children and supervising supplies to the population, and in augmenting them by promoting individual and collective gardening.[37]

Since the war the general position of the unions as 'transmission belts' for the Party and cheer-leaders for production on the one hand, and workers' welfare organisations on the other, has not altered significantly. V. V. Kuznetsov, who had been chairman of the AUCCTU since 1944,[38] reported to a plenum of that body in 1945 on the unions' functions as providers of social and community services, and the plenum devoted its main resolution to the subject. Unions were instructed to attend within the factories to 'improvements in working conditions'; they had to see that managements 'make full use of funds allocated for safety measures', and that they observe legislation for expectant and nursing mothers and juveniles. At the same time, however, meetings were to be held to discuss 'problems of raising labour productivity, Socialist competition, the fulfilment of production plans, and the maintenance of State and labour discipline'.[39]

Since then these two sides of trade union activity have been brought to the fore with alternating emphasis. From the end of the war to Stalin's death in 1953 production took first place. A plenum of the AUCCTU in 1946 decreed that the 'chief task of the unions' should be the 'organisation of the multi-million masses of workers, engineers, technicians and employees for the struggle to fulfil and over-fulfil the 1946–50 Plan . . . on the basis of Socialist competition'.[40] The X Trade Union Congress in 1949 echoed this:[41]

'The congress considers that the most important task of the unions is the further development of Socialist competition for the fulfilment and over-fulfilment of the economic plans, and for the fulfilment ahead of time of the post-war Stalin Five-Year Plan.'

During 1951 the AUCCTU summoned a special All-Union Conference to consider the unions' tasks in supervising Socialist competition. 'The work of all links in trade union organisations', said Kuznetsov, addressing the conference, 'should be subordinated to the task of fulfilling and over-fulfilling the national economic plans . . . '.[42] A year later *Trud* had this to say to its readers, most of them trade union workers:[43]

'The essential duty of the economic and trade union executives is to see to it that every worker and employee labours productively all the 480 minutes of his working day. . . . It is necessary to educate the masses in the spirit of intolerance even to the slightest violations of the [production] schedule. . . . It is necessary . . . to expose the hack-workers, the slovenly workers, the people who have lost the feeling of responsibility for the job entrusted to them.'

'Every instance of the non-fulfilment of norms', said *Trud* a few months later, 'is a danger signal for a trade union official of an unsatisfactory state of affairs in some sector.'[44] Trade union organisations were called upon to play their part in introducing 'technical' (i.e. higher) output norms.*[45]

With the coming of the 'thaw' after Stalin's death and the execution of Beriya, the trade union pendulum swung briefly in the other direction. The trade union Press began to show a demonstrative concern for the defence of the workers' rights and interests. Early in June, 1953, *Trud* declared that economic administrators were used to abusing their authority and ignoring labour legislation, depriving workers of their bonuses and forcing them to work overtime;[46] and the trade union fortnightly periodical was soon afterwards calling for a 'ceaseless improvement of the working conditions of workers and employees', and complaining that many trade unions 'make poor use of their rights of control over the implementation by the administration of labour safety regulations, and sometimes connive at shortcomings in this matter.'[47]

There have been four Trade Union Congresses since the war. The X Congress in 1949 was the first for 17 years; apart from this it was remarkable for little but its unusually obsequious advertisement of the trade unions' subordination to the Party. 'All our successes', said Kuznetsov, 'we owe to the

* *See* pp. 58–63.

Central Committee of the Bolshevik Party, to Comrade Stalin';[48] another speaker echoed faithfully: 'Soviet trade unions are proud and happy that all their activities are daily guided by the Communist Party, by the wise leader and teacher, great Stalin.'[49] The XI Trade Union Congress, in 1954—the first after Stalin's death—heard a report from Shvernik and adopted revised Trade Union Statutes. Neither the report nor the Statutes marked any essential change in the position or functions of the trade unions, but Shvernik's speech showed plainly that the emphasis was once again on production first.[50]

Since the XX Party Congress in 1956 the unions' rôle as defenders of the workers' interests has been re-emphasised, both in Press articles and in official statements. A resolution of a Party Central Committee plenum in December, 1957,[51] stated that improving working and living conditions was 'a most important task' for the unions. Elsewhere, however, the resolution named raising production as the unions' 'central task'. At the XII Trade Union Congress in March, 1959, Grishin defined the task of looking after workers' welfare as 'a most important duty' of the unions.[52] At the same time, the revised Trade Union Statutes adopted by the XII Congress maintain that increasing productivity and plan fulfilment remain the unions' prime function. This was emphasised by Grishin at an AUCCTU plenum following the XXII Party Congress when he listed the protection of workers' interests second to increasing productivity and plan fulfilment as the unions' principal tasks in the period of the 'all-out construction of Communism'.[53] At the XIII Trade Union Congress in October, 1963, Grishin defined the unions' chief task as 'the allround development of the creative initiative of the workers and the recruitment of the broad masses into the struggle to implement the programme of Communist construction'.[54] More recently the 'main content of the work of trade unions' has been described as 'the implementation of the resolution of the Plenum of the CC CPSU introducing the economic and administrative reforms'.[55]

The reorganisation of industrial management instituted by Khrushchev in March, 1957, had considerable effect on trade union structure. A plenum of the AUCCTU held in June, 1957, adopted a resolution which 'envisaged a shift in the centre of gravity of the operative direction of trade union organisations to the *oblasts, krais* and Republics . . .'. The Plenum resolved to 'raise the rôle of the Trade Union Councils . . . to give them more rights and to widen their field of duty'. The councils were to become 'full directing organs capable of carrying on the day-to-day direction of the whole of the local trade union organs and primary organisations'. The councils were to co-operate with the Councils of National Economy (*Sovnarkhozy*) in working out and fulfilling State plans, norm-setting, labour organisation and cultural and welfare services. The duties of Central Committees of individual unions were also re-defined.[56]

With the abolition of the *Sovnarkhozy* at the end of 1965 and the return to central Ministerial control of branches of the economy, the functions of the Trade Union Councils and union Central Committees were further modified and widened.[57]

Changes in the rôle of unions at various levels, consequent on both the 1957 decentralisation of the administration of the economy and the 1965 recentralisation, together with the extension of the rights of factory trade union committees, the institution and subsequent revitalisation of the Permanent Production Conferences and the greater importance to be accorded to collective agreements, discussed below, appear to offer a definite, if limited, increase in the trade unions' authority.

STRUCTURE AND MACHINERY*

Soviet trade unions are 'constructed on the basis of democratic centralism according to the production principle'.[58] 'Democratic centralism', as defined in the Trade Union Statutes,[59] means that:

(*a*) all union organs from bottom to top are elected by union members and are accountable to them;
(*b*) union organisations decide all questions of union work in conformity with the USSR Trade Union Statutes and the decisions of higher union organs;

* Trade Union structure as here described includes changes following the establishment of the *Sovnarkhozy* in 1957, and their abolition and the return to central Ministerial control of branches of industry in 1965. References are to the revised Trade Union Statutes adopted in 1963. Removal of references in the Statutes to the now defunct *Sovnarkhozy*, and also to the bifurcation of the unions into industrial and agricultural wings at the lower levels, abandoned at the end of 1964, must await the next trade union congress, due at the end of 1967.

(*c*) decisions of union organisations are adopted by majority vote of the union members;
(*d*) lower organs of a union are subordinate to higher organs.

The Statutes also enjoin on all union organs the strict observance of 'trade union democracy and the principles of collectivity of leadership', which means that they must:[60]

'regularly convene general meetings and conferences of union members, report back and hold elections, create conditions for the development of criticism and self-criticism in union organisations, inform higher union organs about their work'.

The 'production principle' means that all persons working in one enterprise or establishment belong to the same union; each union embraces the workers and employees in a particular branch (*otrasl*) of the economy[61] Typical names of Soviet trade unions are thus: The 'Trade Union of Workers in Machine-building', 'Trade Union of Workers in the Food Industry', 'Trade Union of Workers in Higher Schools and Scientific Establishments' and so on.[62] 'Branches' of the economy have, however, been more or less narrowly defined over the years, and the number of trade unions has therefore risen and fallen considerably as splits and mergers have taken place. Recently the trend has favoured fewer but bigger unions: the 162 unions of 1937,[63] which grew to 176 at the end of the war, had fallen to 66 in 1951[64] and to 43 in 1954.[65] In May, 1957, there were 47.[66] The following month a plenum of the AUCCTU recommended, in the light of Khrushchev's reorganisation of industry, the amalgamation of a number of branch unions. Shortly afterwards the Presidium of the AUCCTU arbitrarily reduced by amalgamation the number of branch unions from 47 to 23.[67] By 1960 the number had been further reduced to 22.[68] In December, 1965, the number increased to 24 when the union for workers in the electric power stations and electrical industry split into two to form the 'Electric Power Stations and Electrotechnical Industry Workers' Union' and the 'Radio and Electronics Industry Workers' Union';[69] and a shipbuilding industry workers' union hived off from the machine-building workers' union.[70]

Co-ordination between the organs of different trade unions in the same area is effected by 'Councils of Trade Unions' (*Sovety Profsoyuzov*, or *Sovprofy*). These area Councils are elected by Republican, *krai* or *oblast* Inter-Union Conferences.[71] Branch union committees from *Raion* up to central are elected by union conferences or congresses at the appropriate level. 'Directing organs' of trade unions (i.e. committees and councils), and delegates to congresses and conferences, are elected by secret ballot, union members having the 'right to nominate candidates and to reject or criticise any of them'. The elected organs then choose from their membership a chairman, secretary and members of a presidium.[72] Elections may be held prematurely at the request of at least one-third of the membership, 'and also by decision of a higher union organ'.[73]

The 'supreme organ of the trade unions', according to the Statutes, is the All-Union Congress of Trade Unions, which has to be elected not less frequently than once in four years. (This did not prevent 17 years elapsing between the IX Congress in 1932 and the X in 1949, over five years between the X and XI, nearly five years between the XI and XII and over four-and-a-half years between the XII and XIII.) 'Norms of representation' at the congress are established by the AUCCTU.[74] At the X Congress one delegate represented 25,000 members, and delegates were elected by branch union congresses and by any enterprises employing 25,000 unionists or more.[75] At the XI Congress the procedure was slightly less democratic; delegates represented 30,000 unionists each, and were elected exclusively by union congresses.[76] Delegates to the XII Congress were elected by branch union congresses and Republican and regional inter-union conferences. 1,332 delegates represented 52,780,700 trade unionists—which works out at one delegate for every 39,925 members.[77] At the XIII Congress delegates were similarly elected, but representation considerably improved. (This was attributable entirely to the Congress being held in the Kremlin Palace of Congresses, which accommodates nearly 6,000 people. The building was opened in time for the XXII CPSU Congress in 1961.) 4,001 delegates represented about 68,000,000 trade unionists (i.e. one delegate for every 17,000 members).[78] In practice, delegates to the All-Union Congresses have tended to come from the full-time trade union apparatus and from the labour aristocracy rather than from the rank and file. Of 1,322 delegates to the XII Congress 39·8 per cent were workers, all of them 'production innovators'* or advanced workers. 36·4 per cent were full-time

* *See* p. 80.

trade union workers and 44·3 per cent were spare-time active union workers. 65·8 per cent of the delegates had higher or secondary education. 37·3 per cent were members of the USSR or Republican Supreme Soviets or local Soviets.[79] The delegates to the XIII Congress included 2,848 skilled workers and professional staff from industry, transport, construction and agriculture, 2,005 other workers, and 365 engineering and technical officials. 250 delegates were Heroes of the Soviet Union and Heroes of Socialist Labour, 55 had received Lenin and Stalin Prizes and 1,512 had been awarded medals of various kinds. 1,327 were deputies to Soviets. 1,447 had received higher education and 1,160 secondary education. 60 per cent were Party members and candidates.[80]

The Statutes prescribe that the Congress:[81]

'(*a*) hears and confirms reports of the AUCCTU and the Central Revision Commission;
(*b*) confirms the Statutes of Trade Unions of the USSR;
(*c*) defines the immediate tasks of trade unions, hears reports of central planning and economic organs and outlines measures for union participation in the struggle for fulfilment and over-fulfilment of national economic plans, and for upsurge of the well-being and cultural-political level of workers and employees;
(*d*) defines the tasks of the USSR trade unions in the international trade union movement;
(*e*) elects the All-Union Central Council of Trade Unions and the Central Revision Commission.'

In fact, at the congresses of 1949 and 1954 the agenda, laid down in advance by the AUCCTU, had been confined to hearing the reports of the AUCCTU and of the Revision Commission, adopting changes in the Statutes, and electing the AUCCTU and the Revision Commission;[82] in other words, the headings under which general policy might be discussed were omitted. At the 1959 Congress the first item on the agenda was broadened to include 'the tasks of the trade unions of the USSR in connection with the decisions of the XXI Congress of the CPSU':[83] Similarly at the 1963 Congress it included 'the tasks of the trade unions of the USSR in the period of the extensive construction of a Communist society.'[84]

The most important function of the congress, in these circumstances, is the election of the All-Union Central Council of Trade Unions (AUCCTU), the body that 'directs all trade union activity between congresses of the trade unions of the

USSR'.[85] The AUCCTU is described as the 'single centre of the unions of the USSR, the headquarters of the Soviet trade union movement'.[86] According to the Statutes it:[87]

'(*a*) determines the immediate tasks of unions generally, and also in particular fields of union work;
(*b*) participates in the elaboration of national economic plans;
(*c*) directs Socialist competition and the movement for Communist labour;
(*d*) hears reports by union committees and councils, and also by Councils of National Economy, State Committees, Ministries and departments, on questions of production, labour, and cultural and welfare servicing of workers and employees;
(*e*) submits to legislative organs draft laws and decrees, takes part in the preparation and examination by the Government of draft resolutions on wages, social insurance, labour protection and the cultural and everyday servicing of the working people; supervises the observance of Government laws and resolutions on these matters; issues instructions, rules and explanations concerning the operation of adopted labour legislation;
(*f*) exercises the direction of the State social insurance system and the workers' health resort service;
(*g*) arranges All-Union cultural, sport and other mass measures;
(*h*) directs the activity of the All-Union Society of Rationalisers and Inventors, the Council of Science and Technology Societies and the voluntary trade union sports societies and the development of tourism;
(*i*) establishes trade union schools and courses;
(*j*) approves the budget of the trade unions and the State social insurance budget;
(*k*) defines the general structure of trade unions and their staffs;
(*l*) represents Soviet trade unions in the international trade union movement and, in their name, enters into international union associations;
(*m*) regularly informs the trade union organisation about its work;
(*n*) has its own Press organ—the newspaper *Trud*—and the publishing house *Profizdat*; issues trade union magazines.'

The Statutes provide that the AUCCTU shall meet in plenary session not less than once every six months.[88] Between plenums power resides in the AUCCTU Presidium,[89] which is elected by the first plenum of the AUCCTU held on the morrow of a congress; a Secretariat, 'for current work of an organisational and executive nature', is elected at the same time.[90] After the XIII Congress in 1963 a Presidium of 15 persons was elected, together with a Chairman and seven Secretaries.[91] These eight officials comprise the inner directing core of the Soviet trade union system, the Chairman being the leading figure. He has always been a prominent Party member, often with little or no trade union experience, appointed or removed at the will of the Party leaders. When Shvernik became head of the trade unions in 1930, he had been in trade union work only since the previous year.[92] Kuznetsov, a Party member since 1927, was hastily elected Chairman of the Central Committee of the Union of Workers in Ferrous Metallurgy a few months before he took Shvernik's post in 1944.[93] Shvernik returned to the post after Stalin's death, until in March, 1956, he was succeeded by V. V. Grishin.[94] Grishin had been engaged in Party work since 1941 and since 1950 held increasingly important Party posts in the Moscow region. He became a member of the Party Central Committee in 1952 and since January, 1961, he has been a Candidate Member of the Presidium of the Central Committee, now known once more as the Politburo.[95]

The AUCCTU includes the following departments: Organisation and Instruction, Production Work and Wages, Housing and Welfare, Mass-Cultural, Labour Protection, International,[96] State Social Insurance, Physical Culture and Sport, and General.[97] There are also 11 permanent commissions under the AUCCTU (for economic and legal questions, etc.),[98] which 'help the Presidium and Secretariat of the AUCCTU to resolve, with the broad involvement of the public, questions within the competence of higher trade union organs'.[99] The AUCCTU also has a Central Council for Tourism.[100]

Individual branch unions have little or no autonomy *vis-à-vis* the AUCCTU: their Statutes may 'reflect the peculiarities', but must 'conform' to the USSR Statutes.[101] More significantly still, individual unions are born and die at the will of the Party conveyed through the AUCCTU. The multiplication of unions which took place in the early 'thirties was carried out in this fashion: in 1931, for instance, *Trud* reported that 'a special committee and the AUCCTU Secretariat have reached the conclusion that it is necessary to divide a number of unions',[102] and Kaganovich later revealed that the initiative had emanated from the Party Central Committee.[103] When further steps were taken in the same direction three years later, Shvernik stated that the question had been raised 'by the Central Committee of the Party and by Comrade Stalin'[104] and a plenum of the AUCCTU, summoned for the purpose, unanimously approved a plan to divide the existing unions into about three times their previous number.[105] If the process is reversed the motive force is the same: in 1957, following the decentralisation of industrial management which involved the dissolution of a number of central Ministries, the AUCCTU ordered the amalgamation of most unions, reducing their number by half.

Nevertheless, according to the USSR Trade Union Statutes, the 'highest directing organ' of a union is its congress,[106] which is held every two years, and bears much the same relationship to the union Central Committee as the USSR Trade Union Congress does to the AUCCTU. It is the Central Committee, elected by the congress (but the Central Committee determines the congress's agenda and the number of delegates),[107] which directs the activity of the unions between congresses. The Central Committee of a union is responsible both to the union congress and to the AUCCTU; it meets in plenary session not less than once in six months; for day-to-day direction it elects a Chairman, Secretary and members of a Presidium.[108] A Central Committee's duties are laid down in some detail. It:[109]

'takes part in drafting and examining jointly with central planning and economic organs current and long-term plans for the development of the given branch of industry, economy, culture, housing and cultural and welfare construction;

'organises Socialist competition among enterprises of a similar type in different economic regions, develops the movement for Communist labour, generalises and popularises the advanced experience of enterprises and production innovators, exercises control over the introduction into production of achievements of science and technology;

'takes part in drafting and considering new systems of wages to be introduced in specific industries with a view to stimulating the growth of labour productivity;

'takes part in fixing wage scales and rates and drafting standard regulations on incentive wage systems; co-ordinates the branch rates and qualifications handbooks and also branch (departmental) output norms;

'verifies the implementation of approved wage systems;

'studies and popularises the experience of leading industrial enterprises in introducing technically based output norms;

'hears reports by economic bodies on the situation in the organisation of labour and production, wages, norm-setting and labour protection, the production training of cadres, the fulfilment of plans for housing and cultural-welfare construction;

'establishes obligatory rules and norms and safety techniques and industrial hygiene for the given branch of industry; participates in drafting legislation for a particular branch of industry on working hours, rest days and holidays, on protection of the labour of women and juveniles, on norms and periods for wearing special clothing and footwear;

'studies the cause of industrial disease and accidents and plans measures for healthier working conditions;

'takes part in deciding questions of social insurance covering the whole of the particular branch of industry, and of cultural and welfare services for workers and employees;

'directs the activity of the Science and Technology Society, promotes the development of the mass movment of worker inventors and rationalisers, convenes conferences of workers, technicians and engineers of the particular branch of industry at which they exchange experience of work, takes part in the issue of popular industrial and technical literature, directs the work of voluntary sporting societies of particular branches of industry;

'studies the activity of trade union committees, hears reports on their work, generalises and popularises the positive experience of the work of trade union organisations, decides questions of trade union membership and trade union services;

'publishes the trade union's newspapers, periodicals and printed matter;

'maintains and develops fraternal contacts with kindred trade unions in foreign countries, participates actively in the international association of trade unions of the particular industry, promotes in every way the strengthening of international working-class solidarity.'

In November, 1965, the rôle of union Central Committees was ostensibly increased by a resolution of a plenum of the AUCCTU[110] defining the unions' part in carrying out the economic reforms introduced the previous month. However, since most of the new provisions regarding the functions of union Central Committees repeat or only slightly modify the provisions in the Statutes cited above it is reasonable to suppose that committees had previously failed to carry out their obligations to the full. New duties of Central Committees include: the establishment of branch indices for temporary incapacity of workers; the promotion of the training of cadres of workers and employees and the raising of their qualifications; jointly with trade union councils, the selection, placing and training of leading union officials.

Below the branch union Central Committee a series of intermediate links—Republican, *krai, oblast,* town and/or *raion* committees—stretch down to the 'primary organisations'. These intermediate committees are elected by general meetings or conferences at the appropriate level.[111] Depending on the presence of the industry concerned in a particular region, each union has such committees as may be required for the various Republics and *krais,* as well as at the *oblast, raion* and, if necessary, city levels. Where the industry represented by a union is not well developed there may not be a committee for the Republic but only one for a district or city. In Georgia, for example, in 1959 only 19 unions were represented at Republican level, and ten in Uzbekistan.[112] In 1965 there were 20 unions represented at Republican level in Azerbaidzhan.[113]

The base of the branch union hierarchy is the 'primary organisation', which comprises the union members working in any one enterprise, State farm or establishment, or studying in any one educational establishment. The general meeting of these union members, which, like the congresses and conferences higher up the scale, is said to be the 'highest body' of the organisation,[114] elects annually a committee or, if the membership is less than 15, a trade union organiser (*proforganizator*).[115] These committees are known generically as Factory-plant and Local Committees (*fabzavmestkomy,* or *FZMK*).* Local (as opposed to factory-plant) committees are formed in non-industrial establishments; in higher educational establishments they are called 'trade union committees'.[116] The tasks laid down for a primary organisation, which naturally fall mainly on the shoulders of its committee, are manifold and are listed in the following order:[117]

(*a*) mobilisation of all workers and employees in the enterprise, building site, State farm or establishment for fulfilment and over-fulfilment of the State plan, strengthening of labour discipline and development of Socialist competition and the movement for Communist labour;

(*b*) elaboration and putting into effect of practical measures aimed at steadily raising labour productivity, the maximum

* For convenience these will be referred to hereafter as Factory Committees.

utilisation of internal production reserves, improving the quality and lowering the production costs;

(*c*) enlisting workers and employees into active participation in questions of the activity of the enterprise and establishment, in the administration of production and social matters;

(*d*) organising the popularisation of advanced experience, the latest achievements of science and technology, the development of the mass movement of rationalisers and inventors; raising the level of general education and technical knowledge of the working people;

(*e*) daily concern for the improvement of labour protection, the improvement of the material position and everyday servicing of workers and employees; carrying out among working people and their families mass cultural, physical culture and sports activity, the development of tourism;

(*f*) fostering in workers and employees high political consciousness, dedication to the public interest, honesty and truthfulness, high moral qualities, the struggle against anti-social manifestations and survivals of the past in people's minds;

(*g*) fulfilling obligations taken under the collective agreement;

(*h*) implementing decisions of higher trade union organs and resolutions of general meetings;

(*i*) enlisting all workers and employees into membership of the trade union;

(*k*) development of criticism and self-criticism, educating trade union members in a spirit of intolerance of shortcomings, of manifestations of bureaucracy and the issuing of false returns, mismanagement and waste, and a negligent attitude to public property.

In addition to fulfilling these tasks on behalf of the primary organisation the Factory Committee has specific functions to perform. These functions have been considerably broadened since 1958[118] and under the Statutes it now:[119]

'represents the workers and employees of the factory establishment or organisation on all questions of labour, living conditions and culture;

'concludes a collective agreement with the management of the enterprise, organises supervision by the masses over, and takes measures towards, its fulfilment; takes part in drafting the production and financial plans of the enterprise and the plans for industrial and housing construction; as well as building cultural-welfare institutions and facilities, it participates in establishing new and revising existing output quotas, in setting rates and in fixing grades for workers; sees that the wage system and the system of settling accounts with the workers are correctly implemented and that wages are paid punctually; guides the work of the permanent production conferences;

'jointly with the management organises Socialist competition, sums up its results and determines the winners; approves the estimate of awards to be paid to workers and employees out of the enterprise fund and other funds, and also the lists of workers entitled to individual bonuses or in need of financial assistance;

'actively promotes the development of public forms of workers' participation in solving production questions, guides the Councils of the Science and Technology Society and of the Rationalisers and Inventors Society; exercises control over the introduction of new techniques, inventions and rationalisation suggestions; provides for the workers' raising their production qualifications;

'grants allowances out of the social insurance fund, sends workers and employees for treatment at health resorts, to rest homes and tourist camps, checks the standard of the public health services for the working people, takes part in fixing pensions, disposes of the funds of the trade union budget in accordance with the approved estimate;

'provides workers with cultural and welfare services, promotes physical culture, sport and tourism, helps to organise physical culture exercises during breaks in work; organises public control over the fulfilment of plans for the construction of houses and cultural-welfare facilities, and over the work of trade and catering establishments;

'jointly with the management of enterprises and establishments allots living space to the workers;

'calls general meetings and conferences of workers and employees; hears reports by heads of enterprises and establishments on the fulfilment of the production plan and of the commitments taken under the collective agreement, measures taken to improve working conditions and the material welfare and cultural services for the workers and employees and takes steps to eliminate shortcomings;

'organises the fulfilment of the decisions of higher trade union bodies, enlists trade union members into active social work, sets up permanent and *ad hoc* commissions in particular fields of trade union activity and approves their composition;

'the Factory Committee elects a Chairman and Deputy Chairman from among its members.'

These detailed rights of Factory Committees have not always been strictly observed and in February, 1960, the Presidium of the AUCCTU found it necessary to issue a resolution instancing infringements of the regulations issued in July, 1958, and calling on trade union councils to draw them to the attention of Councils of National Economy, factory managers, etc.[120]

The Factory Committee operates through a number of specialised commissions, with the following functions: Wages and Norms,[121] Mass Production Work,[122] Labour Protection,[123] Social Insurance,[124] Pension Questions,[125] Housing and Living Conditions,[126] Work among Children and Young People,[127] Mass Cultural.[128] The committees also provide the 'workers' side' on the Labour Disputes Commissions* [129] and representatives for the Permanent Production Conferences.† [130] They also have Commissions and Groups of Public Control to supervise trade and public catering establishments.[131]

While the Factory Committee is the 'basic' unit in the trade union hierarchy, it is not the lowest. The Statutes provide that Shop Committees may be set up by Factory Committees and Trade Union Bureaux by Local Committees respectively; these committees and bureaux have much the same functions as the Factory-plant or Local Committee on a lower level.[132] The lowest links of all, however, are the Union Groups (*profgruppy*), which exist, according to the Statutes, 'for the better servicing of union members working in one brigade, unit, assembly, section, etc.'. The lowest union officials are the Group Organiser (*profgrupporg*), who is elected for one year by the group by open vote, and his assistants, the Production Organiser, the Insurance Delegate (*strakhovoy delegat*), the Cultural Organiser (*kultorganizator*), the Public Inspector of Labour Protection and the Physical Culture Organiser. The Group Organiser, according to the Statutes:[133]

'actively supports advanced production initiatives of workers and employees, assists in bringing out and widely developing their creative initiative, concerns himself with the dissemination of highly productive work methods among the workers of his group;

'together with the foreman or brigade leader, organises Socialist competition for the fulfilment and over-fulfilment of production tasks, the improvement of the quality of production, the saving of materials by every worker, and develops the competition for Communist labour;

'carries out among workers and employees activity to instil a conscientious attitude to labour and public property;

'convenes general meetings of trade union groups and assists the

* *See* pp. 180–182. † *See* pp. 182–184.

factory, works, local and shop committees in carrying out safety measures and providing workers with welfare and cultural services;

'recruits all workers into membership of the union and collects membership dues from members.'

Beside the branch union hierarchy there are at the Republican, *oblast* and *krai* levels the inter-union Trade Union Councils (*Sovprofy*) already mentioned. In 1960 there were 149 of these Councils, 76 of them in the RSFSR.[134] The Councils' importance has varied over the years. In the late 'twenties and early 'thirties they experienced a decline and by 1937 had apparently ceased to exist.[135] They were re-established in 1948 'at the initiative' of the Party Central Committee.[136] In 1957 the Councils acquired increased importance as a result of the decentralisation of the administration of industry: in August, the Presidium of the AUCCTU issued detailed regulations laying down their new functions.[137] They were to be the 'competent bodies which carry out the direction of all the activity of trade union organisations of the Republic, *krai* or *oblast*'. Many of the questions previously dealt with by branch union Central Committees were transferred to the Councils.[138] In November, 1965, their functions were redefined by a resolution of a plenum of the AUCCTU.[139]

Under the 1963 Trade Union Statutes the 'highest trade union body' in a Republic, *oblast* or *krai* is the inter-union Conference or Congress (in a Republic). Delegates to Conferences and Congresses, which are held once in two years (Congresses are held every four years in four Republics, the Ukraine, Belorussia, Kazakhstan and Uzbekistan), are elected at trade union meetings of enterprises and at branch union meetings at various levels. In Republics subdivided into *oblasts* delegates to Republican Trade Union Congresses are elected at *oblast* inter-union Conferences. Congresses and Conferences hear reports by the Trade Union Council and Auditing Commission, specify the immediate tasks of trade unions in the area, hear reports by planning and economic bodies on plan fulfilment and discuss labour and welfare questions. They elect Trade Union Councils and Auditing Commissions and also delegates to the USSR Trade Union Congress.[140] The Trade Union Council:[141]

'directs all the activity of trade union organisations in the territory of a Republic, *krai* or *oblast*;

'takes an active part in the work of Councils of National Economy, Ministries, departments and planning bodies; in drafting and securing the fulfilment of national economic plans; represents the trade unions of the Republic, *krai* or *oblast* in the corresponding Soviet and economic organs on questions of production, wages, labour, culture and the living conditions of workers and employees;

'carries out activity to mobilise workers and employees for the all-round development of industrial and agricultural production, the fulfilment and over-fulfilment of State plans, directs the activity of trade union organisations towards the broad enlistment of workers into the administration of production;

'organises and directs Socialist competition and the movement for Communist labour in the Republic, *krai* or *oblast*, and jointly with Soviet and economic bodies summarises the results and determines the winners of the competition, organises the study and dissemination of advanced experience;

'jointly with the appropriate economic bodies registers collective agreements and supervises their fulfilment;

'exercises control over the observance of correct relationships of wages levels in branches of industry and enterprises, over the correct application of existing wages systems; jointly with economic bodies takes measures to improve the organisation of labour and fixing of norms, to raise the qualifications of cadres;

'guides the work of the Republican, *krai* or *oblast* Scientific and Technical Societies and Inventors and Rationalisers Societies;

'exercises control over safety arrangements and industrial hygiene, the implementation by managements of labour legislation, sees that funds for special clothing are spent properly and that the workers get their clothing at the proper time;

'participates in planning the allocation of funds for the improvement of working conditions, guides the work of technical inspectors;

'jointly with local planning and economic bodies drafts current and long-term plans for the construction of housing, trade and public catering establishments, cultural, welfare and communal enterprises;

'guides the work of trade union organisations in implementing the State social insurance scheme, supervises the management of health centres, holiday homes and tourism, approves the plan for the allocation of passes to these institutions and sees there are no abuses; supervises the organisation of the working people's medical service;

'exercises control over the correct allotment of living space in houses built by factories, State farms and establishments, takes part in allotting living space built by local Soviets of Workers' Deputies; controls the work of urban transport, communal and trading enterprises and takes steps to eliminate any shortcomings that come to light;

'hears reports by economic bodies on the situation in production, wages, the organisation of labour and labour protection, safety arrangements, the fulfilment of plans for housing and cultural and welfare establishments and takes measures to improve the work of enterprises, State farms, establishments and trade union organisations in the sphere of developing Socialist competition and the movement for Communist labour, social insurance, material welfare and cultural services for workers and employees;

'guides the cultural mass and physical culture work of trade union organisations, sets up cultural, sports and other trade union centres;

'selects and appoints leading trade union personnel, provides for the training and instruction of trade union officials and active trade unionists;

'generalises and spreads the experience of trade union work and issues printed matter on trade union activity;

'provides trade union members with legal advice;

'supervises the financial activity of trade union bodies in operating the trade union and State social insurance budgets, secures the utilisation of the budgets;

'within the established limits and model lists defines the structure, establishment and salaries of trade union organisations and establishments run by them, and reviews their economic and financial activity;

'maintains international contacts with trade unions in other countries;

'the Republican Trade Union Council submits draft laws and decrees on labour, services and culture to the legislation bodies of the Republic.'

Trade Union Councils meet in plenary session not less than once in four months and elect a Presidium consisting of a Chairman, Secretary and members to carry out routine work. *Oblast* or *krai* Councils are responsible to an Inter-Union Conference and the AUCCTU (in Republics, to the Trade Union Council). The Republican Council is subordinate to the Republican Congress and the AUCCTU.[142]

From early 1963 to November, 1964, the unions, like the Party, were reorganised on an industrial and agricultural basis. This mainly involved the establishment at *oblast* and *krai* level of separate industrial and agricultural trade union councils, and of industrial and agricultural Bureaux at Republican level and at the centre. This measure was reversed following the reunification of the Party in November, 1964.

Trade union membership is open to all employees of the State, that is 'all workers and employees working in enterprises, transport, building, State farms, institutions or organisations, and also students at higher, specialised secondary or other technical or occupational educational establishments'.[143]

The official figure for trade union membership in 1966 was 'over 80 million',[144] representing an increase of about 17 million since 1961.[145] In 1965, 94.7 per cent of workers and employees were union members.[146] Before the war the membership percentage stood at about 85 per cent;[147] but in the postwar years it declined until in 1951 it was only about 75 per cent.[148] The recovery from this position was achieved by a mass campaign to recruit new members initiated in the autumn of 1953, and accompanied by a reduction in membership dues.[149] It is nevertheless remarkable that several million Soviet workers refrain from joining the trade unions. An ILO Mission to the Soviet Union in 1959 was informed that 7 per cent, or approximately 4 million workers and employees, were not union members.[150] An earlier reason was given by Shvernik to the XI Trade Union Congress in 1954: 'Workers do not join the trade unions because their organisations work badly and are not concerned with the needs and requirements of workers and employees.'[151]

The trade unionist's rights, duties and privileges are laid down in the Trade Union Statutes. His rights are prescribed as follows:[152]

(*a*) to elect and be elected to all trade union bodies, and to conferences and congresses;

(*b*) to take part in the discussion of questions considered at meetings of trade union members;

(*c*) to put before trade union bodies questions concerning the activities of the trade union and economic bodies and put forward suggestions for improving their work;

(*d*) to criticise at trade union meetings, conferences, congresses and in the Press the activities of trade union and economic bodies, Soviet institutions or their personnel, irrespective of the posts they occupy;

(*e*) to approach any trade union bodies with requests concerning any question of production work, material welfare and cultural services, and also to appeal to it to protect and uphold his rights where the management does not fulfill a collective agreement or infringes labour legislation;

(*f*) to be present in person in all cases where trade union bodies pass an opinion on his work or conduct;
(*g*) to be a member of the trade union mutual aid fund.

The trade unionist is thus entitled to question not the basic principles of Soviet trade unionism but only 'the improvement of trade union work'. Furthermore he not only has no right to discuss the all-important question of Party dictation; he may not even criticise the day-to-day activities of Party organs in relation to the unions. His 'rights' are meagre indeed and so obviously essential to any form of labour organisation that the need for their enumeration would cause surprise if one were not aware of the uniquely *un*-trade-unionist nature of Soviet unions.

By contrast the trade unionist's duties are exacting and important. He is 'in duty bound:[153]

'(*a*) to work honestly and conscientiously, raise labour productivity, strive for the creation of the material and technical base of Communism, the further upsurge of science and culture of the Soviet State, for the fulfilment of production plans and the tasks of the enterprise, workshop or brigade, to take an active part in Socialist competition;
(*b*) to strengthen and safeguard public Socialist property as the basis of the might and prosperity of the Soviet Homeland and the source of a prosperous and cultural life for all working people;
(*c*) strictly to observe State and labour discipline, make full and rational use of working time for highly efficient and productive labour, struggle against all infringements of labour discipline;
(*d*) to raise his political consciousness, general educational and cultural and technical standard, production and business-like qualifications, master the techniques of his own job and advanced methods of work;
(*e*) to be thrifty and economical, reveal shortcomings in production work and struggle for their elimination;
(*f*) to struggle to strengthen the healthy way of life, against various anti-social phenomena and other survivals of the past, to observe the rules of Socialist community;
(*g*) to attend trade union meetings, carry out public assignments given him by trade union organs;
(*h*) to observe the Statutes of the Trade Unions of the USSR, and to pay his membership dues punctually.'

The disparity between a trade unionist's rights and his duties has clearly been officially recognised, and to make it acceptable substantial material advantages over non-union workers are granted to the trade unionist, who:[154]

'(*a*) receives benefits from the State social insurance funds in a larger amount than do non-members in accordance with the legislation;
(*b*) enjoys priority in the distribution of passes to rest houses, sanatoria and health resorts, and also of passes for children to crèches, kindergartens and Pioneer camps;
(*c*) receives free legal aid, provided by the trade union organs;
(*d*) receives, when necessary, material assistance from trade union funds;
(*e*) has the use, as also have the members of his family, of the trade union's cultural and sports facilities on terms established by trade union organs;
(*f*) for active public service depending on his trade union membership record, a union member is awarded trade union certificates of merit and is accorded other marks of encouragement.'

Trade union dues, as written into the Statutes, are as follows:[155]

Members earning:

Less than 50 roubles a month	5 kopeks per 10 roubles.
From 50 to 60 roubles	40 kopeks.
From 60 to 70 roubles	50 kopeks.
Over 70 roubles	1 per cent of earnings.

Unemployed pensioners and students without grants pay 5 kopeks a month.[156] Entrance fees are 1 per cent of earnings or grants, or, in the case of students without grants, 10 kopeks.[157]

COLLECTIVE AGREEMENTS

Collective Agreements between trade unions and employers, which had had some reality in the 'twenties, especially during NEP, fell a victim to the Five-Year Plans, and ceased to be concluded from 1934 until 1947. A movement in the late 'thirties to restore them came to nothing because, as Shvernik put it:[158]

'when the Plan is the decisive principle in the development of our national economy, wage questions cannot be settled outside the Plan, out of connection with it. Thus the Collective Agreement as a form of regulating wages has outlived itself.'

This statement was no less true in 1947, when Collective Agreements were reintroduced 'on the initiative of Comrade

Stalin',[159] and it remains true today. Soviet Collective Agreements have nothing to do with fixing wages. In the words of a Soviet authority on the subject, writing in 1948:[160]

'The present-day Collective Agreement usually includes norms regulating the remuneration of labour (rate systems, with coefficients and grades, progressive scales, etc.). These norms, however, are not the result of the Collective Agreement contract. They originate from the appropriate State authorities.'

There was, in other words, no collective bargaining on the question of wages, and all that the collective Agreement did was to register something decided by the State planning authorities. The same writer explained why it was thought worthwhile putting these clauses into the Agreements at all: 'The inclusion of such norms in Collective Agreements is intended . . . to facilitate the mobilisation of workers and employees in the campaign for the Plan.'[161]

Indeed, the main object of reintroducing the Agreements at all was to find a new form of pressure on the workers to produce more. It was done, in the words of the relevant decree of the Council of Ministers,[162]

'to ensure the fulfilment and over-fulfilment of production plans, a continued increase in the productivity of labour, improvement in the organisation of labour, and also an increase in the responsibility of economic and trade union organisations for improving the material living conditions and cultural services for the workers, technical staff, and employees of enterprises'.

There has been some limited improvement in the position with the enhancement of the trade unions' status, begun in 1957. As has already been mentioned the trade unions now participate in formulating new wages structures at national level, a function shared by branch union Central Committees and to a lesser degree by Trade Union Councils. Collective Agreements are concluded annually between factory committee and the factory management. Under the decree of July 15, 1958,[163] the factory committee 'exercises systematic control over the punctual fulfilment of measures envisaged by the collective agreement'. It also hears reports from managements on the progress of fulfilment of obligations taken under the Collective Agreement. However, this by no means ensures complete observance of the Agreement on the part of managements. In so far as they concern wages, Collective Agreements refer to the rates of pay, categories of skill and regulations currently in force in the given branch of the economy: they sometimes contain detailed wage scales but do not include provisions regarding hours of work, holidays and other basic conditions which are settled by legislation, formulated with trade union participation.[164]

Since the introduction of the economic reforms in October, 1965, which give greater freedom of action to management, an attempt has been made to increase the importance of the Collective Agreement. In a report to an AUCCTU plenum in November, 1965, Grishin complained that agreements had tended to be carried over from one year to the next without much amendment or indeed any check on their implementation.[165] He said:

'The main content of the Agreement must become concrete measures for improving the organisation of labour and production, the creation for workers of conditions for productive labour, the speeding-up of the rate of technical progress, raising workers' material interest in the results of personal labour and the general results of the work of enterprises.'

Grishin attached considerable important to the informing of every worker, through factory meetings, of the contents of Agreements and to supervision of their implementation.

In March, 1966, a new definition of the Collective Agreement was issued in a resolution of the USSR Council of Ministers and the AUCCTU.[166] Article 2 of the resolution, on the duties of managements and workers' collectives, provides for the inclusion in Agreements of clauses on plan fulfilment, improving the use of funds and materials, norm-setting and labour productivity, Socialist competition and the training of cadres. They must also include reference to improving the 'organisation of wages' (though not, of course, the setting of wage rates). Clause 3, defining the duties under the Collective Agreement of managements and union committees, provides for workers' participation in management through the Permanent Production Conferences, the improvement of labour protection and the provision of bonuses for leading workers. Their interest in housing and welfare is also indicated. Clause 4, on labour and wages, states that Agreements must contain, *inter alia*, 'concrete normative provisions on labour and wages worked out by managements and union committees within the rights accorded to them'. Appended to the Agreements must be various plans and lists relating to technical improvements and various aspects of labour protection agreed between both sides (clause 6). Procedure for concluding and registering Agreements is laid down by the AUCCTU and State Committee for Labour and Wages (clause 7) and supervision of the implementation of the Agreement rests with the unions (clause 10).

The workers' specific interests, then, form only a secondary part of the Collective Agreement. In this respect it is of interest that the obligations laid on management differ in nature from those laid on the trade union. The responsibilities of factory committees are entirely moral, in other words they relate to such matters as labour discipline, welfare, education and so on. The managements' responsibilities are generally legal in character. In the case of violation of statutory or contractual provisions on industrial safety and health members of management are liable under Article 140 of the RSFSR Criminal Codex to fines of up to 100 roubles, dismissal or up to five years' imprisonment, depending upon the seriousness of the consequences of their negligence. Similarly deliberate violation of labour legislation by a member of management is punishable by dismissal or up to a year's corrective labour (Article 138). The Trade Union Committee's obligations, on the other hand, are of 'a social, moral-political character', and the only responsibility for their non-fulfilment borne by the Trade Union Committee is 'moral-political responsibility to its electors and superior organs'; 'disciplinary responsibility' comes into the picture only in the case of the individual worker, where his violation of his obligations under the Agreement also involves an infringement of the Rules of Internal Labour Order.[167]

There is ample evidence, however, to show that these provisions, which should weight the scales in favour of the workers on this particular point, have often failed to do so. The number of cases brought against managements is not great, although reports of managements violating various aspects of labour legislation are frequent. As has been shown in the previous chapters, the Collective Agreements have in practice provided little protection of the workers' interests.

The fact is that the oft-repeated theory that there is no conflict of interest between management and workers in the USSR finds no support in the continued need to urge trade unions to see to it that managements adhere to their obligations: many managers, given half a chance, take the easy way out, and the workers' interests suffer.

LABOUR DISPUTES

From 1922 to 1957 most labour disputes were settled in the first instance by the so-called Rates and Conflicts Commissions (*rastsenochno-konfliktnye komissii*, or *RKK*). The 'rates' side of their activities disappeared with the growth of planning and 'State norm-setting': in 1933 the Presidium of the AUCCTU adopted a decree deeming 'incorrect' the practice whereby in many factories norms and rates introduced by the management were 'confirmed' by the *RKK*; the *RKK's* duties should in future be confined to 'familiarisation of the workers with the norms, mobilisation of workers for their fulfilment, and similar tasks; norms and rates could be considered *per se* only if they violated the Collective Agreement.[168]

When, therefore, *RKKs* were abolished in January, 1957, and replaced by Labour Dispute Commissions (*komissii po trudovym sporam*), the change in nomenclature did no more than recognise a real situation which had existed for some time. Moreover, so far as the Commissions themselves are concerned, their position and scope have not been altered substantially. They consist, as before, of equal numbers of representatives of the management and the Trade Union Factory Committee.[169] They are the court of first instance for the examination of *all* labour disputes between workers and management except:[170]

(*a*) the dismissal, reinstatement and transfer of certain responsible workers and employees, and the imposition of disciplinary penalties on these persons. The list of responsible persons, appended to the decree, includes the heads of enterprises, chief engineers, etc., and also the heads of workshops, senior foremen and foremen, etc.;
(*b*) the imposition of disciplinary penalties on persons who come within the scope of the statutes on discipline (i.e. on the railways, river and sea transport, etc.);
(*c*) the establishment of salaries and wage-rates;
(*d*) the alteration of the personnel establishment;
(*e*) the computation of the worker's period of labour service for the purpose of social insurance or other rights and privileges;
(*f*) the provision and allocation of housing, and also 'the satisfaction of the everyday needs of the workers'.

Of these exceptions, the first two refer to groups of employees from whom a standard of discipline higher than average is expected, and whose conflicts with authority are therefore dealt with in a different, more hierarchical fashion, by reference to the next superior rung on the ladder. As regards the third point—wages and salaries—enough has been said about the unions' part in setting wage rates and the absence of collective bargaining at factory level on this issue to make further comment unnecessary. The fourth point means no more nor less than that redundancy is not a possible subject for a labour dispute in the USSR. Nor, apparently, is the important question of establishing correctly a worker's length of service, on which the amount of social insurance, etc., to which he is entitled depends (union rights in these matters were strengthened by AUCCTU decisions of January 5, 1962[171]—*see* subsection on Welfare, pp. 185ff). In the case of supplements to wages, the length of service is established by a special Commission, including a representative of the Trade Union Committee,[172] but for social insurance purposes, length of service is established by the management, the trade union being merely instructed to exercise control over the correctness of calculations.[173] The last exception, concerning housing and everyday living conditions, introduces an alteration in legislation in that previously *RKKs* were competent to deal with disputes on these issues if they arose from the management's failure to fulfil its obligations under the Collective Agreement or Labour Contract;[174] now they are excluded from the Commission's scope altogether. But the Factory Committee is jointly responsible with management for supervising the building and allocation of housing to workers and employees. As we have seen, Factory Committees have Housing and Welfare Commissions to assist them in this task, though in 1963 the AUCCTU Presidium found it necessary to issue a decree designed to improve the work of union organisations in the RSFRS in the distribution of housing.[175]

Among the points that do come within the jurisdiction of the Labour Dispute Commissions, the following are specifically named in the decree:[176]

(*a*) the application of established output norms and rates, and also labour conditions ensuring the fulfilment of output norms;
(*b*) dismissal or transfer to other work;
(*c*) payment for idle-standing or rejects;

(*d*) payment for doing work of different qualifications;
(*e*) payment of unfinished work on piece-rates;
(*f*) payment for time of absence from work;
(*g*) payment for overtime;
(*h*) the right to a bonus and its amount as envisaged by the established system of payment;
(*i*) payment when norms are not fulfilled;
(*j*) amount of payment for probation period;
(*k*) monetary compensation for unused leave;
(*l*) the issue of special ('protective') clothing and special food, and, in appropriate cases, the payment of monetary compensation in lieu;
(*m*) deductions from wages for material damage caused to the enterprise, establishment or organisation;
(*n*) the payment of discharge grants.

The most substantial change introduced by the decree concerned appeals from the Labour Disputes Commission's findings. Previously, if the *RKK's* decision was unacceptable to either side, an appeal had to be lodged with the next higher organ of the trade union, such as the *krai* or *oblast* committee, and beyond that as far as the Union Central Committee.[177] Under the new decree the first court of appeal for the worker is the Trade Union Factory Committee itself; and beyond that he goes to the People's Courts. The workers' position was further clarified by a Decision of the USSR Supreme Soviet Presidium of January 27, 1959.[178] Under this, workers dismissed by management with the agreement of the Trade Union Factory Committee take their cases direct to the People's Court without appealing to the Labour Disputes Commission or the factory committee. This procedure has resulted in the reinstatement by the courts of many workers wrongfully dismissed with the consent of the Trade Union Factory Committee.[179] The management can also appeal to the People's Courts, but only on a point of law, if it thinks that the Trade Union Committee's decision is contrary to existing legislation.[180]

PERMANENT PRODUCTION CONFERENCES

One of the recurrent themes of Party and official propaganda has long been the need for the manager of an enterprise to 'rely on the collective', to 'draw the workers into participation in the work of management', 'to develop the workers' creative initiative'. The main means by which trade unions are expected to play their part in achieving these aims is by holding 'production conferences' (*proizvodstvennye soveshchaniya*).

Such conferences, for which there were few set rules, proved, however, singularly ineffective. In December, 1957, a resolution of a Party Central Committee plenum on the work of trade unions endorsed the persistent criticism of the 'production conferences' which had occurred over the previous two years:

'At many enterprises the rôle of production conferences is played down, they are hurriedly convened without the necessary preparation and are held chiefly in brigades and sectors. Factory and workshop meetings are rarely held, which restricts the opportunities of workers and employees [to take part] in solving questions concerning the activity of the workshop and factory as a whole.'[181]

The resolution proposed that Permanent Production Conferences should be set up: they were duly instituted the following July by a joint decision of the USSR Council of Ministers and the AUCCTU.[182] Under this decision Conferences are set up at enterprises, building sites and workshops with over 100 employees: where there are fewer than 100, general meetings of enterprises are held instead. The Conferences, elected at general meetings of enterprises, are composed of workers and employees, representatives of the Trade Union Factory Committee, management, the Party and Komsomol organisations, primary organisations of the Scientific and Technical and the Inventors and Rationalisers Societies. Conferences elect a Presidium of from five to 15 members, including a chairman and secretary to conduct current work.

The Permanent Production Conference:

'directs all its activity towards securing the successful working of the enterprise or building site, the fulfilment and over-fulfilment of the production plan, the development of Socialist competition, the all-round increase of labour productivity and the spreading of the experience of innovators and advanced production workers'.

It also: takes part in drafting and discussing long-term and current production plans; examines questions concerning the organisation of production, labour and wages, and improving the quality and lowering the cost of output, takes measures against wastage, idle-standing and for the more efficient use of equipment; discusses organisational and technical measures, such as the introduction of new machinery; supervises plans for industrial, housing, cultural and welfare building and the use of capital investment funds; suggests improvements in general factory administration; supervises the improvement of labour protection; examines questions concerning the training of workers and raising their proficiency, the correct use of workers and strengthening labour discipline.

The Conference, which works 'under the direction of' the factory union committee, is convened 'in accordance with need', but not less frequently than 'once or twice a quarter' for enterprises or building sites, and once a month at workshop level. Two-thirds of the members of the Conference constitute a quorum and decisions of the Conference require an absolute majority of votes. The Conference must report on its activities to a general meeting of the enterprise not less than once in six months. Members of the Conference may be replaced at the behest of those who elected them.

By 1965 there were throughout the USSR over 125,000 Permanent Production Conferences with almost 5 million members; 40 million people were taking part in the work of Conferences every year.[183] In the five years 1959–63 10,400,000 proposals were put before the Conferences, of which 7,900,000 were implemented.[184] These figures in fact reveal a sharp falling-off in this aspect of the Conferences' activity since the initial burst of enthusiasm: in 1959, the first full year after the new regulations, over 8,200,000 proposals were put before the Conferences and 5,750,000 implemented.[185] In 1964 only about 1,500,000 proposals were put before the Conferences.[186]

The limited success of the Permanent Production Conferences in their new form was reflected in Khrushchev's proposal in November, 1962, to set up Production Committees (which would nevertheless have been similar to the Conferences). In fact, this did not get beyond the establishment of a few pilot schemes, and the idea was tacitly dropped. In December, 1964, a Volgograd Party official, writing in *Pravda*, called on Party organisations to 'make a thorough study of the work of the Permanent Production Conferences and take steps to ensure that all the valuable proposals and suggestions advanced by the workers receive support'.[187] In a leading article in July, 1965, *Pravda*[188] stressed the need to revitalise the Conferences, which met infrequently and were disregarded by managements. The number of workers taking part had fallen. *Pravda* observed that the 1958 Statutes were already outdated and that proposals to give the Conferences the right to examine important questions and participate in the selection of managerial personnel should be seriously considered. Over a year later a resolution of a plenum of the AUCCTU called on union councils and Committees to 'activate' the Production Conferences.[189] So far, however, no increased rights have been granted to them.

The Permanent Production Conferences have to a limited extent raised workers' participation in management and eliminated many of their forerunners' shortcomings. However, their evident lack of success may be fairly attributed to the fact that they afford participation only in relatively minor matters and have served mainly to assist managements to increase output and productivity.

WELFARE

The trade unions' concern with the workers' material welfare is manifested in three main ways. They are responsible for administering the State Social Insurance, including temporary disability benefits. For this purpose every trade union group should elect an 'insurance delegate'.[190] Social Insurance Commissions are formed by the Trade Union Factory Committee in enterprises employing at least 100 workers, and Commissions are formed in workshops where there are also union committees. Factory Commissions formed on a voluntary basis from workers and employees, engineering and technical workers and insurance delegates, are directly responsible for administering the social insurance funds.[191] Secondly, the Trade Union Factory Committee, operating through its Pensions Commission (instituted as a result of a USSR Council of Ministers and AUCCTU decision of January 2, 1962, 'on broadening trade union participation in deciding workers' and employees' pensions questions') 'jointly with the management prepares documents on the length of service, earnings and other documents' needed by the worker to obtain a State pension, and generally sees that workers receive their proper pensions.[192] Thirdly, the Commission on Housing and Living Conditions of the union committee (redefined in 1963 by a resolution of the Presidium of the AUCCTU[193]) 'assists the union committee to work out and implement measures directed towards improving the housing and living conditions of workers and employees' and exercises control over the construction of housing and other facilities.

The trade unions also take an active part in the drafting and implementation of health measures by local Soviets and economic bodies.[194]

No less importance is attached to the trade unions' 'cultural' activity. The trade unions, according to their Statutes,[195]

'educate the working people in a spirit of Communist consciousness and ideological outlook, Soviet patriotism, Communist attitude to labour and public, Socialist property, inculcate in workers and employees the high moral principles embodied in the moral code of the builder of Communism; help union members to raise their ideological-political and general educational level. . . . The trade unions organise their own Press, set up clubs, houses and palaces of culture, Red Corners and Libraries, sports and tourist bases, pioneer camps, develop mass amateur art, physical culture, sport and tourism among workers and employees, direct voluntary sports societies of the unions; take part in the preservation and strengthening of public order; help the family and the school in the Communist upbringing of children.'

On January 1, 1966, the trade unions had 19,635 clubs and houses and palaces of culture, 31,171 film projectors, 30,746 libraries with a total of 225 million books, 20,810 stadiums, swimming pools and other capital sports facilities and 155,071 sports grounds.[196] In 1964 there were 175,164 Red Corners and and in 1965 5,000 People's Universities with 2 million members.[197] The Clubs, according to a 1964 resolution of the AUCCTU Presidium on Clubs,[198] are explicitly stated to be 'guided by the requirements of the Communist Party of the Soviet Union in the field of inculcating Communist consciousness: they further the formation of a Communist outlook among the working people, the overcoming of survivals of the past in people's minds . . .'. Similarly, libraries, according to another 1964 resolution of the AUCCTU Presidium,[199] must 'persistently promote among the masses of the people's literature explaining Party and Government policy, books and periodicals concerning the education of the working people in the spirit of the moral code of the builders of Communism'. The Clubs work in close contact with the *Znanie* (Knowledge) Society, factory committees, the *Komsomol*, sporting and other societies.[200] Among its other functions the club:

'holds lectures, reports and talks on various branches of knowledge, thematic evenings, pep talks, question and answer evenings, debates, meetings with veterans of labour, advanced production workers, men of science, technology, literature and the arts;

'sets up People's Universities, lecture halls, rooms and Corners of atheism, associations for lovers of music, the cinema, painting, radio, photography, practical hobbies, etc.;

'organises choirs, music, ballet groups, etc.;

'puts on amateur concerts and shows . . . holds dances . . . film shows . . . exhibitions . . . ;

'organises the cultural servicing of the working people in parks, etc.;

'in conjunction with the schools carries out work among children . . . spreads pedagogical knowledge among parents;

'gives practical help to Red Corners, workshops, sectors . . . and organises the workers' cultural facilities.'

The trade unions, and particularly their 'cultural' institutions, play an increasing part in the Communist education of the workers. 'The basic content of all the trade unions' work', says a popular trade union handbook, 'is the broad explanation of the domestic and foreign policy of the Communist Party. . . .'[201] A recent trade union officials' handbook emphasises that the unions, 'being primarily an educative organisation', take part in one of the Party's main tasks, 'educating the new man, able to work in a Communist manner. . . . This activity is an integral part of the ideological work of the Party'.[202] The rôle of trade union clubs as educative and enlightenment centres is growing. The number of clubs, houses and palaces of culture has grown by nearly one-and-a-half times since 1950, while the number of libraries has nearly doubled.[203] More than 7 million lectures are given every year and attendances at People's Universities have doubled since 1960, while the number of 'universities' has nearly trebled.[204]

While preserving and developing the 'best popular traditions and customs' the trade unions encourage in every way the creation of new traditions and rites, such as youth weddings, coming-of-age celebrations, birthdays, receiving an internal passport or other 'significant events in a person's life'.[205] On the other hand scientific-atheistic propaganda occupies a prominent place in the work of clubs,[206] which were called on (in February, 1962) to 'devote more attention to inculcating in workers a Communist attitude to labour and to the struggle against survivals of the past in people's minds . . .'.[207] The following September the Presidium of the AUCCTU again called on the unions to devote greater efforts to atheist and anti-religious propaganda, 'directed towards unmasking the ideology of active religious groups, societies and sects'.[208] In June, 1963, it once again called on the unions 'to develop more actively scientific and atheistic knowledge' and 'persistently unmask the reactionary essence of religion and the harm of religious survivals . . . .'[209] The need for such improvement is readily apparent from Grishin's statement at the XIII Trade Union Congress in 1963:[210]

'Sometimes lectures on atheistic themes are given before audiences in which there is not a single believer whilst explanatory work is not conducted among believers . . . In Taganrog there are in the same building a . . . factory club and a Baptist prayer house. They get along together peacefully in one house. The presbyter of the sect says the club doesn't bother them. "The atheists watch films in the club and we in our house say prayers and give praise to God." '

A Party Central Committee decree of early 1960 on improving Party propaganda work[211] called for more attention to be devoted to the work of trade union clubs, which 'must become . . . genuine centres of propaganda and agitation'. As a result of the decree, which emphasised the need for more attention to be devoted to the propaganda of economic knowledge, Trade Union Factory Committees greatly expanded their activities in this direction and organised popular lecture courses and the study of economics, and set up universities of technical progress and economic knowledge.[212] Two decrees of the Presidium of the AUCCTU, dating from the time of Zhdanov's ideological purges after the war, exemplify the use of trade unions for popularising specific Party propaganda campaigns. The first, of August, 1947, obliged trade union bodies:[213]

'tirelessly to propagate the ideas of Soviet patriotism, and to demonstrate its manifestations in concrete examples;

'to propagate widely the enormous attainments of the Soviet State during the 30 years of its existence, to nurture in Soviet people a feeling of pride in the great achievements of Socialism, and to explain the superiority of the Soviet over the capitalist system;

'to wage an irreconcilable struggle against all manifestations of servility and idolatry towards things foreign . . . ;

'to carry on a decisive struggle against the influence of reactionary, decadent bourgeois culture and ideology'.

Trade union organisations were to give active assistance to workers in scientific establishments, institutes and so forth 'in studying Marxist-Leninist theory, the history of our Party, and the biographies of the great leaders, V. I. Lenin and J. V. Stalin'.[214] The second decree, of March, 1948, was addressed directly to trade union clubs and Houses and Palaces of Culture. Its declared aim was 'to turn all clubs and Houses and Palaces of Culture into real centres of mass political and cultural work'. To this end the 'basis of the content of all Club work must be the historic decrees of the Central Committee of the CPSU (b) on ideological questions: "On the periodicals *Zvezda* and *Leningrad*", "On the repertoire of dramatic theatres and measures for its improvement" [etc.].' Among the club activities—to be based, presumably, on these decrees—were choirs, dramatic, musical and choreographic groups, and societies for visual art, technical knowledge, photography, chess, draughts and other interests; these groups were to be provided with 'qualified, politically literate leaders'.[215]

These decrees were omitted from the 1956 and subsequent Trade Union Workers' Handbooks. In 1955, however, trade union clubs and libraries were criticised for 'functioning in isolation from the tasks facing the collectives of enterprises, poorly propagating the advances of science and technology and not disseminating the advanced methods of work and achievements of production innovators'.[216] Clubs, Palaces of Culture and libraries were ordered to 'make closer contact with production, and actively to promote a higher cultural and technical level in workers'. The clubs' tasks were defined as 'educational work' directed to 'raising the Socialist consciousness of the workers, and to promoting the strengthening of labour discipline'. This shift of the clubs' propaganda drive from ideological orthodoxy to increasing production has continued since the XX Party Congress. An examination of clubs organised by the AUCCTU in 1961 had the task of:

'seeking ways to improve further the activity of cultural institutions, raising the ideological standard of education and mass cultural work strengthening contact with life and the tasks of production collectives. Workers in clubs, palaces and houses of culture will expand the propaganda of the advanced experience of shock-workers and collectives of Communist labour and scientific and technical achievements'.[217]

The revised (1964) regulations on clubs specified, in addition to the provisions cited above, that the clubs' daily activity is 'inseparably linked with life, with the concrete tasks of the collective of the enterprise . . . in fulfilling economic plans and

Socialist obligations, the development of the movement for Communist labour, the dissemination and introduction of advanced production experience, the raising of workers' cultural and technical standard'.[218]

The trade unions' other 'cultural' activities—libraries, Red Corners, amateur art groups, physical culture and sport—are all equally geared to propaganda purposes. Amateur art, for example, is said 'to play a considerable rôle in the Communist education of the working people'.[219] Libraries, under their 1964 regulations, conduct 'broad propaganda of Marxist-Leninist doctrine, the policy of the Communist Party and Soviet Government . . .'.[220] Red Corners, described in their 1964 regulations as 'cultural centres where mass political work is carried on . . .',[221] set up in factories and workshops, etc., 'participate in explaining the internal and external and foreign policy of the Communist Party and Soviet Government . . .', propagate advanced industrial practice, and so on.[222] Physical culture and sport, equally, are 'an important means for the Communist education of the working people . . . [by] strengthening their health and training them for labour and defence of their Socialist Motherland'.[223] In no branch of Soviet life, perhaps, is the all-pervading influence of Party propaganda more clearly evident than in the multifarious activities of the Soviet trade unions.

SOURCES

N.B.—Undated citations of works of which more than one edition is listed in the bibliography refer to the most recent edition there listed; earlier editions are cited with the date in brackets.

1. Lenin, Vol. 5, p. 421.
2. Deutscher, p. 22.
3. *K.P.S.S. v Rezolyutsiakh*, Vol. 1, pp. 538ff.
4. Lenin, Vol. 33, p. 168.
5. Stalin, *Problems of Leninism*, pp. 164–7.
6. *Deutscher*, pp. 78f.
7. *Ibid.*, p. 79.
8. *K.P.S.S. v Rezolyutsiakh*, Vol. II, p. 72.
9. *Ibid.*, p. 554.
10. *Ibid.*, p. 556.
11. Lozovsky, p. 15.
12. *B.S.E.*, 1st edn., Vol. 47, col. 422.
13. *K.P.S.S. v Rezolyutsiakh*, Vol. III, p. 72.
14. *Ibid.*, pp. 64–73.
15. *B.S.E.*, 1st edn., Vol. 47, col. 422.
16. USSR Laws, 1933, 40:238, art. 1.
17. *B.S.E.*, 2nd edn., Vol. 35, p. 161.

18. USSR Laws, 1934, 43 : 342.
19. *K.P.S.S. v Rezolyutsiakh,* Vol. III, pp. 230f.; *B.S.E.*, 2nd edn., Vol. 35, p. 161.
20. *Pravda,* December 11, 1935.
21. *Loc. cit.*
22. *Pravda,* April 8, 1937.
23. *Trud,* March 26, 1937; cf. also *Pravda,* March 21, 1937, and *B.S.E.*, 2nd edn., Vol. 35, p. 161.
24. *Trud,* March 26, 1937.
25. *Lozovsky,* p. 17.
26. *B.S.E.*, 1st edn., Vol. 47, col. 422.
27. Shvernik at the XVIII Party Congress, 1939, quoted by Deutscher, p. 116.
28. *Trud,* September 15, 1938.
29. *K.P.S.S. v Rezolyutsiakh,* Vol. III, p. 364.
30. *Trud,* April 24, 1939.
31. *B.S.E.*, 2nd edn., Vol. 35, p. 161.
32. *Ibid.*, p. 161.
33. *B.S.E.*, 1st edn., Vol. on USSR, cols. 1751f.
34. *B.S.E.*, 2nd edn., Vol. 35, p. 161.
35. *Ibid.*, p. 161f.
36. *B.S.E.*, 1st edn., Vol. on USSR, col. 1751.
37. *Ibid.*, col. 1752.
38. *Pravda,* March 16, 1944.
39. *Trud,* May 11, 1945.
40. *SpravochnikProfsoyuznogo Rabotnika* (1948), p. 15.
41. *Trud,* May 11, 1949.
42. *Izvestiya,* August 22, 1951.
43. *Trud,* August 18, 1952.
44. *Ibid.*, December 19, 1952.
45. *Loc cit.*
46. *Trud,* June 5, 1953.
47. *V Pomoshch Profsoyuznomu Aktiva,* 1953, No. 9, p. 2.
48. *Trud,* April 21, 1949.
49. *Ibid.*, April 27, 1949.
50. *Pravda,* June 8, 1954.
51. *Pravda,* December 19, 1957.
52. *Trud,* March 24, 1959.
53. *Pravda,* November 25, 1961.
54. *Trud,* October 29, 1963.
55. *Postanovlenie VII Plenuma VTsSPS,* in *Trud,* November 5, 1965.
56. *Trud,* June 13, 1957.
57. *Trud,* November 5, 1965.
58. *B.S.E.*, 2nd edn., Vol. 35, p. 162.
59. *Ustav Professionalnykh Soyuzov SSSR,* in *Spravochnik Profsoyuznogo Rabotnika,* pp. 116–36, art. 13.
60. *Ibid.*, art. 24.
61. *Ibid.*, art. 14.
62. *Spravochnaya Kniga o Professionalnyk Soyuzakh SSSR.*
63. Lozovsky, p. 19.
64. *Russia Today,* August, 1951, p. 6.
65. *Trud,* June 10, 1954.
66. *Sovetskie Profsoyuzy,* 1957, No. 5, p. 3.
67. *Partiinaya Zhizn,* 1957, No. 16, p. 31.
68. Ogolev, p. 24.
69. *Trud,* December 16, 1965
70. *Trud,* December 18, 1965.
71. *B.S.E.*, 2nd edn., Vol. 39, p. 524.
72. *Ustav Professionalnykh Soyuzov SSSR,* arts. 36, 44.
73. *Ibid.*, art. 19.
74. *Ibid.*, art. 21.
75. *Trud,* October 15, 1948.
76. *Trud,* January 10, 1954.

77. *Trud*, March 26, 1959.
78. *Trud*, October 31, 1963.
79. *Trud*, March 26, 1959.
80. *Trud*, October 31, 1963.
81. *Ustav Professionalnykh Soyuzov SSSR*, art. 26.
82. *Trud*, October 15, 1948, and January 10, 1954.
83. *Trud*, March 24, 1959.
84. *Trud*, October 29, 1963.
85. *Ustav Professionalnykh Soyuzov SSSR*, art. 28.
86. *B.S.E.*, 2nd edn., Vol. 9, pp. 348f.
87. *Ustav Professionalnykh Soyuzov SSSR*, art. 29.
88. *Ibid.*, art. 31.
89. *Ibid.*, art. 30.
90. *Loc. cit.*
91. *Trud*, November 3, 1963.
92. *B.S.E.*, 1st edn., Vol. 47, col. 422; *ibid.*, Vol. 62, col. 105.
93. *B.S.E.*, 2nd edn., Vol. 9, pp. 348f.
94. *Tass*, March 16, 1956.
95. *Pravda*, January 19, 1961.
96. *Entsiklopedichesky Slovar Pravovykh Znaniy*, p. 62.
97. *Trudovoe Pravo*, p. 74.
98. *Spravochnaya Kniga o Professionalnykh Soyuzakh SSSR*, p. 54; *Sbornik Postanovleniy VTsSPS*, January–March, 1966, p. 11.
99. *Entsiklopedichesky Slovar Pravovykh Znaniy*, p. 62.
100. *Spravochnik Profsoyuznogo Rabotnika*, p. 419.
101. *Ustav Professionalnykh Soyuzov SSSR*, art. 60.
102. *Trud*, January 17, 1931, quoted by Schwarz (roneo), p. 93.
103. *Ibid.*, p. 94.
104. *Trud*, September 6, 1934.
105. *Pravda*, September 9, 1934.
106. *Ustav Professionalnykh Soyuzov SSSR*, art. 33.
107. *Loc. cit.*
108. *Ustav Professionalnyk Soyuzov SSSR*, art. 36.
109. *Ibid.*, art. 35.
110. *Trud*, November 5, 1965.
111. *Ustav Professionalnyk Soyuzov SSSR*, art. 16.
112. *The Trade Union Situation in the USSR*, p. 75.
113. *Ezhegodnik B.S.E.*, 1965, p. 105.
114. *Ustav Professionalnykh Soyuzov SSSR*, art. 45.
115. *Ibid.*, art. 47.
116. *B.S.E.*, 2nd edn., Vol. 44, p. 478.
117. *Ustav Professionalnykh Soyuzov SSSR*, art. 46.
118. *Postanovlenie Plenuma TsK KPSS* of December 17, 1957, in *Pravda*, December 19, 1957; *Ukaz Prezidiuma Verkhovnogo Soveta* SSSR of July 15, 1958, in *Spravochnik Profsoyuznogo Rabotnika*, p. 161.
119. *Ustav Professionalnyk Soyuzov SSSR*, art. 48.
120. *Spravochnik Profsoyuznogo Rabotnika*, (1962), p. 159.
121. *Spravochnik Profsoyuznogo Rabotnika*, p. 108.
122. *Ibid.*, p. 54.
123. *Ibid.*, p. 231.
124. *Ibid.*, p. 339.
125. *Ibid.*, p. 342.
126. *Ibid.*, p. 364.
127. *Ibid.*, p. 404.
128. *Ibid.*, p. 426.
129. *Sbornik*, p. 455, art. 5.
130. *Spravochnik Profsoyuznogo Rabotnika*, p. 49.
131. *Ibid.*, p. 367.
132. *Ustav Professionalnykh Soyozuv SSSR*, art. 49.

133. *Ibid.*, art. 50.
134. Dvornikov, Dzhelomanov and Shtylko, p. 16.
135. They are not mentioned by Lozovsky, pp. 19–29.
136. *Pravda*, October 16, 1948.
137. *Spravochnik Profsoyuznogo Rabotnika*, p. 143.
138. Dvornikov, Dzhelomanov and Shtylko, p. 16.
139. *Trud*, November 5, 1965.
140. *Ustav Professionalnykh Soyuzov SSSR*, art. 33.
141. *Ibid.*, art. 38.
142. *Ibid.*, art. 39.
143. *Ibid.*, art. 1.
144. *Trud*, September 28, 1966.
145. *Pravda*, November 25, 1961.
146. *Spravochnik Profsoyuznogo Rabotnika*, p. 112.
147. Lozovsky, p. 19; *B.S.E.*, 1st edn., Vol. on USSR, col. 1753.
148. L. N. Soloviev, Deputy Chairman of AUCCTU, *Tass*, December 4, 1953; Sovinform for Abroad, January 9, 1952.
149. *Trud*, October 18, 1953.
150. *The Trade Union Situation in the USSR*, p. 72.
151. *Trud*, June 8, 1954.
152. *Ustav Professionalnykh Soyuzov SSSR*, art. 2.
153. *Ibid.*, art. 3.
154. *Ibid.*, art. 4.
155. *Ibid.*, art. 52.
156. *Loc. cit.*
157. *Ustav Professionalnykh Soyuzov SSSR*, Art. 53.
158. Aleksandrov (1949), p. 166.
159. *Loc. cit.*
160. V. M. Dogadov, quoted in *Soviet Studies*, Vol. I, No. 1, p. 84.
161. *Loc. cit.*
162. *Spravochnik Profsoyuznogo Rabotnika* (1949), p. 139.
163. *Sbornik*, p. 57.
164. *The Trade Union Situation in the USSR*, p. 58.
165. *Trud*, November 2, 1965.
166. *Sbornik Postanovleniy VTsSPS*, January–March, 1966, pp. 7–10.
167. Aleksandrov, p. 219.
168. *Postanovlenie Prezidiuma VTsSPS* of January 2, 1933, in *Trudovoe Zakonodatelstvo SSSR*, pp. 320f., art. 3.
169. *Polozhenie o poryadke rassmotreniya trudovykh sporov*, in *Sbornik*, pp. 454–62, art. 5.
170. *Ibid.*, art. 11.
171. *Spravochnik Profsoyuznogo Rabotnika*, pp. 339–45.
172. *Sbornik*, p. 255, art. 17.
173. *Spravochnik Profsoyuznogo Rabotnika*, p. 340, art. 6.
174. *Sbornik* (1956), p. 291.
175. *Spravochnik Profsoyuznogo Rabotnika*, pp. 355–7.
176. *Polozhenie o poryadke rassmotreniya trudovykh sporov*, art. 10.
177. *Sbornik* (1956), p. 297.
178. *Spravochnik Profsoyuznogo Rabotnika*, p. 267.
179. See, for example, *Trud*, January 26, 1965; *Pravda*, March 12, 1965, September 16, 1966.
180. *Polozhenie o poryadke rassmotreniya trudovykh sporov*, arts. 31, 32.
181. *Sbornik*, pp. 26f.
182. *Ibid.*, pp. 41–3.
183. *Pravda*, July 9 and September 25, 1965.
184. *Spravochnik Profsoyuznogo Rabotnika*, p. 12.

185. Dvornikov, Dzhelomanov and Shtylko, pp. 32.
186. *Pravda*, July 9, 1965.
187. *Pravda*, December 9, 1964.
188. *Pravda*, July 9, 1965.
189. *Trud*, October 2, 1966.
190. *Spravochnik Profsoyuznogo Rabotnika*, p. 344, art. 1.
191. *Ibid.*, pp. 339.
192. *Ibid.*, pp. 342–4.
193. *Spravochnik Profsoyuznogo Rabotnika*, pp. 364–7.
194. *Ibid.* (1962), p. 255.
195. *Ustav Professionalnykh Soyuzov SSSR*, preamble.
196. *Moscow News*, July 23, 1966.
197. *Spravochnik Profsoyuznogo Rabotnika*, p. 378.
198. *Ibid.*, p. 421.
199. *Ibid.*, p. 406.
200. *Ibid.*, p. 422.
201. Dvornikov, Dzhelomanov and Shtylko, p. 76.
202. *Spravochnik Profsoyuznogo Rabotnika*, p. 377.
203. *Ibid.*, p. 378.
204. *Ibid.*, pp. 378–9.
205. Dvornikov, Dzhelomanov and Shtylko, p. 88.
206. *Ibid.*, p. 79.
207. *Trud*, February 6, 1962.
208. *Trud*, September 19, 1962.
209. *Spravochnik Profsoyuznogo Rabotnika*, p. 384.
210. *Trud*, October 29, 1963.
211. *Pravda*, January 10, 1960.
212. Dvornikov, Dzhelomanov and Shtylko, p. 79.
213. *Spravochnik Profsoyuznogo Rabotnika* (1948), p. 485.
214. *Ibid.*, p. 486.
215. *Ibid.*, pp. 487, 490.
216. *Trud*, August 13, 1955.
217. *Trud*, December 29, 1960.
218. *Spravochnik Profsoyuznogo Rabotnika*, p. 421.
219. *Trud*, December 29, 1960.
220. *Spravochnik Profsoyuznogo Rabotnika*, p. 409.
221. *Ibid.*, p. 424.
222. *Loc. cit.*
223. Shvernik in *Trud*, June 8, 1954.

BIBLIOGRAPHY

AEU Journal, journal of the Amalgamated Engineering Union.

Aktualnye Problemy Ispolzovaniya Rabochei Sily v SSSR (Current Problems of the Utilisation of the Labour Force in the USSR), *Mysl* Publishing House, Moscow, 1965.

Aleksandrov, N. G., *Sovetskoe Trudovoe Pravo* (Soviet Labour Law), State Publishing House of Juridical Literature, Moscow; editions of 1949, 1950 and 1954.

Aleksandrov, N. G., Kiselev, Ya. L., and Stavtseva, A. I., *Trudovye Prava Rabochikh i Sluzhashchikh v SSSR* (The Labour Rights of Workers and Employees in the USSR), State Publishing House of Juridical Literature, Moscow, 1956.

Aleksandrov, N. G., and Moskalenko, G. K., *Sovetskoe Trudovoe Pravo* (Soviet Labour Law), Juridical Publishing House of the People's Commissariat of Justice of the USSR, Moscow; editions of 1944 and 1947.

Andreyev, V. S., and Gureyev, P. A., *Organizovanny Nabor Rabochikh v SSSR* (The Organised Recruitment of Workers in the USSR), State Publishing House of Juridical Literature, Moscow, 1956.

Artemev, F. A., *Kratkoe Posobie po Zakonodatelstvu ob Okhrane Truda* (A Short Handbook on Legislation on Labour Protection), Publishing House of the All-Union Central Council of Trade Unions, Moscow, 1953.

Baykov, Alexander, *The Development of the Soviet Economic System*, Cambridge University Press, Cambridge, 1946.

Bergson, Abram, *The Structure of Soviet Wages*, Harvard University Press, Cambridge (Mass.), 1944.

Bolshaya Sovetskaya Entsiklopediya (Large Soviet Encyclopaedia), 1st edition, 65 volumes with supplementary volume on the USSR, Moscow, 1926–47; 2nd edition, 51 volumes, Moscow, 1949–58. (Cited as *B.S.E.*)

Byulleten Ispolnitelnogo Komiteta Moskovskogo Gorodskogo Soveta Deputatov Trudyashchikhsaya (Bulletin of the Executive Committee of the Moscow City Soviet of Workers' Deputies), organ of the Moscow City Soviet Executive Committee.

Carr, E. H., *A History of Soviet Russia, The Bolshevik Revolution 1917–23*, Volume 2, Macmillan, London, 1952.

Chigvintsev, I. N., *Zarabotnaya Plata pri Sotsializme* (Wages under Socialism), State Publishing House of Political Literature, Moscow, 1955.

Constitution (Fundamental Law) of the Union of Soviet Socialist Republics, Co-operative Publishing Society of Foreign Workers in the USSR, Moscow, 1937; Foreign Languages Publishing House, Moscow, 1955.

Daily Telegraph, newspaper, London.

Deutscher, Isaac, *Soviet Trade Unions*, Royal Institute of International Affairs, London and New York, 1950.

Dewar, Margaret, *Labour Policy in the USSR 1917–28*, Royal Institute of International Affairs, London and New York, 1956.

Dobb, Maurice, *Soviet Economic Development since 1917*, Routledge and Kegan Paul, London, 1948.

Dvornikov, I., Dzhelomanov, V., and Shtylko, A., *Professionalnye Soyuzy SSSR, Kratky Spravochnik* (Trade Unions of the USSR, A Short Handbook), Trade Unions Publishing House, 1961.

Dvornikov, I. S., Kaftanovskaya, A. M., and Nikitinsky, V. I., *Tovarishcheskie Sudy i ikh Rol v Borbe za Ukreplenie Trudovoy Distsipliny* (Comrades' Courts and their Rôle in the Struggle to Strengthen Labour Discipline), Publishing House of the All-Union Central Council of Trade Unions, Moscow, 1956.

Ekonomicheskaya Gazeta (Economic Gazette), weekly newspaper published by the Central Committee of the Communist Party of the Soviet Union.

Entsiklopedichesky Slovar (Encyclopaedic Dictionary), 3 volumes, *Bolshaya Sovetskaya Entsiklopediya* Publishing House, Moscow, 1953–5.

Entsiklopedichesky Slovar Pravovykh Znaniy (Sovetskoe Pravo) (Encyclopaedic Dictionary of Legal Knowledge (Soviet Law)), *Sovetskaya Entsiklopediya* Publishing House, Moscow, 1965.

Ezhegodnik B.S.E., 1965 (Yearbook of the Large Soviet Encyclopaedia).

Fedotoff White, D., *The Growth of the Red Army*, Princeton University Press, Princeon (N.J.), 1944.

Five-Year Plan for the Rehabilitation and Development of the National Economy of the USSR, 1946–50, Soviet News, London, 1946. (Cited as *Five-Year Plan, 1946–50.*)

Goloshchapov, B. A. (compiler), *Raschety s Rabochimi i Sluzhashchimi* (Settlements with Workers and Employees), 9th revised edition, State Financial Publishing House, Moscow, 1954.

Gosudarstvennye Trudovye Rezervy, Sbornik Ofitsialnykh Materialov (The State Labour Reserves, A Collection of Official

Materials), State Publishing House of Juridical Literature, Moscow, 1950.
Guardian, newspaper, London and Manchester.

Hubbard, L. E., *Soviet Labour and Industry*, Macmillan, London, 1942.

International Labour Review, periodical published by the International Labour Office, Geneva.
Izvestiya (News), newspaper published by the Presidium of the Supreme Soviet of the USSR.

Kapustin, E. I. (editor), *Zarabotnaya Plata v Promyshlennosti SSSR i ee Sovershenstvovanie* (Wages in Industry in the USSR and their Improvement), Publishing House of Economic Literature, Moscow, 1961.
Kazakhstanskaya Pravda (Kazakhstan Truth), organ of the Central Committee of the Communist Party of Kazakhstan.
Kodeks Zakonov o Trude RSFSR (Codex of Laws on Labour of the RSFSR):
1918: RSFSR Laws, 1918, 87/88: 905. (Cited as *KZo*T (1918).)
1922: RSFSR Laws, 1922, 70: 903. (Cited at *KZoT* (1922).)
1931: *Kodeks Zakonov o Trude RSFSR, Prakticheskoe Rukovodstvo* (Codex of Laws on Labour of the RSFSR, A Practical Guide), eds. E. N. Danilova and A. M. Stopani, 2nd edition, State Socio-economic Publishing House, Moscow–Leningrad, 1931. (Cited as *KZoT* (1931).)
1956: Extracts quoted in *Sbornik Zakonodatelnykh Aktov o Trude* (q.v.). (Cited as *KZoT* in *Sbornik*.)
Kommunist (The Communist), periodical published by the Central Committee of the Communist Party of the Soviet Union.
Kommunist Sovetskoy Latvii (The Communist of Soviet Latvia), periodical published by the Central Committee of the Communist Party of Latvia.
Kommunist Tadzihikistana (The Communist of Tadzhikistan), newspaper published by the Central Committee of the Communist Party of Tadzhikistan, the Supreme Soviet and Council of Ministers of the Tadzhik SSR.
Kommunisticheskaya Partiya Sovetskaya v Rezolyutsiakh i Resheniyakh Sezdov, Konferentsiy i Plenumov TsK, 1898–1954 (The Communist Party of the Soviet Union in the Resolutions and Decisions of the Congresses, Conferences and Central Committee Plenums, 1898–1954), 7th edition, 3 volumes, State Publishing House of Political Literature, Moscow, 1954. (Cited as *K.P.S.S. v Rezolutsiyakh.*)
Komsomolskaya Pravda (Young Communist Truth), newspaper published by the Central and Moscow Komsomol Committees.

Konakov, D. M., *Organisatsiya Zarabotnoy Platy i Normirovanie Truda v Promyshlennosti SSSR* (The Organization of Wages and Labour-Norm Setting in Industry in the USSR), State Publishing House of Political Literature, Moscow, 1953.

Kostin, Leonid, *Wages in the USSR*, Foreign Languages Publishing House, Moscow, 1960.

Kotov, F. I., *Voprosy Truda v Semiletnem Plane* (Questions of Labour in the Seven-Year Plan), State Planning Commission Publishing House, Moscow, 1960.

Kulski, W. W., *The Soviet Régime*, Syracuse University Press, Syracuse University Press, Syracuse (N.Y.), 1954.

Kunelsky, L. E., and Begidzhanov, M. G., *Oplata i Normirovanie Truda v Promyshlennosti* (The Payment of Labour and Norm-setting in Industry), *Ekonomika* Publishing House, Moscow, 1965.

Kuznetsova, A. S., *Organizatsiya Zarabotnoy Platy Rabochikh na Promyshlennykh Predpriyatiyakh SSSR* (The Organisation of Workers' Wages at Industrial Enterprises of the USSR), State Publishing House of Political Literature, Moscow, 1956.

Leninskoe Znamya (Banner of Lenin), newspaper published by the Moscow *Oblast* Committee of the CPSU and the Moscow *Oblast* Soviet of Workers' Deputies.

Lenin, V. I., *Sochineniya* (Works), 4th edition, 35 volumes, Marx–Engels–Lenin Institute, Moscow, 1941–50.

Literaturnaya Gazeta (Literary Gazette), newspaper published by the Board of the Union of Soviet Writers of the USSR.

Lozovsky, A. (ed.), *Handbook on the Soviet Trade Unions*, Co-operative Publishing Society of Foreign Workers in the USSR, Moscow, 1937.

Malaya Sovetskaya Entsiklopediya (Small Soviet Encyclopaedia), 10 volumes, State Scientific Publishing House, Moscow, 1958–60. (Cited as *M.S.E.*)

Molodoy Kommunist (Young Communist), periodical published by the *Komsomol* Central Committee.

Monthly Labour Review, periodical published by the US Department of Labor, Bureau of Labor Statistics.

Moscow News, weekly newspaper published by the Union of Soviet Societies of Friendship and Cultural Relations with Foreign Countries.

Mutsinov, G., *Raschety po Zarabotnoy Plate Rabochikh i Sluzhashchikh* (Calculations on the Wages of Workers and Employees), *Profizdat* Publishing House, Moscow, 1965.

Narodnoe Khozyaistvo SSSR, Statistichesky Sbornik (The National Economy of the USSR, A Statistical Handbook), State Statistical Publishing House, Moscow, 1956.

Narodnoe Khozyaistvo SSSR v 1960 godu, Statistichesky Ezhegodnik (The National Economy of the USSR in 1960, A Statistical Yearbook, State Statistical Publishing House, Moscow, 1961 and 1965.

Ob Itogakh Vypolneniya Gosudarstvennogo Plana Razvitiya Narodnogo Khozyaistva SSSR v 1956 godu (On the results of the Fulfilment of the State Plan for the Development of the National Economy of the USSR in 1956), State Publishing House of Political Literature, Moscow, 1957.

Ogolev, N. P. (compiler), *Sputnik Profgruporga* (The Trade Union Group Organiser's vade-mecum), Trade Unions Publishing House, 1960.

Okhana Truda, Sbornik Postanovleniy i Pravil (Labour Protection, A Collection of Resolutions and Rules), Publishing House of the All-Union Central Council of Trade Unions, Moscow, 1963.

Oktyabr (October), periodical published by the Union of Writers of the RSFSR.

Osnovnye Zakonodatelnye Akty o Trude Rabochikh i Sluzhashchikh (Fundamental Legislative Acts on the Labour of Workers and Employees), State Publishing House of Juridical Literature, Moscow, 1st edition, 1953, 2nd edition, 1955. (Cited as *Osnovnye Zakonodatelnye Akty.*)

Partiinaya Zhizn (*Party Life*), periodical published by the Central Committee of the Communist Party of the Soviet Union.

Pasherstnik, A. E., *Pravo na Trud* (The Right to Work), Publishing House of the Academy of Sciences of the USSR, Moscow, 1951.

Pasquier, A., *Le Stakhanovisme* (Stakhanovism), Rousseau, Paris, 1938.

Planovoe Khozyaistvo (Planned Economy), monthly political and economic journal of the State Scientific and Economic Council of the USSR and the State Planning Commission of the USSR.

Pravda (Truth), newspaper published by the Central Committee of the Communist Party of the Soviet Union.

Pravda Ukrainy (Pravda of the Ukraine), newspaper published by the Central Committee of the Communist Party of the Ukraine, The Supreme Soviet and Council of Ministers of the Ukrainian SSR.

Remizov, K., *Organizatsiya Oplaty Truda Rabochikh v SSSR* (The Organisation of the Payment of Worker's Labour in the USSR), Moscow Worker Publishing House, 1960.

Report of the Delegation to the Soviet Union 7th–23rd August, 1956 (n.p., n.d. [National Union of Mineworkers, London, 1957]).

Report of the Delegation which visited the USSR, July 15–26, 1955 (n.p., n.d. [National Union of Mineworkers (Nottingham Area), Nottingham, 1955]).

RSFSR Laws: 1917–38: *Sobranie Uzakoneniy i Rasporyazheniy Raboche-Krestyanskogo Pravitelstva Rossiyskoy Sovetskoy Federativnoy Sotsialisticheskoy Respubliki* (Collection of Statutes and Orders of the Worker-Peasant Government of the Russian Soviet Federative Socialist Republic), People's Commissariat of Justice of the RSFSR, Moscow.

Rumyantsev, A. F., *Povyshenie Proizvoditelnosti Truda i Vnedrenie Peredovogo Opyta v Promyshlennosti SSSR* (Raising the Productivity of Labour and the Introduction of Advanced Experience in the Industry of the USSR), State Publishing House of Political Literature, Moscow, 1953.

Russia Today, periodical published by the British-Soviet Friendship Society, London.

Sbornik Postanovleniy VTsSPS (*Yanvar-Mart*, 1966), *Profizdat* Publishing House, Moscow, 1966.

Sbornik Zakonodatelnykh Aktov o Trude (Collection of Legislative Acts on Labour), State Publishing House of Juridical Literature, Moscow, 1956 and 1961 editions. (Cited as *Sbornik.*)

Sbornik Zakanov SSSR i Ukazov Prezidiuma Verkhovnogo Soveta SSSR, 1938–44 (Collection of Laws of the USSR and of Edicts of the Presidium of the Supreme Soviet of the USSR, 1938–44), published by *Vedomosti Verkhovnogo Soveta SSSR*, Moscow, 1945.

Schwarz, Solomon M., *Labor in the Soviet Union*, Praeger, New York, 1952. (Cited as Schwarz.)

Schwarz, Solomon M., *Trade Unions in the USSR*, roneoed paper, New York, 1953. (Cited as Schwarz (roneo).)

Shkurko, S. I. (editor), *Sovershenstvovanie Organizatsii Zarabotnoy Platy* (The Improvement of the Organisation of Wages), Publishing House of Economic Literature, Moscow, 1961.

Sotsialisticheskaya Zakonnost (Socialist Legality), periodical published by the Public Prosecutor's Office of the USSR.

Sotsialisticheskoe Stroitelstvo SSSR (The Socialist Construction of the USSR), Central Administration of National Economic Accounting of the State Planning Commission of the USSR, Moscow, 1936.

Sotsialistichesky Trud (Socialist Labour), periodical published by the State Committee of the Council of Ministers of the USSR on questions of Labour and Wages.

Sovetskaya Kirgiziya (Soviet Kirghizia), newspaper published by the Central Committee and the Frunze *Oblast* Committee of the Communist Party of Kirghizia, and the Supreme Soviet and the Council of Ministers of the Kirghiz SSR.

Sovetskaya Latviya (Soviet Latvia), newspaper published by the Central Committee of the Communist Party of Latvia and the Supreme Soviet of the Latvian SSR.

Sovetskaya Moldaviya (Soviet Moldavia), newspaper published by the Central Committee of the Communist Party of Moldavia and the Supreme Soviet of the Moldavian SSR.

Sovetskaya Pechat (Soviet Press), periodical published by the Union of Soviet Journalists.

Sovetskaya Rossiya (Soviet Russia), newspaper published by the RSFSR Bureau of the Central Committee of the Communist Party of the Soviet Union and the Council of Ministers of the RSFSR.

Sovetskaya Yustitsiya (Soviet Justice), periodical published by the RSFSR Supreme Court and the Juridical Commission of the RSFSR Council of Ministers.

Sovetskie Profsoyuzy (Soviet Trade Unions), periodical published by the All-Union Central Council of Trade Unions.

Sovetskoe Gosudarstvo i Pravo (Soviet State and Law), periodical published by the Institute of State and Law of the Academy of Sciences of the USSR.

Soviet Studies, periodical, Blackwells, Oxford.

Sovinform, the official Soviet Government Information Service.

Spisok Proizvodstv, Tsekhov, Professiy i Dolzhnostei s vrednymi usloviyami truda, rabota v kotorykh daet pravo na dopolnitelny otpusk i sokrashchenny rabochi den (List of types of production, shops, professions and posts with arduous working conditions, working in which gives the right to additional leave and shortened working day), Publishing House of Economic Literature, Moscow, 1963.

Spravochnaya Kniga o Professionalnykh Soyuzov SSSR (Reference Book on Trade Unions in the USSR), Publishing House of the All-Union Central Council of Trade Unions, Moscow, 1965.

Spravochnik Nalogovogo Rabotnika (The Taxation Worker's Handbook), State Financial Publishing House, Moscow, 1954.

Spravochnik Profsoyuznogo Rabotnika (The Trade Union Worker's Handbook), Publishing House of the All-Union Central Council of Trade Unions, Moscow; editions of 1926, 1948, 1949, 1956 and 1962.

Spravochnik Rayonnogo Finansovogo Rabotnika (The *Raion* Financial Worker's Handbook), Volume II, State Financial Publishing House, Moscow, 1953.

Spravochnye Materialy po Trudu i Zarabotnoy Plate (Reference Material on Labour and Wages), published by the Scientific Research Institute of Labour of the State Committee on Labour and Wages of the USSR Council of Ministers, Moscow, 1960.

Stalin, J., *Economic Problems of Socialism in the USSR*, Foreign Languages Publishing House, Moscow, 1952.

Stalin, J., *Problems of Leninism*, translated from the 11th Russian edition, Foreign Languages Publishing House, Moscow, 1953.

Stalin, J., *Works*, 16 volumes (projected), Foreign Languages Publishing House, Moscow, 1952–1955 (Vol. 13).

Tass, official news agency of the Soviet Government.

The Trade Union Situation in the USSR, Report of a Mission from the International Labour Office, International Labour Office, Geneva, 1960.

Trud i Zarabotnaya Plata (Labour and Wages), periodical published by the Scientific Research Institute of Labour of the State Committee on Labour and Wages of the USSR Council of Ministers.

Trud (Labour), newspaper published by the All-Union Central Council of Trade Unions.

Trudovoe Pravo, Entsiklopedichesky Slovar (Labour Law, An Encyclopaedic Dictionary), State Publishing House of Scientific Literature, Moscow, 1959. (Cited as *Trudovoe Pravo.*)

Trudovoe Zakonodatelstvo SSSR (The Labour Legislation of the USSR), Juridical Publishing House of the People's Commissariat of Justice, Moscow, 1941.

Uchitelskaya Gazeta (Teachers' Gazette), newspaper published by the Ministries of Education of the Union Republics and the Central Committees of the Trade Union of Educational Workers.

Ugolovny Kodeks RSFSR (The Criminal Codex of the RSFSR, introduced in 1961), *Sovetskaya Yustitsiya*, 1960, No. 17.

USSR Laws:

1924–38: *Sobranie Zakonov i Rasporyazheniy Raboche-Kresyanskogo Pravitelstva Soyuza Sovetskikh Sotsialisticheskikh Respublik* (Collection of Laws and Orders of the Worker-Peasant Government of the Union of Soviet Socialist Republics), Administration of Affairs of the Council of People's Commissars of the USSR, Moscow.

1938– : *Sobranie Postanovleniy i Rasporyazheniy Pravitelstva Soyuza Sovetskikh Sotsialisticheskikh Respublik* (Collection of Decrees and Orders of the Government of the Union of Soviet Socialist Republics), Administration of Affairs of the Council of People's Commissars (Ministers from April, 1946) of the USSR, Moscow.

USSR, Questions and Answers, Novosti Press Agency Publishing House, Moscow, 1965.

Vedomosti Verkhovnogo Soveta SSSR (Gazette of the Supreme Soviet of the USSR), organ of the Supreme Soviet of the USSR.

Vestnik Leningradskogo Universiteta (Leningrad University Herald), Economics, Politics and Law Series, published by Leningrad University.

Vestnik Statistiki (Statistics Herald), periodical published by the Central Statistical Administration attached to the Council of Ministers of the USSR.

Vneocherednoy XXI Sezd Kommunisticheskoy Partii Sovetskogo, Soyuza, Stenografichesky Otchet (Extraordinary XXI Congress of the Communist Party of the Soviet Union), State Publishing House of Political Literature, Moscow, 1959. (Cited as *Vneocherednoy XXI Sezd K.P.S.S.*)

Voprosy Ekonomiki (Questions of Economics), periodical published by *Pravda.*

Voprosy Filosofii (Questions of Philosophy), periodical published by the Institute of Philosophy of the USSR Academy of Sciences.

V Pomoshch Politicheskomu Samoobrazovaniyu (Aid to Political Self-education), periodical published by the Central Committee of the Communist Party of the Soviet Union.

V Pomoshch Profsoyuznomu Aktivu (To Assist Trade Union Activists), periodical published by the All-Union Central Council of Trade Unions.

Vsesoyuznaya Kommunisticheskaya Partiya (Bolshevikov) o Profsoyuzakh (The All-Union Communist Party (Bolsheviks) on the Trade Unions), Publishing House of the All-Union Central Council of Trade Unions, Moscow, 1939. (Cited as *VKP (b) o Profsoyuzakh.*)

Vysshaya Shkola, Osnovnye Postanovleniya, Prikazy i Instruktsii (Higher School, Principal Decrees, Orders and Instructions), State Publishing House, *Soviet Science*, Moscow, 1957.

Webb, Sidney and Beatrice, *Soviet Communism: A New Civilization?* Longmans, Green and Co., London; Volume I, 1935, Volume II, 1936. (Cited as Webbs.)

XX Sezd Kommunisticheskoy Partii Sovetskogo Soyuza (The Twentieth Congress of the Communist Party of the Soviet Union), 2 volumes, State Publishing House of Political Literature, Moscow, 1956 (cited as *XX Sezd K.P.S.S.*).

Yagodkin, V. N., *Puti Likvidatsii Tekuchesti Kadrov v Promyshlennosti SSSR* (Ways of Eliminating Fluidity of Cadres in USSR Industry, *Mysl* Publishing House, Moscow, 1965.

Yamenfeld, G. M., Pavlov, V. V., and Dvinov, M. S., *Osnovy Sovetskogo Grazhdanskogo i Trudovogo Prava* (The Bases of Soviet State and Labour Law), State Publishing House of Commercial Literature, Moscow, 1959.

Zasedaniya Verkhovnogo Soveta SSSR, Shestogo Sozyva (Shestaya Sessiya), Stenografichesky Otchet (Sessions of the USSR Supreme Soviet, Sixth Convocation (Sixth Session)), published by the USSR Supreme Soviet, Moscow, 1965.